Long Shadows

Stanley Wally Hoffman

VANTAGE PRESS
New York

FIRST EDITION

Published by Vantage Press, Inc.
516 West 34th Street, New York, New York 10001

Manufactured in the United States of America
ISBN: 0-533-13892-2

Library of Congress Catalog Card No.: 01-126326

0 9 8 7 6 5 4 3 2 1

To my son,
Mark Robin,
who has returned to Africa
and is presently also making it his home

"Our struggle is not against flesh and blood, but against the rulers, against the authorities, against the powers of this dark world and against the spiritual forces of evil in the heavenly realms." —Ephesians 6:12

Contents

Preface

In this book I am picking up the story of our ministry which I left off in *Amid Perils Often* written several years ago, and will continue it from there to share what has transpired since then! First in Uganda, and then in Zambia, where we moved to and are residing presently.

I want to take you with me on several safaris into the bush where we planted churches in remote villages. There you will discover that witchcraft and demon-possession are still very much a part of their lives. Eventually, you discover that churches will be established and lives changed through the power of God's Word.

The accounts in this book do not include any experiences encountered while working in Zimbabwe, Mozambique, Malawi, and Angola. They will be shared in my next and final book, *A Passion for Africa*. That book will also contain those experiences in Zambia not found in this book.

As in all my previous books, this, too, is written in the present tense.

Introduction

The sun is dropping rapidly and before long there will be no more light. Marion and I, at the moment, are high above the Luangwa Valley in eastern Zambia. We are on our way back to Lusaka from Nairobi (via Dar es Salaam), where we spent ten days with Colleen, Tim and their children who are on their way to Canada for six months of home assignment. We are flying Aero Zambia.

Glancing out my window again, I find sunlight still bathing the western side of the hills below us. Not so on the eastern side. Here, shadows are reaching ever eastwardly. The hills are now casting long shadows. There is darkness!

Since moving to Zambia, we have found darkness in many areas, like long shadows, reaching across the countryside wherever we travel. In spite of the gospel being preached in almost every district, there still abound many tribal beliefs. People steeped in traditional customs, witchcraft, juju, ancestral worship, voodooism, black magic, heathen sacrifices, and the like. The light of the gospel shines ever brighter as the years move along but the powers of darkness still cling on in the lives of many worshipers.

Whereas in the countries of East Africa, where we labored for years, we eventually witnessed traditions contrary to the teachings of Christ disappear. If not completely, then at least they were not practiced openly,

xiii

unashamedly, as it is still done here! In Zambia the chiefs and officials encourage their subjects to hang on to their traditions and customs, which makes it difficult for the Christians if some of these traditions contradict the teachings of Christ. Who should they listen to? Who should they obey? The weaker relent while the stronger face hardships from their rulers and elders. Marion and I have come face-to-face with the powers of darkness and have learned that without the Lord's help we would not have been able to reveal His light which the darkness cannot put out!

Speaking out for the Lord in a country that has declared itself a Christian nation has not been all that simple, due to the fact that many are still attempting to live in two different worlds at the same time. Light and darkness just do not mix and therefore God is not blessing them as He would like to. Too many love their customs and traditions. Until these strongholds have been broken down, long shadows will persist and people will continue to walk in darkness.

Long Shadows

One
On the Road Again

Marion and I have just completed itinerating, which took us through Canada and across the United States. During our year on home assignments we shared in at least 90 churches, five Bible colleges and four camp meetings, traveling over 40,000 miles plus thousands more in air miles. Time has now come to return to Uganda and resume our work in that country. We have been packing boxes and stacking them in the container that will be shipped on to Kampala. We have been getting up at six and to bed at midnight for days. It has been tiring work but it all had to get done by today for tomorrow we leave. Before walking back to our furlough apartment, I pray that our things will arrive in Kampala. I believe they will. The sign the Lord gives that He will, is He locks the big sliding door from the inside when I pull it down!

Up at 5:30 in the morning, and try again to phone Colleen and Tim in Kampala but the operator comes on once more to say that the number is still temporarily out of order. This has been the story for over a week!

Marion wanted a time of leisure this morning before our departure for Africa but it is not to be. We do not even get time to go out for breakfast as planned. Instead, we nibble some fruit that, along with the buttermilk, needs

1

finishing. I pack the suitcase while Marion cleans the house.

Then at 10:15 we leave Anderson for the airport at Indianapolis. We fly on United Airways to Chicago where we will catch the KLM flight to Nairobi. While waiting in the lounge at Chicago, I write a letter to Mianitse in Zaire and another one to Esron in Rwanda inviting them to come to Kampala for a meeting. During this time I am paged and asked if we would mind moving from economy class to business class. Would we mind? We certainly would not! And so we have a very comfortable flight across the Atlantic. The Lord had seen our busy schedule the last three weeks and has provided this treat for us. Thank you!

Returning to Africa is like coming home! Not only do we have Tim and Colleen with their two daughters Tiffany and Natasha here in Uganda, but Kirk and Karen with their daughter Ashling are here as well. Due to World Vision being forced out of Sudan, Kirk applied to UNICEF and was accepted. So now he and his family are residing in Kampala. Back in September of last year, while still with World Vision, Kirk and Karen had to fly out of Sudan to Nairobi, Kenya, in order to have Ashling, due to the lack of proper facilities back in the bush where they were stationed. As with Tiffany, Colleen gave birth to Natasha here in Kampala, just last month. It appears Natasha may have my dimple in her chin. Tiffany looks great! She has grown lots and already has quite a vocabulary. Whenever there is an opportunity, she asks Opa to go walking with her. (Opa is grandpa in German.) She takes to me right away, picking up from where we left off a year ago.

There has been progress here in Uganda, thanks to Tim and Colleen's presence and willing spirits during our absence. They have done a splendid job! The church leaders continue to be enthusiastic about their work. I learn that the churches are still being harassed in some districts by rebels and cattle raiders. Many Christians have had to flee while others have been robbed of their belongings, and then there are those who were killed. I am personally saddened to hear that a month ago Stephen, our vice chairman for North Bugisu District, was shot to death in his home by cattle raiders. The hut was then set ablaze! He had been instrumental in assisting us to start the work in his district a few years ago. I cannot hold back the tears as the chairman, filled with emotions, relates the incident. He lives next door and barely escaped with his own life.

I recall the time Stephen took money, instead of allowing me to spend it on lunch for him, when he saw what it would buy for his family. Now he is gone.

The electricity is still very irregular with many power failures that can last all night and at times reach into days. Will it ever be normal? The 3,000 watt generator we brought with us in the container is serving the Stevensons very well, while we keep using the one we had last term.

Tim and Colleen have moved into a house where the High Commissioner for Kenya had lived. During their time there the H.C. had been broken into several different times; the bullet holes in the door and walls are a witness to it having happened. We trust guardian angels will watch over our kids and protect them as they have us. Kirk and Karen live in a house near us as well.

One midnight thieves did try to enter the Stevensons' compound but the watchman next door spotted them and alerted Colleen. Tim was away up-country at the time. She called out to Kirk's watchman to awaken him. This he did and Kirk was soon at the house. A squad car from the UN also showed up in response to Kirk's call on the radio. So the kids had an exciting night! (The UN has given Kirk a radio for security reasons.)

A month later our place also had an attempted entry one night. Both Marion and I were not home at the time. She was visiting the Stevensons while I was out of the country visiting the work in Zambia. Annah, our house girl for the past five years, heard something outside her window. Peering out she saw a man squeezing through the security fence in which he had cut an opening. She screamed and Musa the watchman came running. (Moses, whom she married recently, was in the shower. He used to be our watchman but now assists Tim with projects). The thief ran but his three accomplices remained near the mango tree, which stands outside the fence.

Our workers then told the watchman above us to notify the Stevensons' workers about the thieves. Tim immediately took off on foot with his firearm, along with Kirk who was visiting the Stevensons. They took the short cut across the back fences. No thieves were around, too much activity for them. They returned and Kirk drove Marion home. The UN official living above us made an appearance and summoned the security force. They searched the area and discovered nothing. Finally, all went home and things settled down. The security guard from above us stayed to watch through the night. Marion stayed at home in spite of the kids wishing her to come with them back to the Stevensons.

A few days after our arrival the topic of our morning devotions from *Daily Bread* is "Drink it All!" from Ephesians 1:1–14. There is no limit to the grace of God of which we may freely partake. Our greatest needs cannot exceed

4

God's great resources. So we may drink deeply throughout this term from that well!

Gary and Betty Kellsey, our close friends from Carstairs, Alberta, have accompanied us back to the field and are staying two months to lend a hand in the work as they had done on their first time out two years ago. He assists with the plowing of the church land at Kinyonga with one of the tractors that Tim purchased during our absence. Colleen's cousin Alexander Baum and his wife Cyndie have come for three weeks and are staying with the Stevensons. Tim and Colleen are taking them by road to see Kaiti Mission in Tanzania. Alex spent six years there when his parents Gordon and Eileen were missionaries in the 1960s.

Today, July 25th, a telegram arrives from Marion's brother Jerry stating that their mother has passed away! She died five days ago. Due to the phone being out of order, the news reaches us late. Marion takes her mother's death quite hard. We knew that it would be but a matter of time and she would leave us to join her husband who went ahead five years ago on July 18, 1983. It had been discovered that she had leukemia while we were on home assignment, and Marion tried to be with her as much as possible. But it is never enough. Her prayers will be sorely missed by us all .Lydia Schwartz was a real prayer warrior with a heart for missions. The deaths of both of Marion's parents took place soon after our arrival to the field. There was no opportunity for her to attend either funeral.

A few weeks later I am awakened one night and find a dark figure, resembling a serpent, above my head! It disappears quickly. What does it mean? I had a similar experience while attending Alberta Bible Institute. I was a student there and still single. Ray, my roommate, and I were already in our bunks. I was on the top one and had just dozed off when something awakened me. I was startled by a black figure standing beside the bed and peering directly at me. It was dark inside the room but this shape was even darker. I struck out at it with my clenched fist and the image vanished. Wide awake, I looked over the edge of my bunk to see if Ray was there. He was. I whispered his name. No reply. He was fast asleep. What was it?

At that time I interpreted my experience to mean that Satan had come to distract me as he had tried with Jesus. I was a student at Bible school who was attempting to learn as much as possible of the Scriptures, enrolling in all the Bible and theological courses available. Satan also did not like that I was a part of the group that fasted a day each week and met to pray in between classes and preach after classes, often in the nearby cemetery. Satan, therefore, wished to derail me so that I would not be such a threat to his cause. But he failed miserably in his attempt for I fought back. Physically is not the way to fight him, but that was my response at the time.

Now what about the experience I just had? What is Satan up to this time? The Lord allowed this to happen so as to warn me, I am certain of that. There is something afoot and He wants me to be aware of it. Time will reveal what it is. I must make sure that my full armor is on at all times so as to defeat the enemy when he engages me in battle.

Several months pass by and while on one of my safaris to Zambia, I have a dream between one and two in the morning. I am standing inside of a large building. There are others with me, including Tim. Nearby stands a tall tree. It begins to sway to and fro. If it breaks off, it may fall on top of the building that we are in and smash it to the ground! As we watch, the tree appears to settle down. But then again it starts to rock back and forth, this time leaning over more than ever. With a loud crack, it finally breaks off near the base and falls.

The tree, when it snaps off, twists around just enough so that it is now heading right for us and the building. But, miraculously, at the last second the tree turns just a bit more and brushes by us. It scrapes the side of the roof. Tim and I, along with the rest, rush outside to size up the damage. There is none, only a few scratches on the edge of the roof. We all gather around the fallen tree and stand there gazing at it.

What is the interpretation of this dream? The Lord is showing me that one of our church leaders is going to fall. He will be from the national level, as the tree was tall. The large building we were in is the church. Thank the Lord that when he will fall, the church will not be harmed! Where will this happen? It must be Uganda, instead of Zambia, as Tim is present on the scene.

I pray that this warning has come in time to deter it from happening. May the national leader stand and not fall. As I travel from one seminar to the next, I have time to share this dream, and its meaning, with the national leader who is accompanying me on the journey in his area of Uganda.

They all wonder who it might be. One even asks me, "Is it I?"

I reply, "Is it?" Sadly, he is the very one who is to eventually fall!

The man had a warning earlier from his own son. I shared this in the book *Amid Perils Often,* chapter 13. Had he heeded then, he would not have strayed as much as he ultimately did. As the dream revealed, Francis did repent after the first confrontation. As the tree stopped swaying for awhile, so did he. But, in the end, he backslides and begins to retaliate. No one sides in with him at the meeting, including the missionary who traveled with him on many safaris to plant churches, and he is dismissed as the National Secretary and evangelist for Eastern Region.

It is a sad occasion as I had grown fond of him and his family. But sin is sin. He, of course, repented deeply and in time he was restored into full fellowship after serving his three-year probational period.

*   *   *

Gary accompanies me on several journeys up-country. One of them is to Karamoja to inspect the work there. It has been some time since my last visit and I am very interested to see how it is faring. We are not able to leave Kampala until 11:30, instead of 7 A.M. as planned. This is due to a delay in acquiring sufficient funds for our expenses along the way. This will bring us to Moroto around 6 P.M., too late for the evening service we had planned on having. I check the post office box once more on our way out of town and discover a telegram from Francis Makosia stating that we should take the road via Soroti instead of North Bugisu because of recent clashes between the army and Karamojong cattle rustlers. We certainly will now be arriving in the dark, as this is a longer route.

We eat our lunch while driving as we dare not stop for a meal. Marion has sent along sandwiches, cookies, and bananas. We pass many empty houses between Mbale and Soroti. Their occupants have been moved into the refugee camps at Kumi by the army. A precautionary measure to protect them from the Karamojong raiders and Acholi rebels we are told. It is 5 P.M. when we arrive at Soroti. We keep going. Because of the rains there are many bad spots on the road with ruts and huge holes dug up by army vehicles. We move along slowly.

At dark we reach the border of the Karamoja district near Akisim Mountain. Just inside are the barracks of the military who have been stationed here to keep the Karamojong at bay and we are ordered to check-in with the officer in charge. He tells us that there is no traveling past this point after 5 P.M. because of the danger that we may run into marauding Karamojong. But I eventually persuade him to allow us to carry on. It is past 9:30 P.M. when we finally arrive in Moroto and check-in at Mt. Moroto Hotel, the only hotel in town. We have to awaken the manager as he already has retired for the night. There is no power so we are given lanterns. Time for meals is past but fortunately we are able to purchase a couple of soft drinks, which are not cold, before bedding down ourselves.

The night is cool and we sleep well. Our breakfast is at eight. I am expecting Francis to show up this morning but he does not. We commence searching for him. We drop in at the town office where we had planned to meet at nine. There the clerk informs us that he may have gone home since we did not show up at the appointed time, which was before sunset. He had heard Francis tell someone that he was going ahead to look for us on the road. Then, we find one of the Christians from the church in town and take her along to visit the villages, which I had gone to a year ago. We pick up a chief along the way to help us with the interpretation into Karimojong.

At all three manyattas Gary and I treat the sick with

the medicines I have brought along. We give out three blankets at the first village and two at the second one, where Gary also gives away his cap. There are more young warriors present than on my previous visit. They react nervously whenever I turn the camera on them. Ornaments cover their arms and legs. The razor sharp bracelet used in hand-to-hand combat is one of them. I share the Word of God at each place with many who want Jesus Christ as their Savior. Again as before, I see many needs here. Truly, the fields are white onto harvest but the workers are few.

At six we return to the hotel and have something to eat, our first meal since breakfast as we missed our noon meal. Meanwhile, police personnel have flown in by helicopter and are staying the night. Because of their presence in the hotel Gary and I lose our lanterns to them and are given candles instead. The officer-in-charge has someone watching his front door and back door. There is tight security here tonight.

After breakfast we check out of the hotel and stop at the town office once more to see whether the clerk has heard any more of Francis. He has not, and I decide to return to Kampala. It rained heavily last night and so the roads are all muddy. At the Teso and Karamoja border where there are a lot of big pot holes we find less rain, for which I am glad. We pass through them okay with Gary taking the wheel at times while I do the directing. Farther along the road to Soroti we run into a convoy of troops who were crossing one of the causeways through a swamp. There are seven huge semi-trucks tagging along as well and one has slid off the road, which makes things worse for us. But I manage to keep the Nissan on the road and we creep by them safely.

It already has been dark for some time when we hit a

bad stretch of road not far from Kampala. The highway here is under construction and with some heavy rains last night, the road is greasy and slick. A bus has slid crossways blocking off traffic. We join the long line of stranded vehicles. After a wait of 45 minutes, some smaller vehicles try squeezing between the trucks and the heaps of murraim. They make it. Then I try it. I tread my way through the line-up and reach home finally at 9:30 P.M.! Marion and Betty fared well during our absence. We learned from Marion that it had rained here over three inches in the afternoon! No wonder there was a sea of mud that we had to plow through to reach home.

*   *   *

A return trip to Karamoja has to be cancelled at the last minute when motorists are banned from traveling into that area. Attacking rebels are shooting at vehicles and several occupants have been killed. Foreign workers are not exempt from these attacks.

Two
Journeys to Zaire & Rwanda

Mianitse of Zaire and Esron of Rwanda pull into Kampala by bus and stay with us for a couple of days. We visit and discuss the work in their countries. I am glad they have showed up and we make plans for my next trip there. Colleen types out the letters I have drafted, one for each, which they will need for the Ministry of Justice concerning the registration of the Church in Zaire and in Rwanda. This is our first meeting since arriving back from home assignment. I did see them during the World Conference last year in Seoul, Korea, where I assisted them by interpreting most of the services into Swahili as they still do not know English.

I finally have my visa for Zaire. I had to make five trips to the embassy before they finally had it ready. It is so different in Rwanda. The visa is always waiting for me on my second trip to their embassy. Church leaders drop in the evening and next morning before I can leave to see me about this and that. I thought it would never end. For a week now they have been coming. They pass each other at the gate. It has been hectic! But, finally, I am on my way to the airport at Entebbe. Tim and Marion are seeing me off. I almost do not get on as they have me on standby even though I had been told earlier that my flight was confirmed! The twin-engined Otter has 12 on board and it takes an hour and 15 minutes to reach Kigali.

Esron is there to meet me at the airport. We travel by taxi to town. There is no one around to book me in at the Anglican guesthouse. After an hour of waiting for someone to appear, we try the Presbyterian guesthouse. Here, we find the receptionist present and I am given a room. Then we go to see the advocate who has been working on the church's registration. He thinks that it may cost us $8,000 to get the minister to pass it! "All the churches are doing it," he states when I remark that this is unreasonable.

When we return to the guest house, I have my first bite of food in thirteen hours. At nine I turn in. (It is already ten back in Uganda.) I wake up at six to the sound of a chicken squawking down the hall. It must be a candidate for the noon meal as it is not cackling.

The advocate shows up at 7:30 A.M. as prearranged and he takes Esron and me to see the Minister of Registration. The minister does not have much time for us because of a meeting he must attend and asks that Esron return next week. How many times has that been now? It is a sure sign that there is to be money in Esron's hand when he comes back. There is nothing more left to do here in Kigali so we take off in a taxi for Gisenyi, 166 kilometers away.

In spite of the hairpin curves, we make good time. That is, until we reach the village of Kora, which is situated between Ruhengeri and Gisenyi. Here, Esron wants the driver to turn off and take us to a church nearby. The side road turns out to be too stony for the little vehicle and the driver refuses to go any farther. Esron convinces me that it is only a few meters to the place so we commence walking to it. It is just around the bend, and, just over the next hill. But it is at least two kilometers before we reach the church where the Christians are waiting! I see that the Rwandanese are no different from the Ugandans when it comes to distance. Any reluctance I may have had for walking all this way under the hot sun vanishes when I am greeted heartily by the patiently waiting Christians. After the service many of the believers escort us back to the car. Children eye up the Mzungu (white man) as they scamper along the rocky path beside me, some even daring to touch my arm. They make the most of this rare occasion. When we arrive in Gisenyi, I am put into a rooming house run by a Christian lady.

Mianitse has arrived from Goma, Zaire, which is just across the border from Gisenyi, and will be sleeping here tonight along with Esron. We have something to eat before going into the service, which is held in the church nearby. Many pastors have already arrived. I preach on Philippians 3:10–16. God blesses, and at least 35 come forward for prayer after the message. There is rain tonight. I slip off to bed after a late supper. I should sleep well as the bed has a foam mattress!

The church leaders have come in for a two-day seminar. I teach and preach from morning until late into the night. About 200 crowd inside the church building for each meeting. It gets quite hot during midday. I close the final service with the Lord's Supper. A good ending to our seminar. The meals served by Esron's sisters are top-notch. There is a variety of vegetables and meat. Very tasty! They have been cooking in their parent's home only a few doors away and then carry it to our lodging place. For my bath a basin of water is brought to my room. The first night two drunks interrupt our evening meal. They are the owner's son and daughter. The mother has to finally come and haul them away. Amazingly, the daughter shows up sober in the morning service and I lead her back to the Lord. She attends all the remaining sessions and services.

Mianitse shows up late with the vehicle from across the border. They had trouble with the police as soon as they entered Rwanda, where there are stricter traffic rules. The taxis in Zaire are wrecks compared to those on this side. The driver takes the back roads as we head for the border. He does not slow down for the stop signs because the clunker may stall and we would then have to get out and push, which is how it got started when we left Esron's place. We make it to the border and pass through without any major delay. I am checked into the same lodge that I was in on my last safari. The Baptists own it now. It still looks the same though. No major improvements. The only water tap that works is the cold one on the tub. The toilet bowl runs continuously. Sifa, the women's leader in Zaire, and her friends bring me supper as they did on my previous visits. Mianitse is present but does not eat. I have prayer with them before they leave and carry away their dishes inside of a bucket.

The night was warm. I use the sheet only, no need for the blanket. The bed is hard. I feel the wooden slats beneath the thin foam mattress. I take a cold splash-bath in the tub. There is no mirror on the wall so I use my small one, which fortunately I remembered to bring along. For breakfast, I am eating raw carrots! I actually enjoy them as much as Bugs Bunny does. The women also brought me bread and a tin of margarine but forgot the can opener. So, "What's up Doc?"

A minibus carries Mianitse and me, plus eight others from the church in Goma, to Sake where the seminar is to be held. It is a 27 kilometer drive and we finally reach our destination at ten o'clock. Many of the pastors are waiting and they escort me to the church a kilometer distance up a hill strewn with volcanic rocks and cinders from recent eruptions. Of course, there are a lot of onlookers, probably wondering who this Mzungu afoot might be. But, I am sure there are those who remember me from previous visits.

I preach on 2 Timothy 1:6–14. The Lord blesses the message and 17 come forward for help. I teach for two and a half hours after a 45-minute break for lunch at Mianitse's house. His wife serves a big meal. Before we can take leave for Goma, we must listen to the choirs. They have been patiently waiting for this opportunity to perform for us and sing for half an hour. I am blessed and refreshed by their songs. I am then accompanied by pastors who sing all the way down to the waiting vehicle. Quite a picture we make—a white man leading a group of black singers! We walk past a marketplace full of men and women buying and selling their wares.

I am happy to see a nice looking Land Rover standing there ready to transport us back to Goma. But I soon find out that looks can be deceiving. It has to be pushed before it will start! Not far down the road a tire blows. By the time we get going again it is almost dark. No lights work except for one front park light. The driver drives most of the way with the engine switched off in order to save fuel! A blessing in disguise, for now we do not have to smell the exhaust fumes coming through the floor. Finally, we reach Goma and I find my way to the guesthouse. Sifa and her crew still bring me something to eat in spite of it being so late. Bless their hearts!

During the night I am bitten by fleas. Even though I sprayed the bed with insecticide before crawling into it, they still get me on the side I am lying on. In the morning I am served an omelet along with carrots. It is not until ten before I finally catch a ride to Sake. Mianitse and those who wished to go from Goma are left behind. While he was negotiating the fares for the group, others crowded onto the pick-up ahead of them. Then, when Mianitse himself tries to climb into the cab to sit beside me, a woman who got in ahead of him now refuses to get out. He asks her several times to move but she refuses. What the outcome may have been had there been more time I do not know, for the driver takes off before it is settled! My place is to be at the service in Sake as soon as possible, so I remain quiet or else I too will miss it.

I walk up to the church from the market where the vehicle stopped. I have no one to escort me this time. I find the service has already started. I am on a few minutes later and preach on Matthew 11:1–6. I am nearing the end of my sermon when Mianitse and the Christians from Goma show up. The Spirit is again present during the preaching and many flock to the altar. A good ending to this seminar in Zaire! Before we can close though there are more choir members. Then we meet outside where three men put on a traditional dance for me, spears and all, similar to the one a few years ago. Finally, we eat.

It is 3 P.M. when we walk down to the market to catch a vehicle back to Goma. The Land Rover of yesterday is there but not the driver. We wait an hour for him to show up, and when he does not we book another one. This one proves to be no different! It has a flat on the way as well. There is a five-litre container of petrol at our feet. The engine draws the fuel from it through a plastic hose. Its fumes we inhale all the way. The rattles on it can only be drowned out by the lusty singing of the Christians in the seat behind me. This they accomplish without too much effort. We reach my place of abode at five and find Esron

17

waiting for us. He, Mianitse, and I visit until supper is brought at nine.

I do not sleep as well as previous nights. Thoughts of the immediate needs here in Zaire and Rwanda are overwhelming! How will the Lord provide funds for those government ministers who are waiting to have their palms padded before they will register our churches? They have been stalling for three years now because we have not been accommodating. It is in your hand, Lord, I do not know where else to turn for help!

Today, I vacate the premise here and fly to Kigali. I will not miss this guesthouse as I picked up more flea bites last night. The mold on the walls where I usually eat my meals does not help my appetite. There is jam for the bread this morning and an omelet again. As always the food is placed on whatever serves as a table for me to eat and they all leave the room, including Mianitse. It must be their custom of showing respect. At Gisenyi in Rwanda, Esron would at least stay and eat with me. No comparison with the food either—like coming from the Hilton to McDonalds! Mind you I am not complaining. Just being observant. Praise the Lord, anyhow!

I fly out of Goma to Kigali on Air Rwanda, a seven-seater with six passengers. It is a nice flight over the countless hills of Rwanda. The country is known by the natives as the land of a thousand hills. When the first man, Tutsi, came here from the north he exclaimed, "This is Rwanda!" This means: "This is the whole world!" As he carried on southwards he reached what is now Burundi and exclaimed, "This is Burundi!" or "This is another world!"

From my window I can see the Kagera River below me. It winds its way through the hills until finally the waters run into Tanzania, where they end up in Lake Victoria. I do not spot any bodies floating downstream. But, because of the unrest in Burundi which began last month, many corpses without heads and with hands tied together have been pulled from the rivers that flow into Rwanda from Burundi. It has been reported that thousands have already died! My desire is to go there one day and plant the church in that land.

Over to the north lies the volcanic range, home of the mountain gorillas. Three extinct volcanoes share common borders with Rwanda and Uganda. A fourth, the farthest west, shares its peak with a third country, Zaire. There is another one, beyond this range, in Zaire which is very active. It erupts every few years, the last one being in 1987 when its lava reached Sake.

Esron is waiting for me at the airport with a taxi and we drive into Kigali where we check into the Presbyterian guesthouse again. They do not serve meals here so we eat at a nearby restaurant. It is a relief to ride in a vehicle that does not have to be pushed as in Zaire, where every one I rode in never started on its own! Quite a difference between the two countries.

I enjoyed the night of rest. The room I am in is spacious. There are three wooden bunk beds with thick foam mattresses and a mirror above the sink! Windows are screened to let in cool air and keep out mosquitoes. No bathroom, of course, that is downstairs. I settle for a splash-bath in the sink. (No, I do not actually crawl into it!)

Before going to the airport, Esron and I drop in to see how the advocate made out with the minister concerning the registration of the church. We find that he has not met him yet. So, that is that! At the airport I discover that my flight to Nairobi on Kenya Airways is going to be two hours late. So I sit around and visit with Esron until noon. Then he leaves. Finally the plane arrives and I am on my way. Who said that outreach work is easy? Must be the one who has not done any!

*   *   *

I had intentions of taking Gordon Schieck and Richard Yamabe to Zaire as well but we fail to come up with the dollars that the embassy requires. The visas are now $70.00 each and it must be cash! We had tried five different banks and they all refused to sell us the dollars. So now it will be to Rwanda only. Mianitse and the Christians will have to cross the border if they wish to meet the visitors.

Richard Yamabe was one of my professors when I attended Alberta Bible Institute. He was also the dean for a while. Gordon Schieck and his wife Mina were missionaries to India for many years. They are now involved with raising funds for projects in foreign lands. They have come to see whether they may be of assistance. Hopefully their trip to Africa will bear fruit. Tim had already talked to them about the projects for Uganda.

We leave Kampala at 6:30 A.M. and twelve hours later we reach Kigali, Rwanda. At the Presbyterian guesthouse we find Esron who has just arrived as well. He did receive my telegram which I had sent him three days ago informing him of our coming. We visit with him for a while before retiring for the night. It has been a long trip.

It rains pretty well all night. After some food we carry on to Gisenyi where our meetings are to be held. On the ridge between Kigali and Ruhengeri travel is slow. Not only is there rain on the heights, but heavy clouds obscure the road. Visibility is almost nil, making it well near impossible to stay on the highway, which is anything but straight! But we reach Gisenyi safe and sound. It was quite a drive! Here at Lake Kivu the sun is shining.

There is a service planned for us where the people have been waiting for hours! Richard preaches the message. I translate it into Swahili while Esron puts it then into Kinyarwanda. Many come for prayer afterwards. Then, after eating the meal they have prepared for us, we visit with Esron and Mianitse who has arrived from Zaire. We are spending the night in a house where the owner is away.

After breakfast this morning, we are transported 20 miles up into the hills where there is a church at Gahondo village. There are over 20 of us solidly packed into the van. The service is held outside on a hilltop. I preach this time and at least 20 come for repentance and healing. We return to Gisenyi. All afternoon Gordon is busy with Esron and Mianitse discussing projects for these two countries. I am present to translate for Gordon. Before I can actually retire, Mianitse and Esron present their reports and needs to me. When I finally do retire, I cannot fall asleep until 1 A.M. Lord, provide the necessary funds. I do not know where to turn for them. They are needed for the work here in Rwanda and Zaire!

The service starts at 10 A.M. and ends at 1 P.M. Some of the Christians have come across from Zaire. The church is full, and hot! There is a lot of inspirational singing before Gordon preaches his sermon, which Esron and I again translate. Over 20 come forward for prayer. We then meet with the leaders and pastors for some teachings. Finally, I visit with Esron and Mianitse. This lasts until 10 P.M. when we are asked to come and eat. It's rather late but we oblige, except for Richard who has gone to sleep.

As soon as we are awake, people start dropping in to say their goodbyes. Before we leave Gisenyi, Gordon still meets with Esron and Mianitse to finalize the projects that had been chosen earlier. We arrive back in Kigali at 2 P.M and check in at the guesthouse for the night. When I open my case, I discover shaving foam all over my stuff! The lid had come off during the drive. It's a good thing it does not stain. Before it gets dark we prepare for our return to Uganda in the morning.

We learn that 18,000 have been massacred in Burundi while nearly 60,000 have fled to Rwanda. None wish to go to Zaire. The presidents from the three nations met in Goma two days ago to discuss the problem.

I am up early and leave at 6 A.M. for Kampala. It is foggy in the low patches as we drive through the hills. The temperature at the border is only 47 degrees! That is cold! The crossing takes a little longer today and it is 7:30 P.M. before we reach home. Marion and Mina fared well during our absence. There has been shooting at nights, Marion says. But, that is the norm here in Kampala!

*   *   *

Marion and I make plans in March to visit the churches in Rwanda and Zaire but the Ugandan authorities refuse to allow our vehicle to travel there. Since the beginning of the year there has been a ban on vehicles leaving Uganda for Rwanda, Zaire, and more recently Tanzania. We have songbooks, tracts, quilt blocks, and other items for the churches there which necessitate traveling by road. We are praying that He will open a way for us to still get there before we move from Uganda to Zambia.

The opportunity comes a few months later. But this time Marion is unable to accompany me, I pack the guitar, songbooks, and tracts into the Nissan Patrol for the trip to Rwanda and Zaire. Robert Edwards and Eliezer Mdobi from Tanzania are coming along with me. We leave at 8 A.M. There has been a fuel shortage here in Kampala for days. At Mbarara, halfway to the border, we stop to fill up and find there is no fuel anywhere in town! I end up at the UNICEF workshop where Kirk's friend, Reid Brown, works. He is off for lunch so we wait for him to return. We eat our lunch, which Marion has sent along, at this time.

When Reid returns he is able to find a 20-litre jerry can of diesel for us. There is no more. The fuel situation looks bleak. Do we carry on? What if there is none at any of the filling stations farther down the line? We decide against chancing it and turn back to Kampala. I will check tomorrow whether there is a flight to Kigali. At 8:30 P.M. we pull in and find Marion already in bed. She gets up and prepares something for us to eat.

I hear on the morning news that George Adamson was killed by a band of Somali poachers in a Kenya game park where he resided. He had been a game warden for years in northern Kenya and was recognized as an expert on lions. Wildlife conservationists in Africa have lost a great man! His wife Joy, a renowned artist, is best known for her book on Elsa, *Born Free,* which sold several million copies. It was also made into a film. Colleen met her one day when Joy Adamson came to speak at Rift Valley Academy on wildlife conservation. She preceded her husband, George, in death, brutally murdered by thieves while she was out camping.

After breakfast Bob and I check on a ticket to
Rwanda. We are in luck. There is a flight at one o'clock.
When it is time to leave for the airport, Tim drives us
there. Eliezer is not going along now. The plane is a
20-seater Twin Otter. We take along the guitar, communion trays and cups, but not the songbooks and tracts. It
is too much weight for our luggage allowance. The flight
over Lake Victoria is smooth but then gets a bit rough
when we enter the clouds over the mountainous range of
Rwanda. We land safely in Kigali at 1:30 P.M. local time.

Bob and I have a bite to eat before carrying on to
Gisenyi by road. The taxi gets us there by dark. We find
Esron and Mianitse at the church and I introduce Bob to
them. I am turning the financial responsibilities of
Rwanda and Zaire over to Robert Edwards at the end of
this year 1989. He has recently been appointed Regional
Director of Africa. The Lord willing, I hope to return then
with Marion for our farewells. I have made many friends
and will miss them. And I certainly will remember the experiences I have had traveling in their vehicles and sleeping in their guesthouses, especially in Zaire. There are
presently 176 churches in Rwanda with 6,400 members
and 313 churches in Zaire with 10,000 members.

There is a service the next morning in Gisenyi with
Bob bringing the message after the singing, of which
there was plenty. We pray for the 30 who come forward.
There are plays after the service where youth act out several biblical scenes. In the evening we meet with the pastors and, finally, with just Esron and Mianitse to discuss
the finances. There is still so much pending to pay! It
seems there is no end to requests for the completion of the
church registrations in their countries. What is left are
the signatures of the presidents in Rwanda and Zaire!

Next morning a taxi takes us to Sake in Zaire where

a service is planned. The church is full with about 450 in attendance. About 50 are prayed for after Bob's sermon. More songs from the choirs. During this time I hand out the guitar to them. The son of Mianitse will be in charge of it. After the meal, we return to church and meet with the pastors. Before dark a taxi returns us to Gisenyi. We spend the evening talking with Esron and Mianitse. We finish our business by 10:30 P.M. and get to bed an hour earlier than the night before.

De Klerk, the president of South Africa, is meeting Mobutu, the president of Zaire, in Goma this evening. We found the main street blocked off when we came from Sake and had to go around a side street in order to get to the border. Museveni, the president of Uganda, is supposed to fly in tomorrow for this meeting.

Bob and I leave Gisenyi with a taxi and reach Kigali in time for our flight back to Entebbe. There are eight passengers flying today, three more than the day we came. It is a smooth flight all the way. Marion, Colleen, and Tiffany are waiting to pick us up at the airport. Then it is on to Kampala where we enjoy a scrumptious meal at the Stevensons later on in the evening. Kirk, Karen, and Ashling are present, as well as the Wiebes who have just arrived from Canada to open the new Leadership Training Centre. Before leaving I tuck Tiffany into bed and tell her some stories. She says sweetly, "I was waiting for you, Opa!"

Three
Journeys to Zambia & Malawi

I am on my way to Zambia. When I reach Nairobi I take a taxi from the airport and drop off at the CPK guesthouse. The only bed they have available for me is in a room with an Australian who is visiting some missionaries. I book in as it is getting too late to hunt for another place. Before turning in I call Colleen at Kampala as Marion is not at home. She tells me that all is well. I soon regret having agreed to share a room with someone else. The big Australian tosses around all night on his bunk, which has broken springs that squeak and jingle at his every move!

I walk downtown early and try to purchase some dollars in cash and travelers' checks at the Standard Bank, but by 11:30 I still have not been served. A ten-minute transaction takes all day out here! They had to phone Kisumu where our account is and are still waiting for an answer. I cannot wait any longer as I need to be at the airport pronto. My flight leaves at 1:15 P.M. for Zambia, where I will be for a week visiting the church in that country. I am going with $50 cash in my pocket! According to my calculations I will spend the whole amount for airport tax alone—when I depart today $20, then when I leave Lusaka $10, and finally when I leave Nairobi for Entebbe $20. Now, what about all the other expenses? I will need the Lord's help to be able to stay the week I have planned. It should be interesting!

While waiting in the departure lounge, the loudspeaker blares out the news that the flight to Lusaka will be delayed. An hour later the announcement is the same, "Kenya Airways regrets the delay for technical reasons." All my rushing around in town this forenoon was for nothing! I ask the airline to send a telex to Ndola airport where they are to inform the delegation who are coming for me from Kitwe that I will not be arriving until tomorrow morning.

Three hours later, the Boeing 70 finally lifts off for Lilongwe and then Lusaka. Soon Mt. Kilimanjaro and Mt. Meru come into view through my window. Their peaks rise above the clouds. Then we notice the temperature in the cabin getting hotter instead of cooling off. It reads 94 degrees on my watch. Apparently the air conditioner is not working. An hour into the flight, the plane banks to the right and the sun now is on our left. The pilot announces that we are heading back to Nairobi due to technical problems. Shame, as we were halfway to Lilongwe! Passengers who were sleeping and had not heard the announcement now stare in disbelief as they gape at Nairobi below them. One remarks, "Since when has Lilongwe grown that much!"

We are made to wait an hour in the departure lounge before they finally scrap the flight. It is now to fly the following day. I ask the airline to send another telex to Ndola advising my party that I will now be arriving a day late. I hope they get it in time. The passengers are all transported into town and booked in at the New Stanley Hotel for supper and the night. What a day this has been! Or, should I say, has not been!

In the morning I try to call Marion and then Colleen

but get an out of order reply from the Kampala operator for both places. At 11:30 the Kenya Airways bus returns us to the airport. After we have been ushered back to the room which has become very familiar to us, we are told that the plane will not leave as scheduled. Unbelievable! Instead of 1:15 it leaves finally at 3:15. This time we make it all the way to Lilongwe, Malawi. An hour later we are on our way to Lusaka. I arrive in time to catch the plane for Ndola with only half an hour to spare! Fortunately, it had been delayed as well.

At 8:30 P.M. I arrive in Ndola and find no one waiting for me at the airport. I check with the staff on duty whether a couple of telexes came from Nairobi and learn that none came. Not one of the messages I sent had arrived! What now? I peer out into the darkness. Maybe my party from Kitwe is late. One by one the passengers leave. I cannot even hire a taxi and book in at a lodge as I have no Zambian currency. I am really stranded!

Looking around me in desperation, I notice that there is still one passenger remaining in the arrival area. He is a young chap just returning from South Africa where he attends school. When his sister arrives to pick him up, he invites me to come along to their parents' farm for the night. When we arrive, I am given something to eat. It was very hospitable of them, taking in a stranger without any notice at all! They came out from Britain in 1965 to farm and have been here ever since. Because of them I have a roof over my head and a nice bed to sleep in tonight. God bless them!

I wake up to a cool morning. The temperature is much lower here at night than in Uganda. I walk around a bit outside. It's nice to hear the birds. The countryside reminds me a bit of Tanzania. Mrs. Gibbons and her son Andrew give me a lift to the main road where I catch a ride with a Zambian to Kitwe. He drops me off at Nkana Hotel where I have been booked in on previous occasions by the church leader here in Kitwe. Marion was with me on one of those times. I find no one waiting for me in the lobby and also discovered that I am not booked in either. What's up?

I walk to the place where we usually choose a taxi to go to one of our church leaders' places, but I cannot recall the name of the market where I am to be dropped. so I return to the hotel. While I was away, a man did come to inquire whether I had arrived. He left his number which I am to call. When I do, I am told he is out so I wait. And wait. I should be used to this. Finally, mid-afternoon he shows up and directs me to London's house. The name of the market nearby is Kabulanda! I find Rufus present. (I had planned for him to be here when we met three weeks ago in Kampala.) He arrived four days ago by road and rail. Maybe I should try the train next time as well and thus get here in time.

Due to my arriving a day late the trip to Mbala district has to be shelved until the next safari. I had looked forward to going there to meet some of the churches but it is an all-day and all-night trip by bus to get there. Presently, there is only one bus running and it usually is overbooked.

I am able to get some kwacha, Zambian currency, from a missionary in town. This will assist me for a while. This time around I am to stay at someone's house. Evans is one of the church leaders here who has recently lost his wife. Previous to this, his two children died. There is no hot water here so I take a cold bath in the tub before retiring. I am wearing my clothes tonight as there is no sheet on the bed. I do not hanker sleeping on the blanket that is covering the inch-thick mattress on top of the springs without my shirt and pants. I spray the "bedding" well so the fleas will not bite me any more than I have been bitten. I picked up a few while visiting at London's this afternoon.

There are two services today. One in the forenoon and then another one in the afternoon. I preach in both of them. The church here at Kwacha East has no roof and so it got quite hot inside. The temperature went up to 101 degrees today. I learn later that an intelligence officer was present in both services. he had come to investigate what we were up to. I trust he learned something. I talk to Rufus for some time before going to Evan's house. It is now dark.

The service this forenoon is at Nkana East. There is a lot of singing and the metal roof really rings as the building is small. When they ask me to give my greetings I also go into my sermon. I know if I do not do it now, I will not get on for another hour. Sure enough, the service lasts three and a half hours! Most of the 300 present request prayer at the end. Pray for them where they are as there is no room at the altar, although many do squeeze through.

While we are eating some food at one of the homes after the service, a rat emerges from the settee where some of the pastors are seated! It scurries into the next room. Am I the only one who noticed it? If others did, they do not show it. A common sight with them, I suppose. When we have eaten, I have a session with the pastors and church leaders where I teach them more doctrines of our church.

I talk to Mwale, a Malawian, about starting a church in his village. Rufus is to help him. We plan their journey to Malawi where I will meet them. It is two miles back to Evan's place. While walking in the dark, a boy runs up to me, grabs my arm and screams for me to protect him from a bigger fellow who is trying to catch him so as to beat him for calling him "a son of a dog!" Evan asks the teenager to forgive the little fellow. The boy sticks to us until we turn a corner, and then he is gone.

This is my last day in Kitwe and I spend much of it with the Executive Committee. After their agenda has been exhausted, I query the possibility of bringing the two factions together again. During the year I was on home assignment, the church had split when differences developed between the leaders. I remind them that the Mission Board will not recognize two groups in Zambia. Still, London declares he will not work again with Mbumba, the leader of the other faction. There is a lot of work ahead to be done before this problem will go away.

In the morning I receive a note from Rufus, who had a dream cautioning me not to enter into the conflicts between Mbumba and London. A warning that I need to heed!

The bus for Lusaka does not arrive at seven. Nor at eight. We sit and wait. And then wait some more. The only explanation we are given is that it has mechanical problems and they are repairing it. When one does arrive it is already full. Finally, at noon it pulls up and I manage to get inside amidst the pushing and shoving. My seat number is 29, but no one cares about numbers right now, as long as he or she gets a seat. When I ask, "Do we follow the numbers?" I am told, "Just grab any one!" So I do. As the bus pulls out, I wave goodbye through the open window to those who escorted me to the station.

The bus stops several times on the way. There is air in the diesel. It appears when they put in a new fuel pump, they did not bleed it. The passenger beside me exclaims, "They work on the bus for five hours and it stops on the way!" The battery terminal is broken as well so it has to be held until the engine starts. But, we manage to limp into Lusaka by 6:30 P.M. I grab a taxi to Bob Kurtz's place where I have stayed several times previously. I find them away but their worker opens the guesthouse and makes up the bed for me. I walk across to eat at the Ridgway Hotel. I turn in when I get back. It is only nine o'clock but I am tired.

I am on my last leg home now, and lonesome to see the family. I want to hear Tiffany again say, "Come here, Opa!" She likes to snatch me away from the rest into her room where she can have me for herself. She gets me to read to her stories that she has heard over and over.

It was nice to sleep in a half-decent bed again, and without my shirt and pants! I have had to keep them on during the four nights in Kitwe because the bed at Evan's place had no sheets on it. In the morning I check with the Registrar of Societies about the two registrations of our church here in Zambia. I am told that it is up to the church to sort out its own problems. I had hoped to meet Mbumba as he resides here in Lusaka but he does not make an appearance. The flight leaves for Nairobi an hour late and I arrive at 9:30 P.M. An hour later I am booked in at Mennonite guesthouse for the night.

In the morning I try to phone Marion and am told that it is out of order. I try the Stevensons and am told there is a power failure. So that is that! I hope they remember to pick me up. They do. Marion and Tim are there at the airport when I land at Entebbe. I am now home.

*   *   *

After passing the two roadblocks at Entebbe manned

by soldiers, we are at the airport. Marion has come along but will return home in the vehicle with Tim. We will be separated for 12 days this time. There is a long queue ahead of us at the counter but Richard Yamabe and I get through along with Gordon and Mina Schieck. Praise the Lord! The plane leaves only 15 minutes late. Robert Edwards picks us up at the airport in Nairobi and then drops us off at the Fairview Hotel, a remnant from the colonial past. We will be spending the night here.

In the morning I bid farewell to the Schiecks and Richard. Then I walk downstairs to confirm my flight to Lilongwe, Malawi, with Kenya Airways. It is okay today. I catch their bus to the airport. As usual, the flight leaves late, this time by one hour and ten minutes.

I arrive in Lilongwe at 4:30 their time. The taxi drops me off at a guesthouse in town. There is one room available I am told, but it gets taken while I am paying the taxi! Why me, Lord? I phone over to the Anglican guesthouse. It is full. They tell me to call the Catholic Centre. I do and they have room. The taxi drives me out there. It takes him sometime to find the place. Before retiring to my room, I have a shower. There is no towel and I forgot mine so I wait around until I am dry before jumping into bed.

I have come to Malawi to see about planting churches here. I am to meet Mwale from Zambia and Rufus from Kenya at Blantyre tomorrow. I have a fairly good night in spite of the mosquitoes and flying ants in my room. I hear the birds singing outside. This place is out in the country. I eat breakfast with the priests who are staying here. Afterwards one of them gives me a lift to town and drops me off at the bus park. I catch the express to Blantyre. It is a 350-kilometre ride to the south that takes us five and a half hours due to the many stops. There are a variety of various shaped mountains along the way. The country-side is dry compared to lush green Uganda.

There is a stretch where the road runs along the Mozambique and Malawi border. On the left side there are villages and make-shift camps overcrowded with refugees who have fled the fighting in war-torn Mozambique. There are bags of grain stacked at various centres brought in by aid groups. I see a World Vision sign. The buildings that still remain on the right side are ruined and in disrepair. How often have I seen such sights in the Ugandan countryside during her wars? The roofs are gone, the doors and windows missing, and the walls riddled with bullets! Will their owners ever return to them again?

At Blantyre I expected to catch the bus to Namphungo but I find it is not operating. I hire a vehicle which takes me there by way of Kando. The road is rough and the driver takes it slow. I arrive well after dark. From here I had been instructed by Mwale, the Malawian in Kitwe, to carry on to Sabola village where I am to meet him and Rufus. The driver does not know where the village is. We ask around and finally we head in that direction. This road is exceptionally rough on the vehicle. But we do make it after stopping a few more times to ask for further directions as it was most difficult to find the place in the dark. To reach the house of Mwale's relatives, someone has to lead us there as they live on the other side of a washout.

Finally, we have arrived. I ask the driver to remain as no one knows English and I do not know Chewa, the local language. After a few minutes of greetings and introductions, I learn that Mwale is not here! Yes, he is their relative, but he has not arrived as yet. Nor is Rufus around. They were supposed to have come three weeks ago to prepare the people for my visit! What am I to do now? It is 9 P.M. and so dark that I cannot see the faces of the people I am talking to. I would not even recognize them should we ever meet again in daylight. I cannot converse with them without the assistance of the driver who is anxious to be on his way. I must decide quickly!

I cannot remain here. If Mwale and Rufus do not come tomorrow then how will I communicate with these people? And, how will I find another vehicle to take me out of this remote village back to Blantyre? I may end up here stuck for days. That decides it! I bid them farewell and leave with the vehicle that brought me. Many onlookers from the village were already there curious as to why a white man should come to them in the middle of the night! The driver drops me off at Grace Bandawe Centre in Blantyre where a room is available. It is 10:15 P.M.

Sleep like a log until 5 A.M. It gets light early here. Even though I have not eaten since yesterday morning, I feel fine. There is a public holiday here in Malawi so everything is closed in town. There is a big celebration at the stadium with the president, Dr. Banda, in attendance. I spend the day in my room just lazing around. I need the rest after running here and there the last few days. The Lord must have arranged this day! I read the New Testament on Paul the Apostle. What a full life he lived! Am I able to leave as many tracks behind as he did? Lord, help me take your message to many more nations!

A lot of mosquitoes around, even at the breakfast table this morning. Fortunately there is a net above my bed which I used last night. I walk the two miles into town where there are shops. Finally, I have a chance to buy a towel. Now I can dry myself off after bathing which I have not been able to do the last three nights. Also, I purchase some bananas to eat in my room. (They do not serve meals at noon in the centre so I went without one yesterday.) I find it really hot walking back to Grace Bandawe. It is 96 degrees in the shade.

While in town I checked with the Registrar of Societies about registering our church in Malawi. I was told that for a year now the president has banned the registration of any new church organization. So that is that! Enquired then about whether any Church of God similar to ours has been registered in the past. Searching through their files I find none. How are we going to organize a church here now?

Today I am free and spend it writing a chapter for my next book. If I had met Mwale and Rufus at Sabola, I would have been there until today sometime. My bus for Lilongwe leaves tomorrow. I wash some of my clothes. I feel that I am on the verge of coming down with malaria. Double the intake of the anti-malarial drug I am taking, which is Paladrin. Chloroquine is no longer effective in my case and have stopped using it ever since my second bout with black water fever three and a half years ago. The mosquitoes here are the silent kind, and I have been bitten by them every day since coming to Malawi.

Women here curtsy when they greet the men. While waiting for the bus, I am caught unprepared when a woman who greets me curtsies. They also kneel when talking to an elder in their clan. This custom is also common with some tribes in Zambia and in Uganda. Noticeable too in Zambia is the clapping of their hands together, as if in applause, when they greet. This is performed by both men and women. I have seen it done after prayers as well.

The greatest honor, I feel, shown to me by a woman in Africa is the time we were waiting for food to be served. It was in the home of Josephine, the women's leader in

Ndama District of Uganda. The woman who brings us the water basin to wash our hands in is a young Masai woman from Kenya but married to a Ugandan. As I prepare to dip my hands into it, she takes them in her own and gently washes each hand separately.

Why did I allow her to do it? Why did Jesus allow the woman to wash His feet with her tears and then wipe them dry with her strands of hair? Of course, we know why. She wanted to honour the Master and this was the only way she knew how to show all the love and respect she felt for Him. Jesus knew it and did not interrupt her. He did not want to deny her a blessing. I too felt the same way. In her custom, the young woman was showing her love and respect she had for God's messenger. I could not disappoint her by refusing and thus be at fault for her failure to receive a blessing.

The bus trip back to Lilongwe is shorter by half an hour as it does not go by way of Zombo but it takes the new road that is being constructed which is more direct. I again spend the night at the Catholic Centre. I sleep well in spite of the heat and the mosquitoes. One of the priests is being driven to the airport, so I catch a ride. Today I fly on to Lusaka.

Air Malawi rolls down the runway but does not get airborne. There is not enough power to lift it off the ground! So it taxis back to the terminal where they commence working on the motor. We are required to remain inside and wait.

An hour later the pilot tries it again. It is still greatly underpowered but he manages to get off the ground. Fortunately, there are not tall trees or hills at the end of the runway, otherwise we would have scraped them. I glance outside my window and to my amazement I see the wing almost touching the trees as the pilot banks the plane to

37

gain altitude! What if this flight would be fully loaded instead of less than half full as it is now? A heaviness of heart had come over me on my way to the airport so I prayed until it left. Was it this flight?

The plane drones on and we arrive over an hour late. A taxi drops me off at Kurtz's in Lusaka. No one is home. I walk over to the Ridgeway Hotel and call the Baptist guesthouse. They have room and I take another taxi to get there. It is a nice place, the best room I have been in thus far on my travels. I had a light meal on the plane so I do not need supper.

For breakfast I am invited up to Fred and Joy Allen's apartment. They are missionaries from the States and I learn that they know Karen, Kirk's wife. Their son attended RVA and graduated with her. I enjoyed their fellowship. I return to the Ridgeway Hotel in order to meet one of our leaders in Zambia. I had telegrammed him from Malawi asking him to meet me here today. But by 3:15 P.M. he still is nowhere to be seen. It is time to go on to the airport. Kenya Airways is to leave for Nairobi at 6:10 P.M.

After I check through, an announcement declares that our flight will be five hours late! While waiting I do some more writing for the next book. There are seven Asians who can be heard all over the waiting lounge chattering in their language. They are involved in a card game and getting louder, determined to stay awake until the plane arrives. I hear over the loudspeaker that the Ndola flight by Zambia Airways is delayed as well due to technical reasons. A well-worn phrase which I have heard so often while waiting for my flights.

It eventually enters the humorous stage when they continue to delay our flight's departure. The plane finally arrives at 12:45 A.M. That is seven and a half hours late!

We board it half an hour later but then we do not leave until 3 A.M. because of a flat tire which has to be changed. What next? During the long wait we are cooped up inside the plane. The cabin soon heats up because of no air conditioning. Sweat is dripping down our faces and bodies. Is this how the hostages in hijacked airliners feel? We should have been allowed to stay longer in the terminal where we can walk about. Instead, we were ushered out much too soon. Some passengers are grumbling while others joke. I join the latter. By now the whole incident has become too humorous. For me this flight has not yet been delayed as long as my last one was.

I sleep some on the way. At 6:30 A.M. local time we disembark at Nairobi airport. I confirm my flight to Entebbe before taking a taxi to the Mennonite guest-house. I take a bath and rest after unpacking my bag. I wash some clothes. I have been holding out fairly well thus far with clean clothing considering where I have been since starting out from home. I phone Marion but there is no answer. I try the Stevensons and find Marion with them. From them I learn that three days of mourning have been declared to show respect for those who died after a Ugandan Airliner crash-landed in a fog at Rome a few days ago.

Sitting here, the following day, in the departure lounge of the Nairobi Airport, I hear a familiar announcement: "Kenya Airways regrets the announcement that for technical reasons KQ 410 to Entebbe will be delayed until 10:30 A.M. when it is expected to depart." That is one and a half hours late! Then, at 10:30 the loudspeaker blares: "Kenya Airways regrets to announce a further delay in its flight to Entebbe and apologizes for any inconvenience." This has been the airline's habit ever since I have been using Kenya Airways following my arrival for our second term on the field.

The shifting of moods is again recognizable. First, there is grumbling because it is not leaving on time. Then, when the delays continue to multiply and the situation becomes more ridiculous, there is joking. It has become humorous! Many are smoking, more than I have seen before in a waiting room. There is even a pipe and a cigar. They call us to the restaurant for dinner at one o'clock. Then, there is a scramble for seat reservations. An announcement had come that they are changing aircraft and 25 passengers will be bumped as the new aircraft is smaller! Those remaining will be brought later in a twin-engined Faulker.

I get a seat number and board the plane. No one pays attention to seat numbers once inside. Smokers are seated among the non-smokers. We finally land at Entebbe five and a half hours behind schedule! Marion and Tim are there. They waited for me all this time. For me outreach work that is dependent on air travel has become very thorny, to say the least.

Four
The Rigors of Travel

I purposely choose Zambia Airways this time as flying on Kenya Airways the past year has just had one delay after another in their schedule. But, to my surprise, the flight I am scheduled to fly out from Nairobi to Lusaka is not leaving on time either! I am again stuck in the departure lounge with other passengers waiting for the plane to leave. There are a lot of children traveling this time. Some are crying while others are playing with toys on the floor. "Wee! Wee-wee!" It almost looks like a flight for just the family. Then, we are off. Two hours late!

At Lusaka, I end up staying with a couple who now are living in the house where the Kurtzes used to live. They are Randy and Jane Rhoades. He is the director of Youth With a Mission (YWAM). I am sharing a room to-night with a young Zambian who is training for the ministry. Actually, I had planned to stay at the Baptist guesthouse where I have a reservation. But the Allens, whom I met on my last safari, are on furlough and therefore no one is presently operating the guesthouse. Plans sometimes do not turn out as they should! (Don't I know that!)

I am bitten several times by mosquitoes during the night. Nothing new. This has happened nightly for the past several weeks. They are plentiful in tropical Africa during the rainy season. I am told the reason for the two-hour delay of Zambia Airways at Nairobi airport yesterday is that all the luggage had to be removed and checked while at Dar es Salaam. There must have been a bomb scare. This explains the thorough check of our carry-on luggage as we boarded at Nairobi. The most I have ever seen checked in that airport!

I try to phone Kitwe and tell them I am coming on the second bus as I failed to get a ticket for the first one, but the line is out of order. Nothing more I can do. I tried! The bus leaves on time at 1 P.M. It is a seven-hour journey. All the seats are taken. The front window pops out and breaks when we get on the tarmac. Between Kabwe and Kapiri Mposhi, we come across a bus of the same make with a flat tire. They do not have a spare so the driver gives them ours. Passengers from the other bus commence piling into ours. Most of them manage to squeeze inside. The aisle is packed and so is the front. Fortunately, no one smokes along the way. But there is a theft. One lady steals from another woman. Money is taken out of her bag. There is lots of shouting with men mixing into the fray.

We arrive in Kitwe at 8 P.M. No one is at the bus station to meet me. Did they not think that I will be on the second bus if I am not on the first one? I take a taxi to Kabulanda Market. (I remember the name this time.) It is dark and I do not recognize anything familiar. New shops and shelters have been erected since my last visit. A couple of boys try to help me find London's house. They lead me along all kinds of paths that lead through tall grass. I know this is not the right way. I return and try again, this time, without their help.

After a few more queries, I finally recognize the right path and eventually reach his house. London is already sleeping. But he comes out and after a bath I am given a place to sleep in. It is a small room attached to the house that serves as his office. They find me a folding bed but there is no mattress for it only a spread that will have to serve as one. No blanket either so I will sleep in my clothes. The small mosquito net I am given will protect my face against some of them.

Surprisingly, I slept quite well. I spend the forenoon visiting with London. Then at 2 P.M. Rufus wanders in! He was not due until tomorrow, but the Lord had blessed him with good connections along the way. The youth choir sings for us before we move over to Evan's place where I had stayed on my last visit. Rufus and London are going to sleep here as well. I have the same bed as last time. Still no mattress!

Mwale drops in and tells of his trip to Malawi. He actually did go there after I had gone to his village in the dark. There are now two churches in that area where his relatives live. Praise the Lord!

There is a strong wind tonight and it rains heavily. I have to move the bed as it is dripping on my head at 4 A.M. I hear Rufus praying for a long time in the next room. I hear him again at daybreak. He must be burdened with something.

Life is normal this morning outside my window. People are walking about and vehicles are moving on their way. Nothing seems amiss. Yet last night before retiring, a teenager was hustled into a vehicle on this street and then it sped away. A crowd ran after it, past the house here, but failed to stop the kidnappers. I was then informed that this lad will be killed—his tongue, internal and outer organs removed and sold in Zaire! Others have shared his fate.

A delegation has arrived from Mbala district to join

43

those who have gathered here in Kitwe. We start off the assembly meeting with a service where I preach on Matthew 14:22–33. The following day we discuss the new constitution and bylaws which I had prepared ahead of time back in Kampala. It is a replica of the one we have in Uganda. It is adopted and the officers are chosen. London remains as chairman but Lungu is the new legal representative.

We close with a service Sunday morning with alot of choir numbers. I have them put me in the middle of the program for my sermon. As it is I come in an hour into the program. I preach on Ephesians 6:10–18. The Lord anoints the message and the Spirit moves. All want prayer. The choirs continue to sing, for an hour afterwards. It is again a three-hour service! I have found here in Zambia there are many choirs. The youth will sing all day and all night if you will listen!

I find the taxis are in tougher shape than I remember on previous safaris. The one I was in a couple of days ago had no upholstery on the ceiling nor on the sides! They all rattle and seem to be on their last mile!

I wake up early. Thoughts are of home. I guess I am getting homesick, especially for little Tiffy. I do not know how it will be after we move away from Uganda. I will be away from her for months and months. I purchase several Lady Bird books at a shop in town. Now I can read her some new stories when I get back home.

At the post office I place a call to Kampala. After an hour of waiting I have Marion on the line. It is hard to hear her, due to the noise in the room. There are two phones going at the same time. Reminds me of Kampala where everyone in earshot can hear what is being said because the one using the phone has to shout in order to be heard above the noise in the room. No privacy whatsoever!

I leave Evan's house and on my way to the taxi park we meet two policemen with two thieves handcuffed to each other. One officer wants to know why I am not staying with other whites. He then asks me for my passport. It is strange, when Europeans (whites) keep to themselves we are branded racists. And if we stay with Africans (blacks), they suspect us of wrongdoing! What should we do?

The bus leaves for Lusaka at eight o'clock. London and Lungu are along. This bus has a front window missing and when it rains, water comes inside. The door is wired shut after we get on the road. We arrive at 2:15 P.M. without a mishap. I end up at YWAM and sleep in a room in the back end of the servants' quarters as there are eleven young people from Switzerland staying in the house with Rhoades. London and Lungu look up their friends and are spending the night with them.

Kill a mosquito this morning which is full of blood. My blood! Walk over to the Registrar of Societies and there I meet London and Lungu. All the necessary steps are taken and the church's reregistration takes place. Our work done. I check on the price of a new Nissan Patrol and the time it will take to order one from them. It will take three to four months and cost about $25,000. I will need to ask the Mission Board to forward the amount to Japan so that the process can get started. We will need the vehicle as soon as we move here in five months time.

The day has finally arrived for me to return back to Uganda. I shave again at the water tap outside my room. It is too congested in Randy's house with all the YWAM youth. He drives me to the airport. Zambia Airways leaves only half an hour late. It is much better than

Kenya Airways. The plane passes over Mbugwe again and I see the old stamping grounds of yester years. Those years will always remain the highlight of my missionary career. They may not have been as fruitful as they have been in Uganda but it was home because we pioneered the work and lived in the bush. I catch a ride to Flora Hostel after the plane lands at Nairobi airport.

There is no flight to Entebbe until the day after tomorrow so I will have a full day of shopping in Nairobi for things I need which I cannot get in Kampala. While looking for a handle to fit the back door of our Nissan, I witness a lad snatching a handbag from a lady in a vehicle which had stopped for a red light. He had seen it lying on the seat beside her and reached through the window which was partly open. Fortunately, a man standing right there on the sidewalk grabs the thief before he can take off. But the man lets him go after the thief drops the bag! He should have held onto him for the police.

Finally, I am on the flight to Entebbe which leaves 45 minutes late. It is hot inside the cabin all the way. It takes some time for my luggage to come through once I am inside the airport. Marion and Kirk are there waiting for me. She is not completely rid of her pain in the gallbladder. It is nice traveling in Kirk's vehicle back to Kampala as he does not have to stop at the roadblocks because of the UN license plates. The Stevensons come over and we visit. Tiffany wants me to read one of the books I bought her on my trip. This I do gladly. I have been away for 18 days!

*   *   *

Lungu and London are at the airport as I fly in on

time with Zambia Airways from Nairobi. The taxi takes us directly to the Salvation Army headquarters where we will be staying the next four nights. I have scheduled my trip to Zambia at this time so as to also attend the Evangelical Fellowship of Zambia (EFZ) annual conference. This year happens to be their 25th anniversary. I wish to familiarize myself with the work that is being done by other missionaries and churches here in this country.

After breakfast all of us are transported from the hostel to Mulungushi Hall where the conference will be held. It is officially opened with an address by the Prime Minister of Zambia. He and his entourage remain for the noon meal in the dining hall. I attend the sessions that are scheduled throughout the three days and enjoy them. When the conference is over, I move over to Rhoades until my departure for Uganda, at which time Lungu and London will travel to Petauke. I find the house swarming with young people as on my previous visit.

There are two Zambian fellows with YWAM and I bunk with them in the servants' quarters. I continue my visit with Paffett Chomanika and his wife who are from Malawi. They came to participate in the conference and also to complete their course with YWAM. We talk about starting churches in Paffett's country. The Lord surely brought us together! I trust that this is the answer to the beginning of the church in Malawi.

I wander over to Ridgeway Hotel, which is just across the street, for a few minutes. There is a Big Five Tours receptionist in the lobby. I walk over and browse through their brochures. The one on the Luangwa National Park interests me, so I ask the lady behind the desk for their prices. In the course of our conversation she asks me where I am from, and I reply "Canada." She then tells me that she was there for a course two years ago. While there she met a girl from Swift Current, Saskatchewan, and had gone with her to see her parents one weekend. They told her about some missionaries working in Zambia whom she has been trying to meet ever since her return.

Marion has many relatives in that area of Saskatchewan. In fact, while holding services in Swift Current last year during home assignment, the Beisels did inform us that their daughter had brought a Zambian girl with her to visit them. I mention this to her. We stare at each other. Can it be? We introduce ourselves. Upon hearing each other's names, our mouths drop open. Incredible! She is Dora Chanda, the girl Beisels had told us about. We had gotten a letter from her earlier but the address was Ndola and not Lusaka. When I pointed this out, she tells me that her agent transferred her just recently to this place. What a small world! A chance meeting like this must be one in a million.

I manage to complete all the business that I came here to do in Lusaka, including applying for a work permit which I will need in order to reside in Zambia. While on home assignment I had explained my call to Zambia, which I received on my first visit to this Central African country, to the Mission Board. I had pointed out to them the strategical importance of my residing in Zambia so as to reach the surrounding nations with the gospel. They gave their approval to our move.

It is cold this morning, much colder than Uganda, as I shave again at the tap outside. I need to be at the airport by 6:30 A.M. But I need not have rushed, for Zambia Airways leaves one and a half hour late! While on the hour stop over at Dar es Salaam I come down with malaria in the plane. There is a fever and then chills. I shiver all over and cannot control the shaking! The cold bath this morning back in Lusaka must have triggered it.

My back is very sore. It has been for the last couple of days. I thought it was due to the wooden bunk I was sleeping on at YWAM. When I arrive at Nairobi I take the bus to town. The first phone call I make is to Mark in Canada and learn that he will be arriving the first week in June. That is only three weeks away! It has been a year since we last have seen him. The second call is to the Mission Board. I remind them again to send $25,000 to Japan for the new vehicle I will need in Zambia. The answer I receive is that there is no money for it! Sick with malaria, that is the last answer I wished to hear. I am devastated! They say big men do not cry. You want to bet?

The buses are overcrowded as it is the hour when employees knock off from work and head home. I am still running a fever punctuated with chills. I cannot stand around any longer and resolve to walk up to Flora Hostel before it gets dark. It is too dangerous to walk alone at night. By the time I arrive, my shoulders are cramped from carrying my luggage. I perspired a lot during my walk in spite of light rain falling on me all the way.

I am in time for supper but I feel too tough to eat. To stop my shaking, I take a hot shower and crawl under the covers. Bob Edwards drops in and finds me in bed. We visit awhile and he prays for me before leaving. I am low in body and in spirit. I pray: "Lord, renew my strength and lift my soul to a higher plain!"

The night is an uphill struggle. I have a fever most of the time. To compound my aches and pains, my throat is sore this morning. I must have picked it up walking to the hostel yesterday as I was wet with perspiration and the air was chilly and damp. The weather outside today is still cold and rainy which will not help my condition any. Oh, the rigors of being on the road!

I catch a ride to the airport where I board Uganda

Airlines and fly on to Entebbe. Tim is here to pick me up and we drive back to Kampala. I find Colleen, Tiffany, and Natasha at our place and it is time to catch up with what has transpired since we last saw one another ten days ago. Tiffany is overjoyed at seeing me. She is not ready to leave Opa when Mom and Dad are ready to leave. But I need a hot bath and rest, as malaria is still dogging me. Marion wants to talk so we are up late anyway.

Five
Sorcery & Witchcraft

It is only fitting that before I leave, I share a few of the practices that many Ugandans still adhere to that prevent the light of the gospel from ever entering deep into their lives. Christianity will only be superficial if they remain in the shadow of their beliefs in sorcery and witchcraft. May God help them to step out into the light of His Word and then walk faithfully in it!

Sorcery is practiced by either sex in different tribes throughout the country. It is not an art that he or she is born with, but rather, it is learned. It is brought about by envy, hatred, and quarreling. It is also associated with fear, illness (such as dysentery, leprosy, fits, madness, miscarriage, barrenness, impotence), and death. Many believe that there are more women than men who are sorcerers. The reason is that a man has more opportunities to work off his hostilities in fighting, at beer parties and elsewhere. The woman's social world is more restricted, causing her to be more stressed out. A polygamous marriage provides the right kind of atmosphere for sorcery. It is well known that the co-wives of the man practice it against one another. Even in marriages where there is only one wife, husbands will often accuse their wives of sorcery. It seldom exists between a brother and sister as their interests are not the same. But brothers do practice it against each other for they may have contrary interests. Sorcery between the man and his mother's relatives rarely occurs.

An innocent man needs not fear sorcery. It is only effective against the wrongdoer. Rich individuals are more likely to be attacked by their poor, envious neighbours than the other way around. When someone believes he is a victim of sorcery, he consults a diviner to find out whether his assumptions are right. If the diviner confirms that his troubles are due to sorcery, he will indicate who the sorcerer is. He has used the method of deduction in the list of suspects that his client had shared earlier with him in the interview. The diviner will give him some medicine to drink, or make small cuts on his body and rub medicine into them. Bleeding the client by means of a horn applied to his back may also be used by the diviner as a treatment.

A sorcerer is someone who wants to kill those whom he hates. His victim may be one who has stolen from him, or is richer than he. He may kill him by putting poison in his food or drink, a powder made from dried leaves of a plant. Or, he may conceal the poison on the path that the victim will take. Then, he may just blow it in the direction of his victim. When it finds him it will kill him. Most medicines are made from certain plants and trees, but snake venom and crocodile gall are also used. A small horn of a cow, goat, or duiker filled with medicine and hidden in or outside the victim's house will kill anyone who steps over or under it. The sorcerer will also resort to burning the person's house at night with the intention of killing him and his family.

There are cases where a spirit may be involved. It must then be invited to possess the patient so that it can be dealt with. To acquire this, a seance is held, which could go on for days. When the possession has taken place, the spirit begins to speak through its host, informing those present as to who it is, why it came, and what it wants. To begin with, the spirit is urged to leave the person alone. If it does not agree, then it is coaxed to enter into a friendly relationship with its host. The spirit may now require the person to make sacrifices to it periodically for the rest of his life. As well, it may want him to build a shrine for it.

This possession may turn out to be a profitable thing for the host, especially if the spirit is able to foretell the future. He can now become a diviner, even sit at seances where others have been afflicted by a spirit. These are sources of income for him.

What is witchcraft? Again, my dictionary states that it is magic power or influence. So, a witch is a man or woman who is supposed to have magic powers and uses them to do evil. The witch doctor is also a medicine man. The difference between a sorcerer and a witch is in their respective motivations. A sorcerer is set into doing things by what is happening around him, which give rise to feelings of ill will, such as envy, hatred, and jealousy. The witch, on the other hand, harms others in all kinds of ways and is concerned mainly about satisfying his own desires including the eating of human flesh. A man may use sorcery just once in his lifetime while the witch is a continuous evildoer. It is possible for one to steer clear of becoming a victim of sorcery if he is able to avoid arousing the anger of jealousy of others. But no one, no matter how careful he may be, is safe from the attack of a witch.

Who is a witch? No one really knows. You may suspect one or more individuals, but you are not certain. He can be the one you meet daily, one who pretends to care about you. The person next door may be one. Even your own brother, or your wife, who is an ordinary person by day but a witch by night! We experienced this back in Tanzania where the wife of one of our church members was a witch without his knowledge. She almost succeeded in poisoning him had it not been for Marion who was called in time to treat him. Leba recovered and his wife was shunned by everyone from then on. She ended up walking alone, even after she accepted the Lord.

Many do not fear the witches of other villages, but fear the ones in their own community. They believe that witches do not attack outsiders, only those of their own village.

Ugandans are constantly threatened by diseases. They are subject to most of the diseases found in temperate and tropical regions. Clinics up-country are far in between, in many places non-existent. Traditional medicine is often ineffective to cure their ills and pains. Most do not know the causes of their diseases. All they know is that today you are well, and then tomorrow you are sick. The following day you may be dead. Witchcraft offers an explanation for these calamities that have come upon you. It is used to explain why something happens to you at just that time. For instance: why did the snake bite you and not the person walking along the path directly in front of you? Witchcraft provides the answer.

As with sorcerers, witches can cause crop failure, sickness, and death. In fact, many still meet at the end of their mourning ceremony to try and find out who the witch is that caused the person's death. It is diviners and sorcery removers who are most often suspected of being a witch. Because a diviner is known to have power to detect witches, his familiarity with their ways renders him a perfect suspect. We found this belief in Tanzania as well.

There are witches who may use either sorcery or

witchcraft to achieve their evil goals. A witch, who can be either man or woman, is born, not made. There are cases, though, where a witch may make a witch out of an ordinary person by placing a magical potion in the candidate's native beer. Or, by visiting the person in his or her dream. The witch walks about naked at night without a light. He or she wanders about rapping on doors frightening those inside. A trap can be set for the witch, after all they are still human beings, by removing the door off its hinges and then leaning it against the frame. When the witch raps on it next time, it will fall inwards and he or she will be exposed. The occupants will promptly give the witch a severe beating, often proving fatal.

The witch, like an ordinary person, is vulnerable to physical attacks, which is enough to scare him or her away. Ugandans who must walk at night usually carry a strong stick. But it is rare to see anyone walking alone at night, not only for fear of meeting a witch but also to avoid being suspected of being one as well. A witch once discovered will have his house burned and his or her property destroyed. And, in some cases, he or she may be put to death. The witch is never avenged.

It is a deadly insult to accuse someone in public of being a witch, or of using witchcraft on you. Most prefer consulting a diviner who will discover the witch for you for a fee, of course. He will then prescribe counter-magic to nullify the witchcraft. Or he may advise you take a gift to the person whose anger you have provoked. This may mean eating and drinking with him. If the offended person blows his drink on you, he has forgiven you. It is also possible for you to buy magical charms that will protect you against a witch. These charms turn the intended harm back against the witch.

Witches commit incest, one of the worst kinds of all

sexual transgressions. They also feast on corpses of their victims which are dug up, as we discovered in Bukedi district. A witch will eat any dead he or she may find lying about. Burial used to be uncommon, especially in Bugisu, and the dead were discarded in seldom visited areas in their forests. These places were believed to be haunts of witches and were avoided. When we were looking for property near Boliso, a heavy forest was off limits to us. I was informed that it was a place for the dead.

Women, and sometimes men, are also able to have the evil eye. (This was very common among the Wambugwe women in Tanzania.) She is able to do harm by excessive staring. Children, young animals, and gardens are especially vulnerable to the evil eye. Charms, the most common one is a yellow fruit which grows wild in most areas, are hung around their necks or in their gardens for protection. When I first saw this yellow fruit, which looks like a small apple, hanging around the child's neck I believed it to be a cheap form of decoration. But, then I eventually discovered that it was a charm. There is always more to it then what meets the eye here in Africa!

A man often suspects his father-in-law of witchcraft. The reason is that his father-in-law is never satisfied with the dowry (bride price) which is always being increased after marriage. The installments of payment are never ending. The man cannot openly express his frustrations to his father-in-law as their relationship is one of respect. In the event of a quarrel with his wife, she will side with her father. A woman, in some tribes, retains certain birth rights, and marriage does not transfer her completely to her husband's lineage. She is to some extent a stranger in her married home. It is easy therefore for the man to believe that there is witchcraft being practiced on him in an effort to grasp his property.

When things do not go well with sexual reproduction, a newly married woman is likely to blame the spite of her husband's lineage and accuse him of bewitching her. She is likely to go back to her father and convince him to return the dowry that has been paid. She is likely to succeed, for no father will readily admit that a daughter of his is barren. He chooses to believe that her childlessness is the result of witchcraft.

In the polygamous society, it is the rich who can afford more than one wife. He must treat his wives alike, dividing his land equally among them. Each wife receives her own hut. The children too are treated alike. But most agree that the relationship between his wives is often not as harmonious and friendly as it ought to be. Jealousy between them is almost inevitable and the use of witchcraft on each other is quite common. A wife is quick to accuse one or the other co-wives of using love potions, or charms, to lure the husband's affections away from her. No woman at the time of delivery should be attended to by a co-wife lest a portion of the afterbirth be used against her in witchcraft. If a child sickens, or dies, the mother usually blames a co-wife.

Beliefs in spirits and ancestral worship have suffered greatly because of the teachings of Christ in Uganda, but witchcraft beliefs have changed little from olden times. Witchcraft forms an important part in their traditional religion as it provides answers to their supernatural causes of misfortune. With the weakening of other practices, witchcraft has become the main scapegoat for their calamities. The Christian finds it hard to accept witchcraft; they cannot walk hand-in-hand together. They are independent of each other in their beliefs. Because of it, Christianity has in some ways contributed to the persistence of witchcraft beliefs.

Marion visiting with the Stevensons and the Hoffmans.

Tiffany with Ugandan playmates.

Downtown Kampala.

Ashling, Tiffany, and Natasha enjoying themselves.

Kirk standing on the equator.

Near the source of the Nile River.

We sight the elusive forest gorilla in Bwindi.

Tim, Colleen, and Kirk in Bwindi National Park.

Tiffany inspecting the new generator.

Sunset on Lake Victoria.

Ashling with her pet monkey.

Boat used for evangelism on Lake Victoria.

Some TEE books used in training pastors.

Bikes for the district chairmen.

Colleen assisting villagers with food.

Colleen directing supplies for school children.

Murchison Falls on the Nile River.

Tim and Colleen on the rim of the Murchison Falls.

With Colleen and Tim in search of gorillas.

Sailing to an island on Lake Victoria.

A pygmy at service in Rwanda.

Tiffany with a baby chimpanzee.

Dedicating pulpit to her mother's memory.

On the way to Lolui Island on Lake Victoria.

Kirk, Karen, Ashling, Shaina, and Mikaela.

Tim, Colleen, Tiffany, Natasha, Jesse, and Logan.

Visiting with Francis, Moses, and his wife.

With Tim, Mianitse of Zaire, and Rwandan pastor.

Church youth in Zaire.

Youth choir at the Sake Church, Zaire.

Angoli cattle on Ugandan hilltop.

Preaching at a Rwandan service.

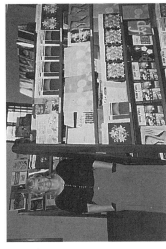

Double-story multi-purpose building in Kasubi.

Colleen in bookroom at Kasubi, Kampala.

Tiffany as flower girl at Anna and Moses' wedding.

Colleen with Mary, the first woman to be ordained.

Church at Boliso, Bukedi District.

Marion sharing in the church service.

A goat given to me on Church Dedication Day.

Farewell service with David Wiebe and Tim.

Six
Winding Down

As I ponder over my leaving Uganda, I come face to face with having to say farewell to those I have come to love, those who through God's guidance have matured into leaders of the church here in Uganda. Looking back over our years here, I find the years have been full of adventures, and many of them filled with danger. I have shared them in my previous book, *Amid Perils Often,* so I will not repeat them in this one. I could not have wished for a field more whiter than the one I found here in this land. At an average we planted one church each week! We now have 320 churches in just six years with 18,300 members. Of course, this took a lot of physical effort and there were many times when I thought I could not go on. I overtaxed my heart often. Piri piri (chilli pepper) was my constant companion on the trips up-country, as I licked that hot stuff in order to keep my heart pumping. No one will really know how close I came to laying down my life for His sake. But He still has more for me to do as I am yet capable to walk with the best of them.

Lest you think that all our experiences have been of a serious nature, let me share one that has a lighter side to it.

Marion and I arrive at Kapiri where we have a congregation nestled against a hill in eastern Uganda. It is a hot and dry day. Gideon and his wife are there to greet us. They are both in rags. This whole area needs the energizing power of the Holy Spirit. There is a spirit of laziness about the place. The people want everything to be done for them. Mud bricks were mortared a year ago for the church building and they have been lying on a pile ever since—waiting for money to come their way so that someone can be hired to erect the church for them. The whole atmosphere is one of not caring.

The big problem here is pombe (native beer). They love to drink and many are drunkards. Their houses are poorly built and many are collapsing. Most follow witchcraft and as a result there is much darkness. We do thank you, Lord, for the toehold we have here, but now we need spirit-filled men who will not tolerate sin. We are praying for His transforming power to change lives here in this dark area.

While sitting under a tree waiting for the evening meal to be served, Marion and I overhear the following conversation between Gideon, the local leader, and Rufus the evangelist, whom we brought along with us.

"I couldn't do more in my TEE (Theological Education by Extension) studies because the ink in my pen dried up," Gideon explains.

"Don't the shops have any more pens?" asks Rufus.

"I suppose they do," Gideon replies.

"When did your ink leave the pen?" Rufus continues.

"I don't remember when the ink left," says Gideon.

"Was it in this year of 1984?" asks Rufus.

The reply is, "Yes, it was in 1984."

"What month was it? Was it in August or September, or October, or this month?" continues Rufus.

"I believe it was last month that there was no more

ink," Gideon says, "so therefore I could not finish my book because the ink was not there."

Rufus questions him further, "So you didn't go to the shop?"

"No," replies Gideon, "the shop probably does not have any pens."

"Have you tried to buy pens?"

"No, not yet."

"All this time and you have not tried?"

"No, not yet."

"When are you going to buy a pen? Until the new year?" Gideon laughs.

Rufus continues, "Are pens so expensive in these shops?"

"No, not too much money."

"Then, to finish your studies you must buy one."

Gideon concludes, "Yes, I think so."

On a weekend at Kinyonga, Marion finds herself sitting and listening to women sharing their problems. One has lost her baby to measles and lets out her grief. Another one's maize is drying up because of no rain. One woman's husband was killed during the recent civil war and they now will have to have a day of remembrance. A cow will be slaughtered and all their friends and relatives will come to grieve the death of her husband. Another woman shares about her recent trip to Kenya where all her things were stolen at the border by custom officials. Still another complains about the prices that have gone up to the point where they now live very simply because they cannot afford even soap, oil, salt, sugar, or tea. They are just surviving. By the time everyone gets done talking, Marion is totally exhausted. She excuses herself and retires to the Nissan for some rest. She has been a channel for the women to share their burdens. She must now lay them at the feet of Jesus if she herself is to have the strength to carry on.

Marion's prayer has always been that her life may be one to bring a breath of fresh air to the monotonous lives of these dear women. Sitting beside their grass-roofed, mud and wattle huts, she has witnessed the simple and ordinary life they live. She has watched them fetch water from a distant stream with pots on their heads, bring back bundles of washed clothes, chop fire wood, peel countless green bananas, shell ground nuts for the sauce that goes with matoke (the cooked mashed plantains), hush the crying babies they have tied to their backs or swing them around to the front for nursing. Marion does have a tremendous task of trying to add joy and light to their lives!

At Boliso in Bukedi District, Marion is asked to assist the chairman's wife with her delivery. While in Tanzania, she had done this often. So while I am busy with the pastors giving them their TEE tests, she sits beside the hut waiting for Selina to begin her delivery. During this time Marion sews together, by hand, blocks of material for the women's work. Young girls nearby are peeling sweet potatoes and cassava, and also shelling ground nuts. Two of the smaller ones are carrying naked babies. One other infant is old enough to sit alone on the ground. Another girl is preparing kuni. Others are approaching with containers of water on their heads, walking gracefully with a sway at their waist. Old ladies of the village roost a short distance away, awaiting the outcome of this public event. A few younger ones are unbraiding their hair so that they can rebraid them into a different style. Birds are singing overhead in a nearby tree. Then, a rooster crows.

It is time to check Selina once more. She is lying on a

sack in the middle of the dirt floor and is ready to commence delivering her baby. Not a whimper or a cry passes her lips as she struggles to bring a new life into the African world. The cord is wrapped around the neck of the infant which Marion quickly pulls over the head. It is another girl, her fourth one. No boy again. There is no excitement when the announcement is made. The father-in-law says, "It would have been better if it was a boy." They promptly name the girl Marion.

We are up at 5:30 and an hour later I leave for Busiro in southeast Uganda. It is a four-hour drive. I find Francis Ouma, the district chairman, and his crew are not yet back with the boats from Jinja. I wait for him. He finally arrives at noon. We eat and visit while someone searches for fuel to put into the engine for the boat. We have to use a motor this time as the wind is blowing in from the wrong direction to sail to Sigulu Island. As we wait, the women show me the quilts they have sewn together from the blocks and patches that Marion and Colleen have given them. Margaret, who used to work for us in our house, is one of those women.

It is sunset when we launch the boat, christened "Safina," which means "the Ark" in the Swahili language. There are 20 of us sailing. It is 45 feet in length and able to carry 40 passengers, I am told. Funds from my Aunt Erica in Canada helped make this mode of transport possible for the gospel to be carried to these islands in Lake Victoria. Our first stop is at Buduma Island where we inform the residents that we will be returning for a service tomorrow. The engine fails us soon after leaving Buduma. We end up paddling until 10 P.M. when the wind changes in our favour. It usually does not do this until well after midnight. The sails are lifted and we pull into our destination an hour later on the west end of Sigulu Island.

There is some singing by the locals before we can call it quits. It is midnight when I turn in with an empty stomach as there was no food ready for us. I am wiped out.

I sleep on my safari mattress on the dirt floor in one of their huts. A rooster gives me his wake-up call at 5:30. He and some of his female friends shared the hut with me. I was so bushed when I turned in last night that I fell asleep in my traveling clothes. I take a shave and a hot bath in an enclosure made from banana leaves. Then we wait around for the wind to swing in our favour. This it does at 10 A.M. Instead of disembarking immediately, the islanders begin asking for medicine, which I have brought along. Then they want a worship service followed by many who request prayer for their needs. It concludes with them presenting me with a live goat to take home. After all this, we are not yet ready to leave as the men are still repairing the sails. No one moves to do a thing until it is time to go! That is, time to go according to my clock as I need to get back to Kampala tonight.

It is not until two o'clock before we push off from Sigulu. The rope to raise the sail is rotten and before long it snaps and the pole falls on top of our heads. I manage to lift my hands in time and catch one end of it. Outside of this incident, the boat sails beautifully. We do stop in at Buduma Island as planned, even though we are running late. I have given in and we walk to where the church is located. I am told it is nearby, but it turns out to be about a mile inland. The members have been waiting since morning to meet us! After the worship service, I am presented with a hen, eggs, and a small wooden replica of the boat "Safina," plus a painting of the boat depicting the missionary coming to them, Bible in hand, with the gospel.

We reach Busiro at 6 P.M. It is now too late to carry on

to Kampala. I will have to leave early in the morning. I treat the sick who show up from nowhere. Then, we have time to hold a worship service where I share the Word of God. There is a short business meeting with the local authorities as well before everyone beds down for the night. I am sleeping in a hut that serves as a dispensary until a proper building is erected. There is much malaria at this place because of the nearby lake. Mosquitoes bombard me throughout the night. Rats scurry back and forth. They enter the cabinet where the medicines are kept. There they set up quite a racket knocking over bottles and boxes. I pull the sleeping bag around my ears so that the rats do not nibble on them and so the mosquitoes do not help themselves to too much of my blood. I wake up in the morning wet with perspiration from being bundled inside the sleeping bag all night. I managed to get just five hours of sleep. I am off to an early start and reach Kampala at ten o'clock.

Talking about rats, Uganda is cursed with them! Everywhere I have gone in this country, I have run across rats. Even on the islands. Here in Kampala we are unable to get rid of them in our house no matter how much poisoned bait we put out. The workmen on the yard tell us that they keep coming over from the neighbours. There is no end to these creatures! One gave me quite a fright one morning at 5 A.M. when I was sitting on the toilet bowl. I heard this splashing below me and I discovered when I took a peek that a rat was trying to get out! How did it get in there? I placed the plunger over it and promptly flushed it down.

There are still troubled areas in northern Uganda which hinder us from moving about freely. Reports keep coming in of killings of Red Cross workers, of a missionary couple, and of one priest and four nuns. This is all taking place in areas where I have travelled recently! But in spite of this, the church keeps growing and miracles continue to take place. Here in Kampala gunfire is heard almost nightly. We are grateful for the continued protection the Lord is giving us. Recently, the house we lived in for five years was robbed. (We moved because the rent had become too steep.) Our guardian angels moved with us! Where would we be without their help? There was a lot of gunfire a few nights ago and we learned that there had been a robbery two houses from us. The thieves who did it ran past the Stevensons' gate, who live below us, without breaking into their place. May their angels as well continue to watch over and protect them in their comings and goings!

In spite of all the vehicles that have been stolen during our time in Uganda, many of those at gunpoint where the occupants also lost their lives, we have escaped unscathed for which we thank God. Only once did our Nissan Patrol receive a major scrape. That happened not in war-torn Uganda, but in peaceful Kenya! Marion and I had driven there to attend a missionary retreat. We stopped in at Kima Mission station for the night which is just north of Kisumu. Here is where the Ludwigs, the Lafonts, Shultzes, and other missionaries lived and worked. There are graves among the trees which remind us that they were here, and then remained here. A large cathedral stands on this compound. It is where the head offices of the Church of God in Kenya is located.

In the morning early, as my habit is, I turn on the BBC for the latest news, especially on Uganda as the local stations do not report what is really happening. I will have to go downstairs to the vehicle as there is no radio in the apartment. As I reach the door to the stairway, which is outside, I hear what sounds like a bomb. It cannot be!

We are not in Kampala! I open the door and prepare to rush down the stairs and find out what caused the explosion. Marion is right behind me and I feel her suddenly grab my arm. She shouts, "Stop, there is no stairway!" In my haste I was looking ahead of me and not down. Without her warning I would have plunged headlong onto a pile of rubble! There are bricks and broken timbers scattered everywhere below us!

Grabbing ahold of what is left of a stairway I lower myself down. What now meets my eyes almost turns me to tears. There stands our Nissan and the front half of the side that is facing the house is all smashed in! The back half barely missed the hurling bricks since it was hidden by the house. Had I parked the vehicle a bit further ahead, the whole side would have received the full force of the explosion. There is a huge gaping hole in the side of the house. What caused this immense damage? The geyser, or hot water heater, had not been switched off by the occupant who stays in the apartment below ours. Apparently the thermostat quit working. Thank God the occupant was not home.

It is incredible what just happened here! Had the geyser exploded a minute later, I would have been inside the Nissan and also received the full force of the blast from those hurling bricks. I would surely have been killed! Not in dangerous Uganda, but on a mission station in Kenya! God must still need my services here below.

We may not have had our vehicle stolen, but now and then some items do turn up missing in our house, especially in the kitchen. Foods, such as sugar, salt, oil, and fruit, are the main victims, with cutlery occasionally missing. Because the house girls live on the compound it is not difficult to discover the loot. Upon questioning them, they usually confess and ask to be forgiven. One, when asked why she did it, replied, "Mkono mrefu!" ("A long arm!") She blamed it on her arm that was too long. I had to turn aside and smother my chuckle as it was quite funny.

Handling a theft by a male proves more difficult. They must be cornered and hit over the head with the proof before a confession can be squeezed out of them. Lying comes easier with them than telling the truth. David, who worked for us on the yard, is a fine example. Marion and I were away at the time when the following incident took place. Tim and Colleen were in our house at the time and he dealt with the following incident.

David is the watchman this particular night. Before going to bed, Tim goes out to check with him on how things are outside. He cannot find David anywhere on the compound. But when he looks inside his room, he finds David fast asleep! Instead of waking him up, Tim picks up the clothes and coat he was wearing and takes them into the house with him. In the morning. Colleen and Tim hear a loud commotion outside. They hear David shouting at the house girls who are laughing at him. Tim goes outside and finds David in his red undershorts. When asked what the problem is, he says that a thief came during the night, tied him up, and stole all his clothes. He will not change his story as to what happened during the night. Tim has him write it down so that the Bwana can deal with it when he returns.

It takes several days before Marion and I return home. By then Tim had to reveal to David that it was he who had taken his clothes that night. This really caught David with his mouth wide open! Until then he had thought that everyone was taken with his story. He began to beg Tim not to reveal to the Bwana what had happened. The clothes were given back to him and all that was left to do was to await my decision on the case. What do I do? This was not his first offense, there were so many before that. This was the last straw as far as I was concerned. David was fired and sent back to Busia, where he came from. He could no longer be trusted.

Because of the decal on the door of our vehicle, which bears the name of our church, we are easy prey for not only beggars, but cheats as well. Now, who is lying and who is telling the truth is what you must quickly decide when he approaches you for help. It does not take me long to respond when I see his leprous hands or elephantiasic feet. (But for the grace of God there go I.) It is a different matter though when the man, dressed in a suit and tie, says he knows you from some government office or border point. His request is usually for a loan which he promises to pay back as soon as we meet again. If he is genuine, he can make it rough for me should I refuse, especially if he is connected with the immigration department. The truth is I will never see him again. He is nothing but a con-artist. I usually discover this after some questions of my own, such as "At which border post did we meet?"

But there is one time while in Nairobi that I am not awake enough and end up a few shillings less in my pocket as a result. I had parked the Nissan Patrol on a side street and then gone shopping. Returning an hour later I find a note under the windscreen wiper. It states that her worker had foiled an attempt by a thief to steal the wheel of our vehicle. Would I be so kind as to reward the lad with a pound? Just then a young man steps forward and says that the note was written by his employer, a British lady, who lives at Karen. Hello! This is a new one! Must be genuine. After all it is only the British who still call the twenty shilling note a pound. I am in a hurry and hand him the money. He disappears down the street.

Then, it hits me! I am parked in front of a bank! I ask the security guard whether he saw anyone trying to remove a tire from my vehicle. His reply is that he has noticed no one. I reread the note and recognize words that only an African would use. Except for the word pound, the terminology is certainly not European. Might as well admit it. I have been had. Sucker!

Upon seeing the Ugandan license plates on the streets of Nairobi, individuals stalk our vehicle and claim to be fleeing from the civil war back in Uganda. They are now refugees in Kenya and need assistance in order to survive. I ask them where they come from, and they are unable to give me the name of their village. And if they do, they fail to speak the language that belongs to the tribe in that area, not even a few words. They do not know that I have travelled extensively in Uganda and am well acquainted with most places and the language they use in that particular tribe. Recognizing that they have been discovered, they leave quietly.

Do we ever try to report or apprehend any of the above culprits? No. It is your word against theirs. The police think you are making too much of nothing. After all, can you not part with some of your riches?

Marion and Colleen are off to Boliso where there is a two-day women's seminar. It turns out well with about 500 women present, plus pastors, youth, and children. There is a mass of people, yet those in charge managed to serve food to everyone. The ladies return home late with four hens and a turkey as gifts from the Boliso women. Marion is ready for a bath and then off to bed. There are other seminars that Marion and Colleen attend in different districts. They leave home, the Nissan loaded with used clothing, material, and quilt blocks to be given to the women's groups. And they always return excited about the progress taking place where they have been! They have not labored in vain.

Marion has to have a second operation which takes place here in Kampala where Tiffany and Natasha were born. The doctor discovers the cause of the infection which has persisted since her first operation three months earlier in Nairobi when her gallbladder was removed. It is lodged in one of the inner stitches which happens to be nylon, and not dissolvable. After the operation she recovers quickly. There is now no more pain or drainage as before. Praise the Lord! She is back to normal and feels great.

Our son Mark visits us for two months. He needs to get acquainted with his three nieces—Tiffany, Natasha, and Ashling. Kirk is still with UNICEF and stationed here in Kampala. Karen has started to teach in the International School. The couple recently donated funds for a central church to be built at Boliso in Bukedi District.

Colleen is busy overseeing the schools up-country plus the day care centre here in Kampala. I accompany her on one of her trips to help distribute powdered milk, supplied by Compassion International, to hundreds of children in two of the schools in eastern Uganda. We had to travel over some bush roads to get there. She also assists the schools with textbooks which are shipped in by containers from various donor countries. Most of the day-care children, as well as many orphans throughout Uganda, are being sponsored by Kinderhilfswerk, Germany. Colleen is a very busy woman! She will be even busier after her mother leaves and the women's work becomes her responsibility. May you, Lord, give her that added strength she needs when the time comes.

Reinhard Berle, the director of Kinderhilfswerk, continues to visit us and the Stevensons. He has been instrumental in helping Colleen with orphans whose parents have died of AIDS and with assisting in the projects that Tim lines up for him. The Leadership Training Centre, funded entirely by the Church of God in Western Canada, is dedicated just before we leave to move to Zambia. David and Myrtle Wiebe, representing the Canadian Board of Missions, are present for the official opening. This two-story structure houses the executive offices, classrooms, a room for the women, one for the youth, and a bookstore. Tim Stevenson spent countless hours in erecting this magnificent building to the glory of God and for the church in Uganda.

Our farewell service is held in the new building and it lasts four hours! I hand out certificates to 12 graduates in the TEE program and pray for three leaders who are getting ordained, one of them being Moses Abasoola. There is a lot of nice singing. I will miss their musical instruments, especially the dungu which is a stringed instrument and comes in various sizes. There is a speech of appreciation before I give my sermon. Following the service there is food and the giving of gifts with more singing. Marion and I received some very nice gifts. It was an enjoyable time.

Now comes the time of packing our things together into crates which are going to be shipped to Lusaka as soon as we have a house there to move into. I am up until midnight each night, and sometimes later. We end up getting all that we want to take with us into ten crates. The day that we leave Uganda, August 30, 1989, we are taken to the airport at Entebbe by Tim, Colleen, and their two children Tiffany and Natasha. We arrive at ten o'clock. Our luggage is 16 kilograms overweight but the lady does not charge us extra. Another nice thing she did for us is give us two seats up front right behind first class. Customs does not go into our luggage. All in all, we are given an excellent send-off by the officials.

It is hard to say goodbye to the Stevensons, even though we will be returning in December when Colleen is expecting her third child. We have been together in the work here for four years, sharing one another's burdens and joys. Now we will be on our own, with neither couple being able to drop in at each other's house for a chat and that proverbial cup of tea. And what about Tiffany, who has been so close to me? I will miss her tremendously! She does not yet know that Opa will be away much longer this time than any of his previous journeys.

ZAMBIA

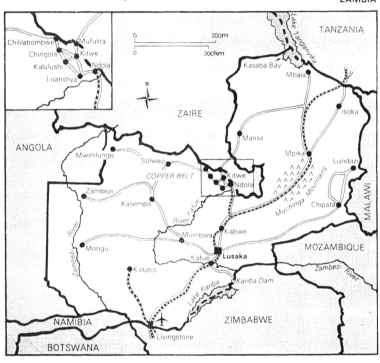

Seven
Shuttling Back & Forth

Marion and I arrive in Lusaka, Zambia, September 1, 1989. On the way I had prayed that the Lord would give us a sign when we reach Lusaka that He will be with us in our ministry. Marion is quite disturbed about the whole affair with Mbumba and London. Upon our arrival at the airport, we find our work permit waiting for us! This is the sign He has given us to show that He will be with us! We are now residents in Zambia. Lusaka is situated on the Great North Road, the very same one that runs by Kaiti Mission, where we resided for 15 years while in Tanzania.

Randy Rhoades of YWAM meets us at the airport and drives us to the Baptist guesthouse where we will be staying until we find a house to rent. He is able to pack us, our luggage, the guitar, and two of our church leaders who came to welcome us, into his small vehicle which has seen better days. The following days we go shopping for groceries and get acquainted with such places as the post office, civic centre, and the bank. The current rate is 16 kwacha to the US dollar. We find everything quite expensive. We had hoped things would be cheaper than in Uganda. The new Nissan Patrol, we discover, will not be arriving until November. That is a long time to be afoot. The taxis are small and well-worn both inside and under the hood.

85

I am finally able to get through to Kampala and talk to Colleen after six days of trying. I tell her of our safe arrival. Tiffany wants to say something so I talk to her. She says she is going to find me and then come on a plane for a visit. I guess she is wondering where I have gone off to. I miss reading her stories. It would be so nice to visit our grandchildren tonight.

We travel by bus to Kitwe where we have several churches. There is a welcome service for us tomorrow. Bob Edwards, the Regional Director who flew in from Nairobi, is with us. We are taken to the Ecumenical Centre for the night by the church leaders. It is a much better place than Buchi Hotel where I was taken last time. A real noisy joint that place was.

There are over 500 present in the Sunday service, which is being held in Buchi Hall. There is lots of singing with choirs from the youth and the women. Marion and I have our turn at greeting the church, followed by a hearty welcome from the leaders. Then we are given some gifts. Finally, Bob gets up to preach and delivers a good message. I pray for those who come forward. Even though the service is very long, we end up still waiting for food to be served. It is evening by now.

The following day we return to Lusaka. The bus we are on is not as good as the one we came with. The seats are very close to each other, there is no leg room at all. The luggage is clogging up the aisle as there are no baggage racks. A very tiring journey, especially for Marion.

While on a stroll one evening, the Lord reminds me that it is His church and that I ought not to fret. We must allow His will to be done and since we have no selfish motives of ours, then why not let Him take care of it all? As well, He reminds me that vengeance is His, He will repay. Marion is fasting today. We have been trying to unite the two factions into one ever since our return from home assignment over a year ago. But London and Mbumba, whom I found already at odds back in 1986 when I first came to plant the Church of God, have resigned themselves not to work together. Marion and I are praying that God will use us as He builds His church here in Zambia.

We keep up our search for a house to rent. It has been four weeks since our arrival and still there is nothing to our liking. We have looked everywhere. The Baptists are having a convention and need all the rooms, including the one we are in, so we must move out for two weeks. With no place to go, we decide to take our vacation and fly to Luangwa National Park and spend a week there. It is suppose to be the best park in Zambia.

We find ourselves surrounded with plenty of wild game. There are elephants, buffalo, hippo, crocodile, and antelope of various species. Also, there are lions, leopards, and hyenas. Three nights are spent at Chichele Lodge and then four nights at Mfuwe Lodge. One elephant visits us at the swimming pool. He makes a false charge when I take a photo of him. Three other lumber by our cabin, near enough for me to touch them. But I don't! I do some writing for my next book when I am not resting or viewing game. Marion and I often find ourselves talking about our children. We would love to see them and hold our grandchildren again. We miss very much Tiffany's hugs! President Kaunda is also spending a few days at his safari lodge situated about a kilometer from where we are staying at Mfuwe. He can be seen viewing game in an open Landcruiser which is being escorted by his guards in several vehicles.

On our return flight in the same twin-engined plane, we meet a couple from Lublin, Poland, who are on a work assignment in Copperbelt province. I talk to the woman as she speaks English, and share with her that my father was born near Lublin. We have a good chat and we are invited to come to Poland and visit them. That is almost an impossibility! My grandparents, John and Alvena Hoffman, moved from Poland to Germany when my father Gustav was two years of age. Then, three more children were to be born before they migrated to Canada in 1912.

While in Luangwa, we met a Greek family who gave us the name of their friend that has a house for rent at Makeni in Lusaka. We catch a lift, as soon as we arrive back, and have a look at it. The house is big, much more than we need, but we are tired of looking at houses which are not up to what we require for the work. We take it and, finally, move into a home after two months of living out of suitcases.

Now that we have a house, we arrange a flight back to Uganda in order to pick up our ten crates of household effects which are waiting for us in Kampala. On the way we disembark at Nairobi to be with Colleen for a few hours. She is on her way to Canada where she is planning to have her baby. Natasha is with her. She has grown and talks some. They will be staying with Tim's folks who are pastoring in Ontario. Tim and Tiffany will be following them in two weeks as he still has some things to do in Uganda.

When we fly into Entebbe, Tim and Tiffany are there to meet us. She is happy to see us and gives us plenty of hugs and kisses. We are back in familiar territory. Power shortage is still the in-thing. Gunfire is also still quite popular. Tonight, we are sleeping in our old bed again. Of course, I read Tiffany a story before she drops off to sleep.

I bring several books with me from Nairobi, and Colleen had bought some Lady Bird books for her as well.

It takes several days before our ten crates are ready for shipping. They had to be banded and then inspected by customs. Finally, the shipping agent picks them up and they are on their way to Lusaka via Nairobi by air. They should arrive about the same time that we will. I spend time with both Ashling and Tiffany whenever I can. Kirk and Karen have us over for meals and we visit. Before we know it our two weeks are up and we pack our bags for our return trip to Lusaka. Tim, who has been busy with the container from Germany, is also ready to leave for Canada. He locks everything up in the house, and then locks the last door. Kirk takes the four of us to the airport. We say our goodbyes to him and leave Uganda behind.

All of us spend the night in Nairobi. Then in the morning it is goodbye to Tim and Tiffany as Marion and I catch our flight to Lusaka. They themselves will carry on to Toronto, Canada, in just a few hours. When we reach Lusaka airport, we find our 10 crates waiting for us. It is a miracle how quickly they arrived! Thank you, Lord.

It takes us all month to get our house looking like a home. We sleep on the floor the first few nights until we find the right bed to buy. With no vehicle we are dependent on a taxi, or on our neighbour who is the landlord, for our transportation. The new Nissan Patrol has already come but it is with Customs until the certificate of duty exemption is granted by their head office in Livingstone. They said it will take ten days but when it comes time for us to fly to Nairobi for the Missionary Retreat 23 days later, it still has not yet arrived! A disappointment, but nothing we can do about it. It will be waiting for us when we get back.

We enjoy the fellowship of the missionaries who are working in Africa like us. After the retreat, Marion and I fly on to Entebbe where Kirk is waiting to pick us up. While in Kampala, we will be staying in the Stevensons' house and using their vehicle to get around. Most evenings are spent with Kirk, Karen, and Ashling, either at their home or with us. There is still no word on whether Colleen has delivered or not. The phone is out of order here at the house, and at Kirk's, so I place a call to Colleen from the post office. She is expecting to go to the hospital tomorrow, the 15th of December. Tiffany is there and says a few words as well. She wants to come back and see Opa and Oma.

The following day, Marion takes me to the airport and I catch the plane to Rwanda. There are only six of us flying in this 20-seater Faulker. I am traveling with two boxes of songbooks containing 250 copies and two boxes of tracts. I wish that I could have taken all of those that I have for Rwanda and Zaire but I would have been too loaded down. It is raining in Kigali. I check through customs and immigration, and then I go through again, since my destination is Gisenyi. It is on the same plane. But before I reach Gisenyi, the plane makes a stop at Kamembe. Across the border is Bukavu, Zaire. Here the Zairean woman and her baby disembark. They were the only other passengers besides myself on this flight from Kigali. Four come aboard here. When we finally reach Gisenyi, I am the only one who gets off. The others are destined for Kigali. Esron and Mianitse are waiting for me. Disappointment is written all over their faces when they do not see Marion. They were expecting her to come along this time.

After visiting awhile, we end up in church where I, of course, speak. The pastors have come and I share on prayer. Many of them after class respond and come forward to be prayed for. Finally at 8:30 P.M. (Uganda time 9:30 P.M.) I receive my supper. I am quite weak by now as I have not had anything since breakfast fourteen hours ago. I am in the same building as I was last time when Bob Edwards accompanied me. Food is served at Esron's father's place and it is very European. It beats eating at any hotel. It is off to bed after this.

When breakfast is done, there is a service in the church. It is their farewell program for me as this is my last visit to them as their missionary. I received several gifts, one is a jar of live flowers! After my words of farewell, I deliver the message. At least 25 come forward for prayer. The service is three hours long. Meet with Esron and Mianitse afterwards to discuss the future of the work here in Rwanda and Zaire. I am closing the financial books with them as Bob Edwards will be in charge next year until another missionary shows up. At four o'clock, I leave with Mianitse for Goma in a taxi. At the border we spend a long time awaiting my turn with the Rwandan immigration officer. He definitely is wearing colored glasses as he intentionally overlooks me and takes care of others even when they show up after me. No problem with immigration on the Zairean side.

I have a good night here at the Swedish Pentecostal guesthouse, except for a mosquito or two. I managed to put one of them out of commission. It is tidy and clean here. Breakfast is brought to me by Sifa and her co-workers. (Last night they brought supper as well for Mianitse and myself.) These ladies are really dedicated! Ever since I have started coming here to Zaire, they have carried the food from where they prepare it to where I am staying. When I suggest to them that I can eat in a restaurant, the women feel offended and will not hear of it!

Mianitse brings a taxi and we travel to Sake. The driver is a chief who resides at Sake and does not charge us. His vehicle has come from Uganda. The one that brought us from Gisenyi yesterday, even though it had a Zairean license plate, was also from Uganda. I have often been told that vehicles stolen in Kampala are whisked off to Zaire and sold there. It is true, in at least these two cases. Mianitse points out several other vehicles that have been smuggled into Zaire. They are easily identified by their steering wheel located on the right hand side instead of the left. In Zaire vehicles drive on the right side of the road, as in America, while in East and Southern Africa they still follow the British system.

There is a four-hour service in the Sake church where around 400 people are present. The guitar I brought with me last time and presented to Mianitse's son is in use along with several simply made instruments. I preach and at least 35 respond to the altar call. It is good to be speaking in Swahili again as it is not common in Zambia. It has been raining much throughout the day, but it let up at the time of the service, especially during the preaching. We eat at Mianitse's house. Then it is back to Goma. The chief's driver takes us there. I rest some before Sifa, Mianitse, and two others come with supper. We visit until nine o'clock.

After breakfast, which again was brought to me, Mianitse and I return to Sake. Today is for pastors only. In the forenoon I teach them for two hours on accountability. In the afternoon I teach from the first book of Paul to Timothy. It again rains heavily at noon and on into the afternoon. We arrive back in Goma at 5 P.M. and visit until Sifa and her crew bring us supper, which they have carried in their buckets for a distance of two to three kilometers! The meals here in Goma cannot be compared with those we receive at Mianitse's house in Sake, as his wife is a good cook. When they leave it is already nine o'clock.

I wake up thinking about Colleen and whether she has already had her baby. I pray that she has and that all is well. We reach Sake in good time. Today is my farewell service so I preach on being remembered for our faith using for my Scripture reading: Hebrews 11:32–40. After I am finished, over 30 come forward to the altar. I pray they all will persevere and go on in their faith in Christ. The service is three hours long. When we get outside the church, they honour me with their tribal singing and dancing which features a lot of leaping in the air. When we leave, many run alongside and behind the vehicle, singing and waving until we reach the main road. It is an emotional exit! Will I ever be back again? I have been invited, but. . . .

I look around the shops for something to purchase for Marion. Not much to choose from as it is mostly material and yard goods that they sell here. Christians from town come to say their goodbyes before I have my supper that Sifa again brings me. It is nine before they leave with Mianitse. I have had a busy day. Tomorrow I return to Gisenyi.

A mosquito bothers me during the night. After biting me several times, I am at 3:30 A.M. finally able to kill it. I get very little sleep. I pack my bag and after breakfast I say good-bye to the women. The taxi drives Mianitse and me to Gisenyi. At the border we are delayed for only a short while. Esron is waiting for us at the church. There is a two and a half hour service where I preach the message. Thirty or more come up for prayer. After dinner there is a two and a half hour class in the church with the pastors and the church leaders. I also teach them here about accountability. It is well received.

Esron finally takes me to his house. This is a first. Ever since I have been coming to Rwanda, he has never invited me. His wife is a nice woman, rather shy, since her husband is such a vocal person. We have a good visit, but I end up eating at his father's house again. I return to my place of abode at nine o'clock. I hear a Christmas carol on my little radio which I brought along. It reminds me that Christmas day is but four days away! Here I am, in the heart of Africa, away from family! No time even to get lonely. It has been a busy safari for the Lord thus far.

It rains during the night. After breakfast we are back in church where I teach the pastors for three hours from 1 Timothy. They participate much more than they did in Zaire. It takes another half an hour to get away due to saying goodbye to them all. After dinner I look in the shops for something to buy for Marion but find nothing suitable. So I return and visit with Esron and Mianitse until supper time. It is ten o'clock before I retire. It has been a worthwhile trip to see the church here in Zaire and Rwanda. May the Lord continue to be with the work and enrich it with His presence.

I woke up before five o'clock. The taxi that is to take me back to Kigali was to have been here at 5:30 A.M. but it isn't. Esron finally goes looking for another taxi and does find one. Before leaving Gisenyi, the driver still needs to fill up with petrol. Finally, the third station we go to is open. In the meantime, the clock is ticking away the minutes! The plane leaves at 9:30 A.M. and it is already 6:45 A.M. when we leave for Kigali. It is a two and a half hour drive. Well, the driver takes the hairpin curves at top speed. My stomach gets wheezy at one point even though I had nothing to eat. He makes one stop for the two pastors who have come along with Esron and me, not to let them throw up but to relieve themselves. More delay! It is foggy in spots on the high ridges, we stop for red lights when we reach Kigali , and reach the airport at 9:30 A.M.! I rush inside to check through but am delayed by the Immigration Officer who is annoyed that I did not come with the taxi who had been booked the day we arrived in Kigali. He and the driver must be in some kind of a partnership. It is disgusting as I am in a hurry to get on the plane! Fortunately the pastors who came along from Gisenyi take over. I sneak past them during one of their shouting matches. And you know what? It has been a rush all for nothing! The flight has been delayed for three hours. It is 2:45 P.M. when I finally arrive at Entebbe airport. Marion is there waiting for me along with Kirk and his family. I learn from them that Colleen had a baby boy a week ago, December 15th. Jesse is his name. I cannot call them as the phone is still out at the house.

We are able to talk to Colleen the following day at Kirk's as their phone starts working in the afternoon. It is nice to hear her, Tim, and Tiffany who comes on the line as well. We spend Christmas eve at Kirk's. Karen makes a delicious meal and gifts are exchanged afterwards. It is a nice evening. We get together again on Christmas day. Colleen calls. They are spending Christmas with Tim's parents who are pastoring in Ontario. We try to get Mark on the phone but he is out. It is not until the next day that we are able to talk with him. He is missing all of us.

I attend the Executive Council meeting. The number of churches have increased to 331 from 320 when we left in August. The Assembly meeting is the following day. A few knots but otherwise a fair meeting. There is a big service Sunday morning where there are a lot of introductions and songs. I give out TEE certificates to the graduates. Eliezer Mdobi from Tanzania brings the message. He arrived this morning with his group, which includes Dismus and his wife Marta, our converts from Mbugwe. Arthur Magezi married Colleen Mdobi in Babati, Tanzania, a few days ago and has come here to Uganda for their reception and for the Mdobis to meet his relatives.

After the service we meet outside for the reception. Colleen puts on her wedding dress for the occasion. She is a beautiful bride. I still remember those days when she as a little girl used to sit on my lap at Kaiti Mission and comb my hair. Now she is a young lady. May she have a wonderful life as she deserves it. While the Tanzanians are here we have Eliezer, Dismus, Marta, and Lydia (Edna's daughter) stay with us in our house. We are up until midnight and wish each other a happy New Year! It has been a very busy ending to 1989! A real nice treat that we can end it with our friends of years gone by.

New Year's Day 1990: We are entering another year. Lord, let it be a blessed one with your presence in our midst throughout. Today, our pastors retreat begins and will last five days. I have Eliezer and Dismus assist me and Marion in teaching some of the classes. It is the largest retreat we have ever had with 158 pastors and national church leaders attending. The Spirit of God is present throughout. I work on the Ugandan accounts as well and get them done. I talk to the Stevensons by phone and bring them up to date on events out here. They are returning to Uganda next month. The last night here in Kampala I am up all night. I am busy with office work until 2:30 A.M., then pack the rest of our things into our luggage. I take a quick bath and Kirk is at the door ready to take us to the airport. We lock up everything, commit the house to the Lord for protection, and leave.

We find the airport deserted. When someone finally makes an appearance, Kirk says goodbye and returns to

Kampala. We are not charged for the luggage being overweight by 57 kilograms. It is Zambia Airways' maiden flight and so we receive royal treatment. Our luggage is not even checked, in fact, it is carried to the plane along with our carry-on baggage. There are 17 attendants present at the airport to assist us! We are the only passengers boarding at Entebbe. We find those inside the plane are Arabic as the flight is returning to Lusaka from Dubai. We arrive in Lusaka half an hour early! That is a first, I believe, in all my flights I have chalked up here in Africa. No problem with customs. It has been a trip with VIP treatment!

Our landlord, Albertos Gregory, fetches us from the airport. We discover our new Nissan Patrol waiting for us on his yard. He picked it up for us. It looks nice! Now we are ready to launch out into the deep and lower our nets for souls in Zambia and to dispel the darkness in this land by sharing the gospel light of Jesus Christ our Lord.

Eight
Lusaka's Welcome Party

Before we moved to Zambia we were warned by the Skinners, PAOC (Pentecostal Assemblies of Canada) missionaries who had resided in Zambia and are now in Uganda, that Lusaka is noted for her thieves. They are even worse than those in Kampala, we were told. Is this possible? Overlanders do not stay overnight in Lusaka but keep moving on down the line. On one of our earlier visits, we personally had witnessed one attempted robbery in Lusaka when we stayed with the Kurtzes, who are PAOC missionaries in Zambia. I shared this experience in my book *Amid Perils Often,* chapter 18. We soon learn that we are not exempt from those very crafty thieves and they manage to relieve us of a few things, much to our chagrin, before we learned to stay a pace ahead of them.

We park our new Nissan Patrol on Cairo Road a block from the Rendezvous store, we could not find a spot any closer, and we do some shopping for groceries. Before long we return to our vehicle and load our things into the back. As we turn into Cairo Road the door behind Marion flies open. She reaches around and pulls it shut. We are curious as to why the door flew open and as soon as I find a place to park I stop the vehicle to investigate. The door locks for our laundry room, which we had purchased earlier, are gone from behind the seat. Also, a pocket knife is missing from the glove compartment. The thief had seen us coming and left hurriedly, failing to close the door properly. Had the door not flown open right away, we would not have known there was a robbery until we had reached home. How had the thief managed to get into the Nissan so easily and quickly? There are no scratch marks on the door anywhere. And, of course, no one saw the thief. Welcome to Lusaka!

Two days later I have an alarm system installed in the Nissan, plus an anti-hijack unit. This should help prevent any further robberies. Or, so I thought. Four months later the following incident takes place.

I am at Barclay's Bank in Longacres where we have our account. After depositing several checks, I withdraw some money in local currency and return to town center. I find a parking spot in front of the Rendezvous. I walk across busy Cairo Road to Phoenix Studio for my pictures, which should be ready for pickup. They are ready and as I am about to step outside, I hear a siren go off across the street. It sounds like mine but it cannot be. Just the same, I rush onto the street and notice that the sound is coming from the direction of the Rendezvous. I weave my way between the heavy traffic that is flowing at this time of the day, still hoping that it is not coming from my vehicle. Halfway across I notice a crowd outside the shop and it appears they are looking at my vehicle. When I finally reach the Nissan, I discover the door ajar on the passenger's side. The glove compartment that I had left locked has been pried open and the money I had just picked up at the bank is gone!

There are at least 20 people in the crowd assembled on the sidewalk. In that group there is one elderly white woman, the Greek owner of Rendezvous, who says in broken English, "Is dis your car?" I reply that it is. "Vaat ever you had in it is now gone!" she adds, I ask her, and everyone else who is staring at me blankly, "Why did anyone not stop them?"

The woman replied, "Can't you see? Dey're all tieves!" Someone in the crowd said, "There were four of them and they had knives!"

A lad steps forward and then describes the one who had opened the door with a wire which he squeezed between the door and the frame to lift up the knob. The intruder, a big husky man wearing a red shirt, then used a screwdriver to pry open the locked glove compartment. The gang must have followed me from the bank. How else did they know I had left money in the glove compartment?

The lad, and a friend of his, informed me that they saw the thieves head off towards the Post Office, which is nearby, and disappear behind it. I ask them to jump into the vehicle and go with me to search for any sign of them. Someone else in the crowd steps up and asks to go along. He tells me that he is a policeman in plain clothes. "Oh, yeah, then why did you not try to stop them?" Of course, I do not say this aloud. I need all the help I can get right now so I take him with us. I drive through the back and side streets of the Post Office and Rendezvous. The thieves cannot be spotted anywhere. They have vanished from sight?

One of the passengers suggests that we drive to the city market where most of the thieves hang out. It is an open market just a couple of streets off Cairo Road. Driving down Freedom Way, we spot a man standing behind a vehicle like mine and he is swaying it back and forth as if to check whether it has an alarm system. The young lad blurts out, "That's one of the men! That's one of the thieves!" We are just across from the city market. The man does not notice when I stop right behind him. Two of the fellows slide out and grab him from behind. Before he knows what is really happening, they have him bundled inside my Nissan Patrol. He does not utter a sound as I drive him off to Central Police Station. Once inside, he finally commences to deny he had done anything wrong. He tells the policeman, who is writing down the charges, that the boy is lying. The policeman slaps the man a few times and shouts at him, "Yes, you are a thief! I know you are part of a gang!" The suspect is then promptly hauled off and locked up in a cell. The officer in charge assures me, "We will get to the bottom of this. You come back tomorrow at ten o'clock."

I make an appearance at ten as I was told and find the lad who had witnessed the theft there as well. I had asked him to return and help me with the case. I also see the thief and he looks none the worse for his ordeal in prison. I thought he may have a few bruises on him as often police use some rough tactics to squeeze the truth out of the apprehended. After taking down the young lad's statement as to what he saw, we are told to leave and return in the afternoon. I do just that and am told there is nothing new. They are still investigating. I am to try again next week.

When I show my face again at the police station, I am told that nothing more has turned up since my last visit. The prisoner has been released due to lack of enough evidence and that they did not have any more food to feed him. Imagine that! I may as well kiss the money that was stolen goodbye. So much for asking the police to help me in finding it and apprehending the thieves who stole it! Does anyone ever get caught?

A few weeks later I am parked on Chachacha Street in front of one of the many hardware shops that are found in this part of town. I have come to purchase a few items at Andees and just when I reach the counter the alarm goes off on my Nissan which is only one door away. I rush outside as fast as I can and to my surprise I see no one running away in either direction! The door is unlocked and only partly open. Marion's white sweater is still on the seat where she had left it when I dropped her off at the hairdresser. My quick response had interrupted the theft.

There is a watchman sitting at the door of each shop along this street as Chachacha is noted for its thieves. No one leaves their vehicles unattended. Most have an alarm system. Yet they carry someone along to help prevent things getting stolen out of their vehicles as the owner himself may not arrive back in time to foil the theft as I just did. I ask each watchman whether they saw anyone at the door of my vehicle. Of course, no one did. I am told the thieves wash themselves with a soap which makes them invisible. More than likely, the watchmen at these shops are on the side of the thieves. The watchman at Andees probably gave the man a sign when I turned to rush outside upon hearing the alarm. It had to be that way. How else could the thief know I was coming?

To prevent a further break-in from occurring, I remove the knobs on each door and shorten the cable they are screwed onto at the bottom of the window so no one will be able to hook them again with a wire from outside. Not even me.

Marion is in need of some curtain material so I drive her to Limbada, a shop across the street from the city market. It being an area where thieves abound, I remain in the Nissan. It is not long before I hear someone tampering with the rear wheel on the far side. I look back over my shoulder and spot through the back window someone's head bobbing up and down. What is he up to? I jump out of the vehicle and whip around the back and find a man kneeling beside the wheel. He appears startled and I ask him what he is up to? He mumbles something about checking the valve stem, that it was a pretty color. I tell him to leave. He makes a move to do so but stops after a few steps. I again tell him to get going! He acts as if I am suppose to chase him. Then, I realize I have been set-up. I hurry back to my side and find the door ajar with my briefcase gone!

I fell for the oldest trick in the book! The man behind the vehicle was to lure me away while his assistant steals whatever you have inside. I feel about as low as a man can get, and sore at myself for not being more attentive. In front of me there are some vendors on the sidewalk selling books, clothing, yard goods, and other items. I ask them whether they saw someone running by them with a briefcase. No, no one saw anyone like that, I look around for a policeman but there is no one in sight. What a sickening and helpless feeling! If crying could help, I would cry. Marion makes an appearance and I tell her what had just taken place.

Dropping Marion off at the house, I return to town and report the theft to the police. After they have opened a docket, two officers wish to be taken to the scene. On the way one says to me, "Don't you know that it is very dangerous to park your vehicle in that area of town?"

I reply, "If that is true then why are not the police patrolling the streets so that it ceases to be so dangerous?" Their reply is that they are understaffed and cannot be everywhere. The first thing the officers do when we arrive in front of Limbada is to approach the vendors on the sidewalk with rifles drawn and commence drilling them whether they know of any thieves in the vicinity. Now why do they not approach them in a more subtle manner?

Upon seeing the rifles, the vendors freeze up and say they know absolutely nothing.

We walk through the marketplace to find my briefcase. The policemen are thinking that just maybe the thieves have already disposed of it at one of the stalls. But we come up dry. The officers soon tire and say they are hungry. This means I take them to eat somewhere, or give them money for food. I give them money. I again am the loser! I had in my briefcase, the house keys, my identity card, driver's license, and the logbook (registration) for the vehicle, plus some money. Another welcome from this fair city of Lusaka!

I begin to work on getting copies of the documents that were stolen. They tell me that it will take some time. I start with the driver's license. At the civic center I discover they are out of application forms. So I head for the printers and purchase several of them. When I return to the civic center, the lady behind the window informs that it is the wrong form. I need forms for duplicate driving permits! For this I am sent to another place. Had to ask around before I locate it. Here I am told that I must have an affidavit. And guess where that is? Back at the civic center! Upon reaching it I discover all I have to do is just pay for it. After doing that, I am sent to another building where I fill in some forms. From there I must go to the magistrate who is in another building for signing. I return to the civic center for the license and find them locking the doors as it is now already 12:30. It is unbelievable what one must go through to get a duplicate driver's license! The onus of getting documents replaced here in Lusaka is all left up to the loser—me. Those dirty thieves ought to be caught and punished for stealing them instead of running around free and easy while I am running my legs off from place to place using up my precious time!

At 2:30 A.M. the following morning, I return to the civic center for my driver's license. But, today I am told to pick it up at the place on Government Road where I had been yesterday. When I reach it, they inform me that the duplicate driver's licenses are out of stock and it will take a few weeks to get a new order. You have got to be pulling my leg! All this running around yesterday and today for nothing! Lord, grant me the patience of these Zambians. I need a double dose.

I inquire at the civic center about the vehicle logbook. They send me to another office where I am told that because it is a duty-free vehicle I have to go to customs. So I trot on over to that office. Here I am given a new one. I thought I was through but, no, I now must return to the civic center for some entries to be made in the logbook. Back I go. The lady behind the window enters the required data, stamps it, and hands it to me. It is done! Whoopi! I now have one of the documents in my hands. Two more to go.

I now head for the building where they issue National Registration Cards (NRC). It is next to the Central Police Station. I find the place crowded with people. There is no way I can get through the lineup today so I have to come back another time. And when I do, I get as far as paying the fee for a replacement. That's all. I am told to come back in the afternoon for it. This I do, and with the help of someone, we push and shove our way through the mass of people to the proper room, only to discover that it is not ready yet! There are so many people waiting for their NRCs, it is unbelievable! And, yet it is believable after seeing the lack of efficiency in these offices.

Ten days later I check again for my new registration card. Learning from the last time, I barge my way to the front of the line and after checking in two different rooms, I discover they have not done anything! They send me with a note over to their Central Office in another part of town. When I reach it, they are unable to find my original application. I am then handed a note which I am to carry back to the place I have just come from! Again, when I get there, I shoulder my way through the mob. I could have saved the effort as I hear those all too familiar words once more, "Come back tomorrow afternoon!" They say they want to check their files again. If they have not done anything in the past two weeks, will they do anything tomorrow? Their offices are in shambles!

When I check again for my NRC, a week has slipped by. This time I stand around for quite a while before I am assisted. And when they do, I am directed back to their Central Office. There I am asked to return at 2:00 P.M. (or at 14 hours, Zambia keeps 24-hour time!). It will be ready by then I am told. Well, after 14 hours I am back to pick up my card. The fellow who had said it would be ready is nowhere around. I am asked to wait for him. After some time of pacing up and down I leave, without a card, as he does not show up. I try again the following day and go directly to the Central Office. My card is not yet ready! One of the clerks then accompanies me back to the place where I have wasted so much of my time and energy. He claims the record of my registration when I first entered Zambia cannot be found. This time it does not take them long and I finally have my NRC! They were able to process it because of the photocopy I had given them. Now why did they not do this right from the start? I guess I need to be thankful for the opportunities to practice my patience!

Marion comes along with me to town and takes in her application forms for a new passport at the Canadian

High Commission and finds the one who deals with it is not in. So we will have to return tomorrow. That's how it goes! The list does not shorten, instead it gets longer by the time the day is done. A person can use up the whole day without accomplishing much, if anything. It's "Come back." "Try next door," "We don't have it," etc.

Today, I am mailing my reports to the Mission Board. First, I buy several large envelopes but when it comes to gluing them shut, the glue will not stick. I go shopping for a glue stick. After several shops of no luck, I buy smaller envelopes and re-address them. But, the same thing happens. The glue on the envelopes does not stick! I end up buying a bottle of liquid glue and hope this will stick. It does. Then, I join a long queue at the stamp counter. There are 21 people ahead of me! What it takes to mail these letters, the Mission Board will never know. And if they did, they would not believe it. It was almost a half day's work!

There is still the driver's license that I need to run down. Weeks have passed since I last checked. And when I do, it is not ready for pickup. It is months later, due to our schedule taking us to Kenya and Uganda, before I pop in again. Nothing! I then leave it for several months as the police do not ask for a driver's license unless you are involved in an accident. And even then I wondered. They are usually more interested in whether you are carrying triangles in your vehicles and if there is white reflection tape on your front bumper. Maybe it is just taken for granted that all foreigners have one, either an International Driver's License or one from where they have come from. Finally, after a few more tries, I receive my duplicate driver's license. How long ago has it been since I began applying for it? I have forgotten.

Needless to say, I am more wary from now on when

strangers come up to me while seated in the vehicle. There are many times when one will point to a tire and say that it is flat, wanting me to step outside to look. They will even point under the vehicle saying there is a lot of oil leaking from somewhere. I ignore them and eventually they leave. The urge is to check it out but I dare not fall for it. If it looks quite real, I drive to a filling station and then step out to check. There is nothing wrong with the tire or the chassis underneath!

The above has happened to Marion on countless occasions as well. She always makes sure the doors are locked when she is waiting for me to return from running an errand. While waiting on one occasion, she witnesses an attempted break-in on a vehicle parked just ahead of her. The man is trying to open the trunk of the car belonging to the owner inside the shop. She presses down on the horn and he looks up at her, not in any hurry to run off. Instead he is annoyed at Marion and comes over to her window and waves his fist at her. She continues to hoot the horn until he finally walks away disgusted that he has been driven off by a white woman. Nary a one, walking back and forth on the sidewalk, had paid him any attention as he tried to break into the trunk!

I am looking for some kitchen tiles and step inside the shop which handles them on Chachacha Street. It does not take long to make the purchase and I am soon on my way back to the vehicle which is parked only a few doors away. I reach the Nissan and when I try to unlock the door, the key refuses to enter. After several failures I am forced to use the door on the passenger's side. I ask an old man who is seated in the doorway of a small clinic whether he saw someone trying to force his way into my vehicle with a key. He answers me and says that there had been one who ran off as soon as he saw me step outside the shop I had been in. "Could you not try to stop him?" I ask him.

He says, "Oh, no, he had a knife!"

"Did you see the knife?" I continue.

"No! But I know he had one," says the old man.

I am disgusted with his answers. There are people in Lusaka who just do not care about helping strangers from being robbed. When I reach home, I open up the lock on my door and find the broken end of a key inside. His just did not fit!

I park across from the bicycle shop. I am sitting in my Nissan waiting for Marion to return when I feel the vehicle begin to shake. I look around and see a man standing behind the rear wheel which is on my far side. He is pointing at the tire and saying something to me which I do not catch. So, here is another one! This time I am not going to be a sucker and fall for the trick. I start the vehicle and put it into reverse. He takes off before I can run into him. Of course, there are passive onlookers who do not make an effort to grab him.

While parked in front of a printing shop on Chachacha Street, someone has the nerve to climb up on the rear bumper and commence untying the ropes that are holding down our luggage on top of the roof rack! I am inside the shop picking up the rubber stamp and pad I had ordered earlier. Mailes and Sarah are waiting inside the Nissan with Marion. When the women noticed some movement of the vehicle, they look back and spot someone through the window standing on the bumper. Sarah and Marion leap out of the vehicle and shout at the man to get down! When he runs off, Sarah takes out after him. It is at that moment I emerge from the shop and realize something is amiss. Marion informs me that a thief had been caught in the process of trying to remove some of our luggage from the roof rack. I call out to Sarah to return and severely reprimand the security guard next door for not warning the women of the thief. It is as if they are curious to see whether the thief will be successful in his mission!

Some are even bold enough to try and force their way into our vehicle. One is almost strong enough to succeed, had I not persevered. Upon reaching the Nissan I unlock the door, throw inside the package of meat I had just bought, and crawl behind the wheel. I reach for the door handle to pull it shut when a tall rugged individual steps up and grabs the door. I ask him what he wants. He does not answer, instead he begins to pull on the door. He has a mean look on his face and I am guessing he wants to gain entrance so as to snatch my money bag, which I have thrown on the seat beside me when I entered. A tug-of-war commences. He is strong, but so am I. When I am about to smash my left fist into his face, he lets go and saunders away as if nothing took place! The onlookers also disperse. No one had offered to help me.

Marion has had a similar experience. She had just enough strength to pull the door shut and then lock it. He had underestimated this white woman's strength. Fortunately, the man was not any larger than she was. She said that after he failed to gain entrance, he just turned and walked merrily on his way. All in a day's walk, I guess.

Recently, while on my way back to the vehicle, which is just off Cairo Road, I feel my money pouch jerked from out of my hand! It takes place so quickly! I often carry my money this way, in a small green canvas bag. Sometimes, I tuck it inside the waist band in front of me. Whichever way I carry my money, I have never been attacked this way while walking. I have heard of others having their

110

money snatched from them, or their pockets picked, but never me! That is, until today.

I could not believe it! I take a quick look to my right as I was carrying the pouch in my right hand. I notice there is no one near enough to have grabbed it. To my left is a burly individual who is crowding me. He must surely be involved! I grab him around the neck in a vise-like grip! His reaction is not one of anger, nor is he annoyed in the least at my strangle hold on him. He only points behind me and shouts in my ear, "He ran that way! He ran that way!" I take a quick look and see no one running, only pedestrians walking back and forth. In my heart I feel that the thief took off in the opposite direction. This one is only trying to divert my attention. Why is no one coming to my rescue? They keep walking as if blind to what is taking place.

Then, I hear my name, "Bwana, this is the one! Here it is!" I look to my left and there is Sarah behind the man on the other side of the one I am still holding. She has tackled him from behind much like a football player would, pinning his arms to his side. From where did she get all that strength? The man is so surprised that he drops the bag. I can now spot it on the sidewalk near the wall of a building. I release my man and make a dive to pick it up. But Mailesi comes to Sarah's rescue and scoops it up before I can get to it. After Sarah releases the thief, he turns to look at her and finds to his surprise that it is a young woman, and not a big muscular man, who has disarmed him! There is a verbal exchange of words now between the unsuccessful thieves and the two women. I, too, blast them with a few words of my own as we walk off towards the vehicle. Sarah will not release the money bag, instead she clutches it to her bosom and complains bitterly how careless I had been. She does not return it to me until we all are safely inside the Nissan.

Sarah, Mailesi Phiri, Monica, and Josephine, all women from the church, had been trailing along behind me at a short distance when suddenly they saw me flailing my arms. The sidewalk is quite crowded with people, but Sarah is still able to recognize my green bag being clutched behind a stranger's back. "That's Bwana's bag!" cries Sarah. The women rush forward to assist the missionary. Sarah spots the pouch being handed to another man. This is when she flies into action. None of the pedestrians comes to our aid. Unbelievable! No wonder thefts are common in Lusaka.

But for the two women, I would have lost my pouch which contained not only money but credit cards, my National Registration Card, and my driver's license. The Lord taught me a lesson today. I am not exempt from thieves welcoming me while walking along on the sidewalks of Lusaka! He allowed it to take place the day when there where Christians here who cared to help me. Yes, they were women who were my guardian angels in disguise.

Nine
Storming the Gates of Darkness

When the earthquake hits at 5:00 A.M. we already are awake since today, February 2, 1990, we are traveling up to Mbala District in the Northern Province for a weekend of teaching and preaching the Word. The tremour lasted ten seconds—quite long for this part! It is 8:00 A.M. before we finally leave Lusaka. We take the Great North Road and stay on it until Mpika where we turn off onto the one that leads to Mbala. Along the way we passed through three road blocks. At one of them, they asked me to open the back so they could check what we were carrying.

We thought of spending the night at Kasama, but when we get there it is only 5:15 P.M. We decided to carry on. It is 7:00 P.M. and dark when we reach Mbala. Here we are told that the place where we are going for our meetings is just 10 kilometers off the main road. We keep going. It turns out to be more than 10 kilometers! The road is rough and very muddy. We climb up an escarpment and splash through ruts filled with water. It has just rained heavily. Finally, we arrive at our destination in the middle of nowhere at 8:30 P.M. The village is Katulo. We travelled 35 kilometers over a bad road to get here. In a few minutes a group of villagers assemble and sing a few songs for us. After prayer we excuse ourselves and prepare our bed in the Nissan Patrol. We tell them not to prepare any food for us as we have been nibbling along the way on some which Marion brought along.

Marion and I have a fairly good night. It is a little uneven because of the space between the folded seats. I need to make a long narrow box to stick in between them. It should then be okay. The Christians heat water for our bath, which we take in a grass enclosure. The toilet is narrow with a small door. I dirty my shirt entering it. The soil here is red and it is a sticky mess when the rain begins to fall. The skies are overcast and it pours heavily all forenoon. I thought it would never stop but, finally, in the afternoon the sun shows itself rather shyly.

Many show up for the meeting this afternoon. I speak on our goals. Marion shares as well. Many questions are asked. It is a good meeting. For supper we are served wild meat, from a warthog killed by the locals. We are told that they don't have permission from the government to hunt, they have it from God! The spokesman goes on, "God wakes us up early in the morning and says, 'Now go!'" Many locals have guns and do a lot of hunting. But, they add, game is already getting scarce. After supper we sit around the logfire and sing. It is an enjoyable evening.

Marion and I wake up to a beautiful sunrise. We hear a francolin in the bush nearby. The service starts at ten. Christians have come from six churches to attend this convention. There are 470 people present. I preach on "Jesus is the Way" and sixteen come forward for salvation. There are no youth at the altar. This is the first place I have been at where the youth do not come forward! There are many of them around and they have large choirs. After dinner there is another service for a second group who have come from four other churches. There are 26 of them. It is threatening to rain and I pray that it will not, at least not until after the service. The Lord answers and it does not rain. Praise His Name! I preach on "Walking with God." Many come forward, including young people this time. Gifts are given by the Christians to Marion, and I receive a stool. They want us to stay until tomorrow, but we must return to Lusaka. There is singing around the fire again. Marion joins them while I finish with the church leaders.

It does not rain during the night. Praise the Lord! It is a bit foggy though, so the grass is all wet. We get up while it is still dark and prepare for our trip back to Lusaka. We do not take a bath, nor do I shave. We pull out at 6:10 A.M. without eating. There is no trouble reaching the main road in spite of the big rain the day before yesterday. At Mbala we discover there is no diesel at the pumps. We carry on to Kasama 150 kilometers down the road. With God's help we reach it and fill up. We are driving on empty by now! It rains between Mpika and Kapiri Mposhi. The second roadblock forces us to step outside and show our identity cards. At Kapiri Mposhi Marion and I have a couple of samosas (Asian vegetables or meat pies) and a drink before completing the last lap of our journey. It is our first bit of food today. We reach home safely at 6:45 P.M. All is well here. Thank you, Lord! We clocked 2,152 kilometers on this round trip! It feels nice to relax in a tub full of hot water.

It is our first trip to the Petauke District in the Eastern Province and I am looking forward to it. We leave at 6:15 A.M. after having a bite to eat. We pass through some hilly countryside along with way. At the Luangwa River there is a roadblock at the bridge. Some troops are on maneuvers and we are asked to slow down. We find Lungu, who had gone on ahead, waiting for us at the Petauke BP filling station. Marion buys some bread at the shops while I fill up with diesel. Here we turn south onto a dirt road

115

and Lungu directs us to his mother's place at Chinzombo village. It is a 48-kilometer drive into the bush which takes us through some washouts along the way. We reach the village in one piece and meet their inhabitants. We hold a service in the church that they have already constructed out of poles and mud. The building is full of people. I preach on getting their names in the Book of Life. Many respond to the call for salvation. Tonight we sleep inside a hut instead of the Nissan Patrol. Before we can prepare our bed on the floor though, there is a frog that needs to be chased outside.

It was cool during the night but we rested well. We wash up before breakfast. As soon as we have eaten, we hold our first service. The church is full again with children sitting on the floor, in fact others are standing outside. Over 100 are in attendance. Marion has the first hour and speaks on "The Two Roads!" I preach on the Church of God in the following hour. Many come forward for salvation at the end of the service. There are those who want healing so we anoint them and pray for them. While in the process of doing this, a demon manifests itself in a woman who is standing at the door. We immediately go to her and commence binding the evil spirit in her. Before we can cast it out, a second woman who is standing just outside the church is thrown to the ground by another demon! What to do? I go to her, leaving Marion and Lungu with the first possessed woman. The demon in her is strong and she rises up from the ground. I hang onto her and at the same time command the evil spirit to come out in the name of Jesus.

Matters continue to worsen. A third woman begins to shriek and thrash about, flailing her arms wildly. There is no one to deal with her as I have my hands full and so does Marion who is being assisted by Lungu. Then I notice her flee into the bush before one of us has a chance to get to her. What was once a peaceful scene just minutes ago has now turned into total pandemonium! People are standing around watching to see how these missionaries are going to handle this mess. Many are laughing, thoroughly enjoying what they are witnessing. I suppose it did appear amusing to them—missionaries hanging onto those possessed with demons! Then, the Lord reveals to me that this is just what Satan wants. To create confusion so as to break up our meeting. But I will not let him succeed. No way!

I stop struggling with the evil spirits in the possessed and call the people back inside the church. There are too many unbelievers out there, that is why we could not control the situation. We return to praying for the sick. To our surprise we discover some of them have demons! They manifest themselves as soon as we lay on hands to pray for their healing. The evil spirits shriek loudly and become violent, throwing the people to the ground! But we are now in charge and they are driven from them in the name of Jesus Christ. After we have finished praying for the sick in body, we call for those who are demon-possessed. They are brought forward by a relative or friend. I then ask them, through the interpreter, which demons or evil spirits possess their bodies. In the process, I discover there are various names for the demons. There is the lion, baboon, monkey, and snake from the animal kingdom. From the religious world, Mary is quite common. There are those they call traditional spirits which reside in streams, hills, trees, and far away places. Then, there are ancestral spirits bearing the names of dead family members. One has a dumb spirit and another one drops over as if dead.

Most have more than one demon, but one woman has

nine of them which means more time is needed to drive them all from the person. Hours tick by as we struggle with the forces of evil. Sweat is pouring down my face, some of it entering my eyes. That does not stop me and I do not back off. Some manage to knock me over backwards. I must be more careful and brace myself for their surprise attacks! Marion, who is standing behind them, tries to hang onto them by their shoulders. But when several demons react at the same time, it takes several of us to hold the possessed. This we have to do in order to keep the person from hurting someone or from running away. There are those who do twist out of our hands when they are possessed with snake demons. It is impossible to hang onto them when they begin to turn and twist around and around on the ground!

But those who resist the most at being cast out we find are the ancestral spirits. They start to weep and stubbornly refuse to vacate their hosts. They claim to have been in them for years, and in some individuals, from their childhood on! No wonder it takes a lot of our spiritual energy to dislodge them. They are deeply rooted. But once I start with them, I do not stop until they have all been driven out. We are able to tell when this happens. They go limp and their eyes open. They look about and recognize those around them. They now give us their names when asked to do so. To make sure the demons are all out, we have the people repeat a prayer of deliverance. If there is one still hiding inside, the demon will react as it cannot abide in those who confess Jesus Christ as their Lord and Saviour. It is then promptly cast out. The names of the delivered are then recorded by the pastors and they are encouraged to attend church regularly. Those wearing charms are asked to surrender them. And those who still have some back in their huts are told to burn them as soon as they reach home.

By the time we are done, eleven souls have been delivered from demon-possession. We are left exhausted! But this is not the end. More show up at the campfire tonight. Before we can retire to our sleeping quarters, we deal with five more demon-possessed individuals. With the help of the Lord, who renews our strength, all the demons are driven out and the people are set free. It has been a full day, to say the least. It is our first time to have faced so much darkness at one time! But we feel satisfied at the outcome. We stood the test and have begun to drive back the powers of the Evil One from this area. What we read about in the book of Acts, we experienced today. There is power in the name of Jesus!

Our throats are still sore this morning from all the praying we did yesterday when casting out the demons. I have never seen so much demonic activity like this before. They were bad in Uburunge, Tanzania, but to have so many manifestations in one afternoon at one place is unbelievable! One of the ladies who was delivered last night has returned with her gourd of charms, which she has gotten from the witch doctor, and wants us to burn them. The Lord has done a miracle in the lives of the new Christians here at Chinzombo! We load up the things that the people have given us. It fills the vehicle. We leave for Lusaka at 8:00 A.M. We stop at Mumbi were we hope to plant a church next time around, and visit with the chief awhile and give him the blanket I had bought for him, plus a Bible. I was told that these are appropriate gifts to give chiefs. We reach home at 3:30 P.M.

On our second trip to Mbala District we leave at 5:00 A.M. Six hours later we stop at the small village of Mufumbushi, 25 kilometers south of Mpika, where a new church has been planted recently right beside the Great North Road. London and Tyson are there waiting for us. I preach inside a building that is not quite completed yet. There are 40 present for the service. I preach on "Jesus the Way" and a dozen come forward for prayer. I give the new leader a Bible and a songbook. I cannot give him a TEE book as they have as yet not arrived from Kenya. I wish they would arrive soon as it is holding up our teaching program for the new pastors. Churches are opening up quicker than we can train leaders! At 13 hours we continue with our safari. Along the way we pick up a soldier at a roadblock between Mpika and Kasama and give him a lift to Kasama. This time we turn off the road before we reach Mbala and London shows us a shorter route to Katulo.

The road is rough and eventually at 6:45 P.M. we arrive in the dark. All along the last few kilometers, we keep hearing through the darkness. "Hoffmani! Hoffmani." When they saw the lights of the vehicle they knew it was us coming. We are given something to eat and then hustled off to a large enclosure that they have erected for this convention. Of course, I am worn-out from the long trip after getting up at 4:00 A.M. But they do not think that this is possible for missionaries to get tired. Marion and I share after the choirs sing several songs. Then they sing some more. Finally, at 21 hours we call it a day. We are sleeping on our mattress in a room of a purposed dispensary. London and Tyson are in the next room.

We wake up to a beautiful morning. It is not as cold here as in Lusaka. The night on the floor was all right. It is much better than it would have been in the Nissan. I get them to widen the entrance to the latrine so that we can go in and out without soiling our clothes. The bathing place is a grass enclosure where some also go to urinate. We can smell it whenever we enter for a shower. Throughout the day Marion and I are busy holding classes. She teaches the women about AIDS and the cooking of a variety of meals instead of just their staple food, which is nsima (maize meal). She also has a worship service with them and ends the day by treating the sick. I teach on baptism and the Sabbath, then conclude with a time for questions and answers. After supper there is a service inside the large enclosure. I am told there are 600 present. I preach on "Being Ready by Living a Holy Life." Many accept Christ after the message. Choirs and quartettes sing until 9 P.M. An hour later we retire for the night.

We are up at six and take our baths with the warm water they bring us. Our breakfast consists of nshima and beans. Whenever Marion and I can, we eat some of the dried fruit that we brought along. It is easy to get constipated out here when we are in meetings all day long without any physical activity, and when we eat meals without any vegetables and fruit.

All forenoon there are classes for both Marion and me. Yesterday she concentrated on the women and today she is teaching the youth about health and diseases. I speak to them on being unequally yoked together with the world. Some of the boys participate, but there is a blockage here. The Spirit is not moving in their midst. In the afternoon there is a choir contest, and after supper they gather in groups around logfires for the service. I preach on "Taking Up Your Cross Daily." During my message I have to reprimand one group for talking and not listening. It appears the young people want only to sing and not learn the Word of God. When I give the altar call many of them come forward. Marion and I do not stay for

121

the singing afterwards but turn in for the night. The choirs keep singing into the night and do not stop until a quarter to one!

It is a short night for us as the ones in the next room are up early. The service gets underway at 9:30 A.M. We observe the Lord's Supper before the message. For juice we are using water that has been colored with a local red flower. I preach on "Spiritual Warfare." A sense of worship is lacking, and we soon know why. While we are dealing with those who have come for prayer, a woman begins to quake. The demons are tormenting her. I command them to come out in the name of Jesus! They react violently and toss her to the ground. It takes all four of us to control her. Eventually several demons leave her, except for two—Katende and Chisha. The latter is the name of one of the nearby hills. They keep refusing to vacate their host, whose name is Naomi. We battle on under the burning sun. I am sweating, dirty, and dusty from kneeling on the ground.

There is a standoff between us and the demonic powers here in Mbala District. I will not give in! Katende and Chisha inform us that they cannot leave because if they do then their commander will severely beat them! So, the devil has regiments and battalions in his army? We fight on in spite of physical exhaustion creeping in. The spirit is willing but the body is weak. Then, they agree to leave if they may be allowed to go into her baby! We decline their offer. They continue and ask whether they can inhabit her husband who, by the way, has three other wives. Again, we refuse. To my surprise one of the co-wives comes crawling up to us on her hands and knees and asks the demons to come into her! She has seen Naomi's plight and has volunteered to help her out. I rebuke the woman and send her away. We do not bargain with the devil!

Katende begins to complain that he is hot and tired, that he needs to go down to the river for water. We agree and send him on his way. Now it is just Chisha. He is much easier to deal with now that he is alone. I command him to go and join his friend. I receive a few more blows on my shoulder and arm, and so do the others who are helping me, before Chisha finally gives up and leaves. It was a three-hour battle, but we won. Thank the Lord for His sustaining power! Without His help we could never have defeated those two demons. We now ask the Holy Spirit to come into Naomi and fill up that vacancy left by the departed demons.

While we were dealing with Naomi, another woman was thrown about by evil spirits. I could not get to her so London dealt with her. He said she had five demons and that all had been driven out. There was a lot of opposition present, as it had been at the service outside the church at Chinzombo in Petauke District. That is why it took so long for Naomi to get delivered. Demons are everywhere out here! We have only scratched the surface. We must continue to fight.

After we eat a late dinner, we have a pastors' meeting and then a district meeting where a committee is chosen. A bike is given to the new chairman of the district to be used for overseeing the churches and planting new ones. Marion and I are beat from battling Satan but we continue with the program of the day. Finally, at nine we turn in. It has been an exciting day. We have stirred up a nest of hornets. Only these hornets are demons! They are going to hate us now, and that is for sure!

We get up five o'clock, roll up our mattress, and load the vehicle for our trip back to Lusaka. Before we can leave though, Marion passes out some medicine to the sick. Then at six, as dawn is breaking, we are on our way. We take another route from Katulo. It skirts the escarpment and connects up with the tarmac road farther down from Mbala. It is a quiet drive through the bush. No birds and animals! Before we left Katulo, someone had come to sell us some wild meat. We had eaten meat from a sitatunga two days earlier. It was nice and tender. These animals are found in the swamps near Lake Tanganyika. It is a few minutes after six when we reach home. We put in 2,121 kilometers this time. So the way through the bush is a bit shorter.

We pack our suitcases and it isn't until 8:30 A.M. before we set out for Petauke District. After we cross the Luangwa River we come across a troop of baboons and some monkeys. We also spot a poacher. It is noon when we reach Petauke town. Here we have a snack and fill up with diesel. Lungu has been waiting for us and we take him along. We use a different route to Chinzombo this time and we arrive at the village mid-afternoon. After we unload our things into the hut they have prepared for us, we eat some of their nsima. Then, we carry on to a nearby village, Chibali, to do some teaching. Many have come and after a few songs, I teach about being a Christian. In the end ten ask to become a follower of Christ. We pray for them and return to Chinzombo with 16 passengers packed inside the Nissan Patrol.

Before supper a woman comes for deliverance. She has heard how so many were delivered during out last visit and wants us to help her as well. We take her into the church and commence casting out the demons that are possessing her. Three different demons come out of the woman—a snake, a lion, and a lying spirit. It was refreshing to see them come out in short order. We also pray for the healing of a sick child who has a high fever. We are off to a good start! It is 9 P.M. when we turn in for the night and crawl into our sleeping bag.

It is after eight o'clock before we can leave for our first place of worship which is at Mwanjawanthu near the Mozambique border. When we arrive we find the teacher and his pupils still in the classroom we are to use. So we pick up two soldiers from the nearby camp and take them along to the border. They keep their automatic rifles ready as we drive along in the bush. When we reach the border we park the vehicle and walk across into Mozambique a short distance. We then stop and pray for peace to come to this war-torn country so that we can one day soon enter with the gospel of Jesus Christ. The two soldiers with us have removed their hats while we prayed. Having accomplished what we came for, we return to the village.

The classroom is full for our service. I preach on "Where Are You?" Thirty of them ask for salvation. Then, we pray for 11 who have come for deliverance. Three of them are only oppressed by evil spirits, but the other eight are possessed with demons. Most of the demons that come out of them are snakes and lions. Others cast out are unclean and foul spirits. Two of them also had monkeys. After the possessed have been delivered, we pray for the sick. One woman has scabies on her arms and another one cannot hear. Before leaving, we ask the Christians to choose their leader and the church committee of seven officers. I give them Bibles, hymn books, and to the new church leader I give a TEE book to study. They feed us yet before we make our departure.

Our next stop is Mumbi where we are preparing to establish a new church. We are two hours late because the casting out of demons took some time. But the chief is in a meeting of his own in the building we are to have our service in, so we end up waiting anyway. At five we finally get started. I preach on "I Am the Way" and nine accept Christ as their Saviour. After the service, we have them choose a leader and a committee as the Christians did at the previous place. They also receive their Bibles, hymn books, and the leader gets his TEE book. I pray for them and we turn our way back to Mwanjawanthu. It is after dark when we arrive. They have supper waiting for us. Marion and I retire to our hut at nine. It has been a full day, and very fulfilling. It is strange but I appear to have some kind of force in me, like a charge of electricity, as tonight and last night sparks jumped from my fingers when I touched something!

We are able to leave early this morning for our first place of worship. When we reach Kasero, no one is ready. It takes an hour before we can start. The meeting is in a classroom. It looks like a very backward place. In fact, it is within the devil's stronghold for the witchdoctor's domain is in the next village. Twenty-nine souls accept Christ as their Saviour after my message. Then, there are eight who want to be delivered from the power of Satan. Two of them are men! It has almost always been women. One of those men wearing long scraggly hair has a mad demon inside of him and is it ever strong! People in the classroom jump out of the way when desks begin to fly around. Some run outside very much afraid of the demon-possessed man. There are five of us hanging on to him so that he does not injure himself or us. He keeps insulting us over and over. His language gets so foul that Lungu quits translating and walks away. But Marion and I keep at it and finally the man is set free from the mad and foul spirits. Praise the Lord! What a battle that was!

This is the largest audience we have had watching us casting out demons. I had to rebuke them several times when they became unruly. I even told those who were laughing hysterically that the demons would come into them if they were not careful! That quietened them down. Demons do look for new hosts to enter into after being driven out of their previous ones. When they leave, they usually take along, especially if they have possessed that person or animal for years, some of their characteristics. That is why a human being can host demons or evil spirits who have at one time resided in a lion, snake, or monkey! They will grunt like a lion, twist like a snake, or screech like a monkey. We have already seen proof of it since coming to Zambia.

We leave at 12:30, after installing a leader and a committee. The leader they have chosen is the other man who had a demon cast out of him! The devil's hold has been broken on his life and we ask the Holy Spirit to use him now. He is enrolled in the TEE course. The next place we go to is back in the bush beyond Manyane near the Mozambique border. The village is in an isolated area and called Sikapala. The people here are backward and very much under the spell of Satan. The service is held under a tree. We pray for four of them who wish to accept Christ after my message. One of them becomes their leader and he receives the TEE book.

Then, we go to a village called Muya for our last service. It is now four o'clock. No one is ready so we end up waiting for the people to assemble. Our meeting is in front of a hunt. They are steeped in sin here as well. I preach on "You Cannot Serve Two Masters." I end up praying for many of them. There is one who is demon-oppressed and two who are demon-possessed. The difference is that one is being tormented outwardly by demons, usually in dreams, and the other is where the demons have already taken up residency in the person. By the mighty and powerful name of Jesus they are set free from the powers of darkness! The leader who is appointed has been a drunkard and has just accepted Christ. Will he make it? If not, then they will have to choose a different one. Right now there is no other choice. We have to start somewhere. Jesus did.

I get back at 7:00 P.M. It has been a full day! I came in contact with a lot of darkness. We felt it everywhere we went. I trust that God will add to what has been done, to make perfect that which is imperfect. Amen.

Our prayer this morning is that God will renew us for the work of this day. The service starts at ten o'clock. The little church building here at Chinzombo is not big enough for the crowd that gathers. There are 357 who have come to hear the Word of the Lord. I preach on "The Armour of God" and many come forward to repent and accept Christ into their hearts. We pray for many who want healing. There is so much disease in these villages. Finally, we deal with those who are demon-possessed. There are eight of them, one of them is a man. Two people take a long time to be delivered. I am worn out and so is Marion. When we have driven the demons out of five people, we stop to pray for added strength from the Lord. He grants it and we carry on with the remaining three. The demons have now been driven out of them all. A demon-oppressed woman is also delivered from her tormentors. There is still one more man who is possessed, but we cannot get through to him. A spirit of unbelief has engulfed him. He finally confesses that he has charms at home. So Lungu tells him to get rid of them and then return for deliverance.

It is 2:30 P.M. when we end this service! I meet with different church leaders yet before going to eat some food. After this we walk at least a kilometer down to a small river to baptize those converts who wish to be baptized. There is a spot in it where the water is deep enough for the candidates to be immersed and I baptize 34 of them after a short message. The water is cold! This is our first baptismal service in this district and it is a real testimony to all who have come to watch. It is dark by the time we get back to our hut. Two women are waiting to be prayed for. Our voices are hoarse from commanding the demons to come out, but we can still communicate properly. Tomorrow we return to Lusaka. This has been a fruitful trip where many got saved, healed, and delivered. The future of the work in this district looks great. It is growing like wildfire!

Three women from Kasero who were delivered yesterday have brought their paraphernalia which they used when possessed. There are charms, ceremonial axes, fly whisks, and bells made from seed pods which they wear around their feet while dancing. Truly, this is a sign that they have found Christ and are giving up their old traditions. Praise the Lord, the shadow of darkness is retreating!

Ten
Driving Back the Forces of Darkness

Satan has been trying to deter us from forging ahead in our search for a deeper walk with God so that we can perform our ministry in a greater way. It is driving us to our knees asking the Lord for His assistance. Marion and I have a season of prayer each night. We must be firmly united as we face all the demon-possession in this land, and engage the devil in an all-out struggle for souls. The warfare against darkness is a very real battle here!

Then one day, Marion and I walk from room to room, opening up closets, and binding any forces of darkness that may be lurking in them. Whenever we detect any demons, and they are there in places, we cast them out in the name of Jesus Christ. Did not Jesus say, "In my name they will drive out demons" (Mark 16:17b)? Then again, "He gave them power and authority to drive out all demons." (Luke 9:1) The previous occupants of this house were Iranians who left behind pictures and writings which disclosed their belief in the powers of darkness. The landlord informed us of their secretive ways, not even allowing him inside to check on his own house! Therefore, the darkness left behind by them needed to be bound and cast out.

This weekend we are in Kitwe District, which is in

the Copperbelt Province, for classes and services. Rufus and Wilson from Uganda are assisting Marion and me. They came in by bus today and will be with us for four weeks. Both were very much a part of the church in Uganda when we served there. It is a joy to see them again! Wilson preaches the message tonight at the church in Kwacha East. They have brought along some mail from Colleen which we read with interest. We are spending the night in a guesthouse here in the town of Kitwe.

In the morning we eat from our lunch box which Marion brought along from home. The four of us are busy with classes all forenoon. It is a hot day and shade is hard to find. The building here does not have as of yet a roof so we are getting enough sun. A lot of people come today and the church is full. There is a district meeting in the afternoon, and a choir contest after that. Rufus is the speaker tonight in the service. Our wedding anniversary today slipped by quietly.

The Sunday morning service does not start until ten o'clock. There was plenty of singing before that. Many come forward, about fifty, after Wilson's message. Three demon-possessed women have to be prayed for. I end up dealing with two of them and it takes an hour to drive them all out. I found the demons quite stubborn. London takes the third person and deals with her outside. When he thinks she has been delivered, a demon reacts as soon as the woman returns inside. Wilson takes over and casts out the remaining one. Before the service closes I speak. I did not intend to but the Spirit is upon me. I exhort them to leave their traditional beliefs behind and to follow Christ with their whole heart. It ends on a high! If the meetings could continue a few more days, I believe the Christians would be helped even more.

We leave Kitwe at 1:30 P.M. and reach Lusaka four

and a half hours later. We find Mark, our son, waiting for us at home. He arrived yesterday and Ritter, the Principal of the American International School, picked him up at the airport. Mark wants to work in Zambia, where his parents are, and wants to teach at the American-International School. Kim, his wife, will follow him in a few weeks as soon as Mark get settled. They were married in Carstairs, Alberta, on June 30, 1990. We flew there for it and I officiated at the wedding. Angelina, one of our workers from Tanzania, flies in this evening and will be with us for two weeks. She was a great help, first as a house girl and then as a pastor, when Marion and I served in Tanzania. Colleen phones us tonight and wishes us a happy anniversary. It's great to hear her voice again.

There is a fuel shortage here in Zambia and service stations all have long queues at their pumps. The prices have doubled! Tomorrow we are going to Mbala for several days of classes and services. Therefore, we need to take along extra fuel or else we may get stranded far away from home. At Kampala we found jerry cans in plenty but not so here. I end up having to drive from one end of the city to the other before I manage to find two of them!

Marion and I pack the clothes we are taking along into an old suitcase, eat breakfast, and then leave for Katulo in Mbala District at 6:15 A.M. Lungu, Wilson, Rufus, and Angelina are with us. We are able to put everyone inside the Nissan Patrol as the mattress, pillows, sleeping bag, and two cases are placed on the roof rack. At Mpika we find a shady tree under which to eat our lunch, which Marion made before leaving home. Here I also fill up the vehicle and the two jerry cans with diesel. It is now 12:30, or as the Zambians say, "Half twelve." We turn off onto the Katito road, the same one that we came out on our last safari, and make good time in spite of the sandy spots along the way. We reach Katulo at 6:30 P.M. The seminar this time will be near the river below at a place called Karonga. There is still a service tonight in which Wilson is the preacher. Marion and I are sleeping in our vehicle tonight while the others are spending it in a building which has separate rooms but no roof.

We spend a cool night in the vehicle. The water they bring us this morning is hot which helps to revive us both. Classes begin just after nine and all of us are kept busy all day teaching. Some meet under large trees while others inside the grass enclosures which also serve as sleeping quarters during the night. In the evening Marion and Angelina give out medicine to the sick while I hold a district meeting. There is a service tonight after supper within the largest enclosure and Wilson again preaches. All attend it, except for me. I need to catch up on some rest. Also, I am not keen on preaching or meeting in the dark. I remember the last time we were here when the youth gathered around their little fires and visited. It upsets me too much. Tonight the choirs sing until midnight and then quit. Praise the Lord!

The night is not as cold as last night and we could keep two windows down a bit for fresh air. I shave at the vehicle with cold water from the water jug. The latrine is just a grass enclosure with no roof. Again, we teach throughout the day until four o'clock. I have to be straight with the youth as they are very rebellious. They talk among themselves instead of listening. I have my hands full trying to keep order. I even have to take away the drums from the children who are playing them during class time! The youth are very bound in darkness here in spite of turning up in large numbers to sing. They have not been taught properly in the past. Marion and Angelina treat the patients between four and six o'clock. There is a baptismal service at five where thirty are baptized. Rufus preaches in the service after supper.

Some sick show up this morning and Marion with Angelina treats them after breakfast. The first service today is at 9:30 and Wilson delivers the message. Many come forward for prayer. Some have come for healing and we pray for them. I also deal with a demon-possessed woman. It does not take long and she is delivered from her demons. Wilson drives the demons out of another one as well. It is very hot in the open enclosure. The place is filled with people. At four I preach on "Judgment Day" in the second service. I feel anointed and God blesses! Again we have many coming for prayer. A demon-possessed woman I deal with has a snake demon and an ancestral spirit. It takes me some time before they are cast out in Jesus' name. The latter had been in her for years. Marion and Angelina treat more patients this evening while I talk to the leaders. We are leaving early in the morning for Lusaka so Marion and I turn in at ten.

I have a dream during the night where Marion and I enter a house which has no lights. When I look outside there is darkness as well. Then, I see a stranger in the next room who acts as though he is the owner of the building. Hands suddenly appear out of the darkness and begin choking me. I sense an evil power and begin binding it in the name of Jesus. It is then that I awaken. What is the meaning of this dream? It does not take me long to know what it is. It means that Satan does not like our invasion of his stronghold here in Mbala District.

The first church to be started in the city of Lusaka is at Garden in early 1990. Marion planted it by teaching some women at the house of Lungu's relative. It soon grew into a congregation where we meet for services each Sunday. When there were too many for the front yard, the group moved into a classroom in the nearby school.

Six months later when we meet at Garden, a woman falls over with demons racking her body just before Wilson is about to deliver his message. Rufus and Angelina are present, as well as our son Mark. It takes place during the singing of a chorus which is quite lively with some women starting to dance. I stop them, as they keep singing in spite of the shrieking woman. I tell them to pray instead. The demon-possessed person is becoming very violent. The worst I have seen thus far. She is very strong and it takes five of us to try and keep her from hurting herself against the school desks as she thrashes about. She bites and pinches, even bites into the Bible which I am holding. When I touch her on the chest with the Bible, she tries to shake it off! I touch her hand and she desperately tries to knock it away. She bites at my hand. I withdraw it in time before her teeth sink into my knuckles! Fortunately her teeth just scratch my skin. It takes about an hour to deliver her from the ten demons that possess her. Without the Lord's help we could not have done it.

While dealing with her, one of the women in church fetches some water and prays over it with intentions to sprinkle it on the demon-possessed woman. I had Marion take away the water from her. It is witchcraft and will certainly not help in driving out any demon! Wilson also deals with one woman, as I have my hands full. She has only one demon and is soon delivered. After the one I was dealing with is delivered, a third woman with two demons reacts. Wilson preaches the message while Lungu and I attend to the possessed person in another room. The first demon comes out readily but the second one is more difficult. The woman becomes like a corpse! She is stiff and makes no movement at all. When we try to sit her up, her whole body comes up straight as a board. I have never dealt with a demon such as this one! When the service ends, to my disappointment we have to leave the woman still with her demon as there is another service planned at Chawama. I will never do that again. (And I haven't!) What a day this has been!

We are up early for our five-day trip to Eastern Province where this time we will be going to Petauke, Katete, and Chipata Districts. There has been rebel activity along the border with Mozambique and people have been killed by gunmen. We had asked the police whether it was safe to go and we were told that it was. After breakfast we start off. Lungu is with us. At the Nyimba roadblock, we pick up Oscar Ndao, the pastor from Mwanjawanthu, who is also a medical worker at the clinic there, to travel with us. Our first meeting is at Mtambata in Petauke District where 578 have gathered, many of them children. There is a school here and it appears they want us to help them. Nothing unusual about that! There are speeches from the teachers and songs by the children. Then I speak about "Seeking First the Kingdom of God." We pray for many afterwards. Then we also pray for the leader and his committee as we are starting a new church here. Marion and I are given a pair of doves and we give them a box of chalk for the school.

Our next stop is at Chinzombo. It is 17 hours when we arrive. The Christians have built a hut for us. it is about eight feet by eight feet square with a grass roof. Very thoughtful of them! There are some rain clouds with lightning and thunder this evening. We receive a shower but that is all. The service tonight is beside a log fire. The choir has improved much in their songs. After my message tnere are several who want prayer. Before we retire there is a meeting with the officers of this church.

Except for only a few insects crawling over our sleeping bag, our night in the hut passed okay. Breakfast is at seven and an hour later we meet in the church for a service. I preach on the qualifications of a pastor and a deacon. There is a district meeting after the service so they need to know what is expected of them. Pray for several sick, and also for a demon-possessed woman. She has two of them, a baboon and a religious one. They are driven out in about fifteen minutes. In the district meeting Oscar Ndao is chosen as the chairman. He and his wife Mailes accepted Christ under our ministry. We pray for the newly elected committee and then leave for Mwanjawanthu.

Here we are served dinner before the service, which is in the classroom again. I preach on baptism as I will be baptizing several candidates afterwards. I pray for some sick, and seven children who are being dedicated by their parents. They are mostly mothers, as the unsaved fathers are not present. I also pray for two couples who wish to have their marriages blessed as they were not wedded in a church. A new pastor is chosen as Oscar is now the district chairman. The pastor is now a woman, Joyce Nkhata. Then, we walk to the Nkanya River two kilometers away and 14 are baptized. The water is actually warm. There is a service tonight beside a logfire. Soldiers from the nearby border post are present. I preach on "If Anyone Loves Me, He Will Obey My Teachings." I pray for several afterwards and for one who is demon-oppressed. There is also a demon-possessed person who is set free from them through the name of Jesus. I close the meeting tonight with a prayer for rain as the crops around here are drying up. I have them join their hands and form a large circle around the fire. The soldiers lay aside their weapons and join us.

We leave Mwanjawanthu at 8:00 A.M. for Songwe in Katete District. Oscar is coming along. After reaching the village, we meet with the headman. He wants us to meet the chief so we travel to his boma which is only a short distance away. The chief has a high-pitched voice and is demon-possessed. He doesn't allow us to plant any church in his chiefdom. "Iyai! Iyai!" ("No! No!") he screams at us continuously in falsetto. We drive on to Katete town and ask the police whether we can hold a service at Songwe. He informs us that we can and to ignore the chief. So we return to the village and hold a service. Only men show up. I preach on "Jesus is the Way." Seventeen accept Christ as their Saviour. Many questions follow, for over an hour. Finally, we are able to get away and look for something to eat in Katete. Nothing. We return to Songwe. I meet the chief going to town on his bike. Luckily, Marion brought along some cheese and biscuits from home so we eat them with the bananas we found here in the village.

It rains heavily in the mid-afternoon. An answer to our prayer at Mwanjawanthu last night! This should revive their crops. Thank you, Lord! We meet again for another service at 4:00 P.M. This time women and children show up. I preach on "Listen to Jesus." Sixteen receive salvation. There are three demon-possessed women present. The Holy Spirit is very much present and the demons are driven out in short order. Praise the Lord! It is a big testimony to all in the crowd. We choose the leader and committee before leaving. I am excited about the results today! Satan tried to keep us out but God opened the way.

We had prayed that He would bind the chief and the powers of darkness here. And He has! Thank you, Lord. The headman gives us some nsima to eat before we retire at 20 hours. Marion and I are sleeping in the vehicle while Lungu and Oscar are saying in a nearby hut.

It is light before 5:-00 A.M. out here. People are passing by so we have to get up. Dress in the vehicle. What a job! We have some tea and cookies which Marion has brought along. Oscar and Lungu had a poor night and ended up by sleeping outside where they were bitten by mosquitos. They had moved out because there were too many lice in the hut. Many come for prayer yet before we can leave. They are the sick and those who need to be saved. One is demon-oppressed and we pray for his deliverance. Finally, we get going and stop at a hut in the bush a couple of kilometers off the main road to pray for a very sick woman. It looks as if she is suffering from AIDS. We pray for two others who are brought to us, one for healing as well and the other for demon-oppression.

After this we travel to Chipata District. We are going to a remote village called Kalume, deep in the bush about 40 kilometers north of the main road. Along the way we come across a dry sandy riverbed and I have to use the 4-wheel drive before I can get to the other side. The people are waiting for us when we arrive. In the service, after my message, most of them come forward for prayer. After praying for them, we choose the church leader and the committee of deacons. Then we are off to another place.

At the village of Mitolo we meet with the chief who turns out to be an agreeable old man. His son is to become the new church leader here. After the sermon, eleven accept Christ as their Saviour. Marion treats the sick with the medicine she has brought along before we leave for our third meeting of the day. It is at Chindola village.

Here I preach on "Where Are You?" and no one comes up for prayer. There is a lot of darkness in this place. Even our contact person is too backward to be a leader here. I tell them we will not be back and leave. On our way back to Kalume where we will be staying the night, we pass through the village of Lufu. Here we stop and pass out tracts. We are asked to come back and plant a church. So, God shut one door and opened another one!

When we reach Kalume there is a demon-possessed woman waiting to be delivered. Tired as we are we take time to cast out the demons in the name of Jesus. Marion assists me as she always does by holding her from behind so that she does not thrash around too much should the demons react violently. We finally have something to eat at 8 o'clock. Food is served in a dirty pot as they do not seem to possess any dishes. It's a good thing it is pitch dark tonight so we do not see what we are eating. The Nissan Patrol is our bedroom again tonight. Oscar and Lungu are bedding down outside on the ground as it is still hot when we retire.

We are up at five o'clock. A mosquito got in last night and we are bitten up. We had to turn the window down as it was too warm inside. They serve us only tea this morning which we have with some of Marion's biscuits. There are no toilets here, nor any enclosures for bathing. When I ask them why they do not build toilets, their answer is that they use the bush. If that is the case, I tell them they should at least have a hoe handy. To this they answer that their pigs are the cleaning crew! Many have bilharzia due to their bathing and drinking from the same water in the nearby stream. They are real backward here! They are also lazy, as they have no chairs, just one or two small stools fit for only children to sit on. We head out at 7:00 A.M. for Lusaka and home.

140

Early one morning as I step outside the house at Makeni, I spot a pigeon lying dead on the sidewalk. I pick it up and give it to our gardener. The bird must have gotten killed when it hit the roof during the night. So the pigeon should still be fit for eating. But shortly after, I hear from Lungu, who lives on the compound, and he said that when they came to prepare the pigeon they discovered it had no insides! He hesitantly informs me that someone is attempting to bewitch me. The pigeon was a messenger of death, used by a witch doctor to deliver some bad omen. It takes effect as soon as someone touches it. That was me!

Several weeks pass by and I am none the worse for having touched the pigeon that I am told was sent by a witch doctor. Then one of our leaders from Kitwe calls in. He informs me that his daughter was killed a week ago by lightning! She was sitting in her sister's house at the time when, for no reason at all since the sky was clear and there was no sign of rain, a lightning bolt entered through the open door killing her instantly. The flash also grazed the right hand of her sister's husband, who was in the house at the time, burning it badly. The man outside the door who was passing with wheelbarrow is killed as well. A man who is visiting us at the time calls me aside and says that this punishment has come about as a result of something he had done. What?

We soon hear that just before the pigeon dropped dead on our yard, the man's wife went to see a witch doctor and asked his assistance in getting rid of the missionary. The method he used is open for speculation. But it is reported that when the man's daughter dies instead of me, the wife returns to the witchdoctor and denounces him for not using strong enough medicine. Little do they realize that God's power is greater than all the powers of darkness put together. He caused the evil they intended for me and returned it onto their own heads!

The Lord is helping us to drive back the powers of darkness. Praise His Name!

A baptismal service.

Marion teaching the women.

Preaching at a village service.

Teaching pastors at a seminar.

Marion helping to shell groundnuts.

Marion handing out used clothing.

Our sleeping quarters at a village.

Marion helping to treat the sick.

Children enjoying nsima and greens.

Cooked grasshoppers with the meal.

Preparing nsima for our meal.

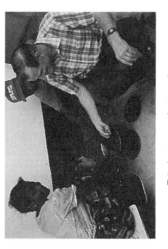

Fried ants ready to eat!

Crossing a river on a pontoon.

Ox cart with a spare ox.

Crossing a stream on a make-shift bridge.

Digging for water in a riverbed.

The Ndaos receiving their Certificates.

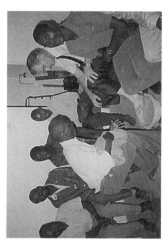

Foot-washing service at Easter.

Pastors receiving TEE books and Bibles.

Communion service at a seminar.

Transporting maize to famine areas.

Passing out the maize to the needy.

Returning to their homes with their portions.

The lame, the leper, and the blind receive help.

African doctors advertising their cure-alls.

African doctors are still very popular.

Our church at Kayama, Lusaka.

One of our churches in a village.

Commanding the demon to come out of her!

Delivered woman surrenders her dancing rattles.

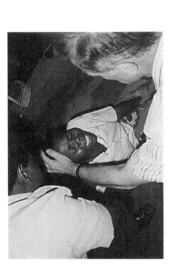

A demon-possessed woman begins to react.

The demons put up a struggle.

A poacher with his muzzle-loader.

An elephant looking for a cool drink!

A ten-foot black mamba.

Nyau dancer of the Chewa tribe.

Drilling for water.

Water pump at the bore-hole.

Reinhard Berle receiving gifts.

Looking after her baby sister.

Eleven
The Devil Fights Back

Colleen calls us this evening and informs us that she and Tim have been given fourteen days notice from the Immigration Department to leave Uganda. It is a severe blow to receive this kind of news from our daughter! She says that no reason has been given for their expulsion order. It appears two of their leaders, who have been stirring up trouble for them with government officials concerning the re-registration of the church, are behind it. God, will you allow this injustice to succeed? After I hang up, Jim and Jeanne Weems from Portland, Oregon, who are with us for a month, join Marion and me in a season of prayer. I cry out to God from the depths of my soul for the future work of Colleen and Tim! I storm the gates of heaven on their behalf. I bind the forces of evil at work in Uganda, and rebuke the devil who is in the lives of those leaders who are involved in this scheme to have our kids deported. "Lord, answer our prayers please!" I plead with a heavy heart.

I call Colleen and Tim at seven this morning to tell them we have been praying for them, and that we touched the throne of God last night. She says that today the Executive Committee will meet with the Vice-president of Uganda and the Foreign Minister to try and revoke the deportation letter from Immigration. I tell Colleen that what hurts her also hurts me. She answers, "I know, Dad." Last night before going to sleep, after Marion and I got through praying for Colleen and Tim, my heart almost broke! My spirit groaned within me and I could not stop for some time. How I wanted to take their place so that they could avoid the anguish. "Lord, please take care of my little girl!"

During the two weeks that follow, Tim is privileged to meet with the Vice-president three times and he grants them permission to stay in Uganda. He sees no reason that they had received the deportation order. In the meantime, we receive a letter on the 28th of March, 1991, from the Mission Board stating that a letter had been received from one of our church leaders in Kitwe. He had written that our services here in Zambia will terminate July, 1992. The Board wants to know what we plan to do after that? This is all news to us! There are some here as well who want to get rid of their missionaries. Lord, you need to help us also. The devil is out to stop the ministry that we, and the Stevensons, are in. We are a threat to him!

I had a dream the night before last that I was ploughing a field and I came across a nest of snakes. They were small so I walked over them. But, then, I saw something dragging along behind me. I lifted the foot and discovered a large snake attached to my heel! The mother snake, I supposed. I stamped on it with such force I woke up Marion and myself. Is the snake that leader?

The letter to the Mission Board has upset Marion and she is up most of the night. Do burdens ever cease? I have learned to leave them with the Lord, but Marion clings to them for some time. While I am sleeping, I have another dream and Marion hears me keep saying, "Yes! Yes! Yes!" In my dream I am driving my vehicle around in

154

an enclosed village, trying to get away from another vehicle which is attempting to head me off at the corners. I succeed finally in eluding the pursuer and wake up drained. I do not usually dream, but when I do I am able to know when it is of the Lord. This one tonight has shown me that Satan is out to corner me but he is failing!

I have been trying to call the Stevensons for days now, but no one answers. Then, I try Kirk's number and he comes on the line. From him I learn that the Stevensons' phone is out of order. No wonder our faxes do not go through either. Our phone has been acting up as well. It goes off for days and then it comes on for a day or two. So our communication with Colleen and Tim during this time of anxiety is next to nil.

Marion and I have started fasting. We want the Lord to work in our lives in a much greater way, and to defeat the enemies of the church in Zambia and in Uganda. The Lord has laid it on our hearts to fast three days and four nights. We do not eat food, only drink liquids. We are listening to the book of Acts. It is inspiring to hear how the Holy Spirit moved in the early Church! Our prayer is that He will move in our lives and in today's Church as well. I try to call Colleen but there is no answer. Their phone must be out of order still. They have their Executive Council meeting today. Our prayer is that God will perform a miracle there and set things aright.

Two days later, and we still are unable to reach the Stevensons by phone. Marion and I are wondering how they fared in their meetings with the Executive and the Council the last two days. I wish they would let us know since I cannot reach them. The operator in Kampala told us that their phone is out of order. After another two days pass by, we receive a call from Gary Kellsey. He wants to know how Tim and Colleen are doing as he heard that

Tim is in prison! I tell him we have not heard that news. The next morning I call Kirk and find the line to East Africa is down. What next? Satan is in charge of a lot of things. At noon a fax comes through from the UNICEF office in Kampala. It is a letter from Colleen. She brings us up to date on what has transpired with them the last five days.

On April 10th, 1991, Tim received a notice to go and see the Commissioner of Immigration concerning his passport. He thought nothing of this and hoped that their work permit would be granted as theirs was expiring on May the 4th. When Tim arrived at Immigration, he was sent directly to the Commissioner's office. He was asked why he had not yet left the country as he had been ordered to do. By their quit notice they were to have left the country on the 27th of March. Tim answered him that the Vice-president had told him to stay. To this the Commissioner blurted out, "Who is the Vice-president anyway?" Then, he placed Tim under arrest and hauled him off to prison.

At 6:00 P.M. Kasto shows up and tells Colleen that Tim has been arrested! She is stunned. He explains that when he had gone to Immigration to pick up Tim, they told him that he had been taken off to prison. They would not tell him to which one. Kasto tells Colleen he will go and find the Chief Inspector of Police and ask him where Tim has been taken to. She herself now notifies Kirk and Karen of Tim's arrest and imprisonment. He calls UN security on his phone and they swing into action in an endeavour to seek Tim's release. But Kirk is told that since Tim was put in under the Immigration Act, only the President or the Minister of Internal Affairs could release him.

It is 9:00 P.M. when Kasto returns and informs Colleen that Tim is being held at the Jinja Road Police Station. She gathers together some books, a Bible, sweets, and a few other things to take to him. Kirk then drives her to where Tim is being held a prisoner. It is now eleven o'clock. There she finds him already sleeping along with 27 others, all occupying the same cell! It is devastating to see him like this. Colleen asks the policeman on duty if he could allow Tim to come out of his cell so that she can visit with him. The officer refuses, saying that this is a delicate case. Kirk, noticing that the man had been drinking, tells him that if he does not comply he will call the Chief of Police on his phone and brief him that the officer on duty is drunk. Upon hearing this, the man brings Tim out and seats him behind the desk. This is where they now can visit with him.

While he eats the snacks Colleen has brought, they plan the actions they will take tomorrow. Tim fills them in of what had taken place prior to his imprisonment. He also shares with her that the prisoners, when they heard that he was a missionary, had asked him to preach. They produced a tattered Bible and he preached from it a sermon after singing some songs. They then asked for prayer. Some of his cell mates are hardened criminals. It is after midnight when Tim is returned to his cell and Colleen with Kirk leave the police station.

Because their phones are out, Colleen is unable to reach us in Zambia, nor his folks in Canada, to relay the urgency for prayer. During this most trying time Kirk and Karen are a great support to her, plus David Reames and Bob Edwards, Missionary Board representatives, who came two days earlier to attend the Executive Council meeting. In the morning Colleen, the two Missionary Board representatives, all the Executive Council members, some U.N. personnel, and the Canadian Consulate are all present outside the Jinja Road Police Station. It is a sight to see! The police cannot believe their eyes at the large delegation that has come to the aid of the missionary they are holding. Eventually the Commissioner sends for Tim and they all follow in a convoy down to the Immigration Department. All day they work on Tim's release. The Minister of Foreign Affairs and the Vice-president are both involved in procuring finally his release at 5:00 P.M. that evening.

The Commissioner tells Tim that he still wants him deported from Uganda and hangs onto his passport. In reality Tim is now under house arrest. He cannot leave the country until all the investigations are over with. When Tim is returned to Kasubi where the Executive Council is meeting, he is lifted up and carried to the altar in front and placed upon it. The Council members then offer up a prayer of thanks to God for Tim's release! In the meeting that follows, the Council defrocks and expels the two men that are responsible for Tim's imprisonment and for trying to harm the bylaws of the Church. It appears they got the Commissioner to collaborate with them in their scheme to get rid of the missionaries by refusing to renew Tim's work permit.

In her fax, Colleen asks us to call Tim's folks in Ontario, Canada, and inform them of what has transpired in the last five days. Marion and I also call Gary Kellsey in Alberta and bring him up to date. The following day we decide to fast again. Marion and I want God to move in on the enemies of His Church, especially in Uganda. We are standing on Isaiah 41:9–13 and on Isaiah 54:15–17. Wonderful promises that speak of God's care and protection for His servants. Marion types out a letter for Tim and Colleen encouraging them with the above Scriptures, and faxes it to Kirk since their line is still out. It takes several attempts, and two days, before it finally gets through to them where it is readable! The devil even tries to keep the Word from reaching our kids in Uganda. Unbelievable!

It is our third day of fasting. We begin listening to the book of Philippians on audio tape. After a season of prayer, I involve myself in some office work. At ten o'clock Edith, our new house girl who knows very little English, appears in the doorway of my office waving her arms and trying to say something but no words pass her lips. She motions for me to follow her into the living room. I find Marion, lying on the floor and there is a pool of blood beside her head! I had heard a thud but thought nothing of it as she was showing Edith places to clean and dust. I rush to her side and cradle her head in my lap. Is she dead? No, she is unconscious. I see where the blood is seeping from a gash on the forehead, and place my hand over it to stop the bleeding. There must be a fracture as the skull appears indented! I commence calling on the Lord to heal her and not to take her just yet as I still need her. "Lord, Please spare her life!" I plead.

To my left I can see blood and some hair where Marion's head had struck the cement step leading up to the dining area. She had stepped on top of a bedside stand to show Edith where she is to wash on top the windows and then as she turned around to step down, the top came loose and tilted, slapping her on the lower part of the back. This sends her flying ahead, hitting with her tail bone the stool she had used to get onto the stand. The stool then tipped causing her to land on the side of her forehead. It looks bad!

I continue to plead with the Lord for Marion's recovery. I hold her close and kiss her blood-smeared face. My hand is still pressing down on the cut. I do not stop knocking at heaven's gate. An hour passes by. Then, Marion be-

159

gins to stir. Thank you, Lord, for hearing me! She weakly asks me not to move her as her back is paining. The hands and feet are getting numb as well, she adds. Then, she begins to shiver. I carry on praying, calling on the Lord to restore her fully. Marion joins me in praying. We now unite our faith and trust God for a miraculous recovery to take place. She does not want to be taken anywhere, she wants only God to heal her.

I ask Edith, who has been standing by all this time horrified at what she is witnessing, to fetch Lungu. He arrives and helps us in praying for a miracle. Two of the other workers make an appearance and stand around to watch what will transpire. Finally, at twelve noon Marion asks to get up. I had just finished reading where Jesus healed the crippled and the lame. By this time the shivering had stopped and the numbness was gone. She stands up and begins to walk back and forth in the living room, her hands raised high above her head and praising the Lord! I rejoice with her, but the rest stand around staring at her face covered with blood and wondering whether the white lady had flipped. A thing like this just does not normally take place! Truly, it is a miracle. God has answered prayer. He has extended Marion's days here on earth so that she can still assist me in driving back the darkness in this land. Thank you, Lord!

I wash away the blood on her face and in her hair as best as I can. Then, I tuck her into bed. I call up Mark and Kim and share with them of what has just transpired. She comes over and patches up the gash on Marion's forehead with some butterfly adhesive strips she has brought along. Kim has had some experience in dressing wounds from working in a hospital in Calgary, Alberta. She suggests that we have her checked at one of the clinics. So we place Marion on the back seat of the vehicle and drive to

Monica Chiumya Clinic where a Polish woman doctor examines her. The X-rays reveal that the back, even though badly bruised, has no broken bones. But the skull has a crack on her upper left-hand corner of the forehead. She has had a narrow escape from death! The doctor scolds Marion for crawling up on a stool at her age. "That's what you have workers for!" she declares, I silently agree.

Marion is much better the following morning. Praise the Lord! She had a good night of rest and her cut on the forehead is closing up nicely. A miracle! She will not need any stitches. I wash her head and her hair again as there is still some blood on them. She takes a shower and gets up for breakfast. I have broken my fast as well. I am down to 165 pounds. I lost about ten pounds due to the two fasts we have had back-to-back. They were three and a half days each. As the week progresses, Marion steadily improves. She is taking heavy doses of Vitamin C to help along the healing process. The eye that had turned black is now about back to normal. On the seventh day after the accident, she is able to dress herself on her own. The swelling on the bottom of her back and buttocks is gradually receding but there remains plenty of purple coloring yet. The cut on her forehead is almost healed. The dizzy spells still persist though, but that is normal for such a nasty skull fracture she has just received.

We are still praying that God will reward the righteous and punish the wicked. A new verse comes to us today as we listen to Second Thessalonians this morning before prayer. It is in chapter one and verse six: "God is just, He will pay back trouble to those who trouble you." Thank you. We will stand on it! Kirk sends a fax and informs us that the Commissioner for Immigration has asked Tim to submit his work permit, and an air ticket out of the country, to his office immediately. Five days later Kirk phones us as our power is off and the fax that he's trying to send cannot come through. He reports that Tim is still around. The Vice-president has again stopped the Commissioner from deporting Tim. But he still has Tim's work permit, air ticket, and passport in his custody. The UNICEF Representative is setting up an appointment for Tim to talk to President Museveni himself. So it is going all the way to the top! Kirk went on to say that the Criminal Investigation Department (CID) will now be investigating the whole matter. Reinhard Berle is coming and will probably also involve the Ambassador from Germany. Kinderhilfswerk has assisted in many projects because of the Stevensons being in Uganda.

Two days later, Tim's folks phone us and want to know whether we have any latest news on Tim. They had heard that he was to have been out of Uganda yesterday? Then we have a nice surprise this evening when Colleen calls and talks to us about an hour! Their phone is finally working. It is nice to hear her again. Tim still has not seen the President. It is all on hold. The Commissioner has been told to cool it. A decision will be made once the investigations have been completed. She appreciated the Scriptures which we had sent her earlier. They have been a great comfort to them, she adds. We then give her 2 Thessalonians 1:6. God is just and He will have the final say. We believe that and will continue to stand on it! The devil can rage and roar but he will not win this battle.

We call back a week later and Colleen bring us up to date on the situation in Uganda. She tells us that they are still being harassed by the two men who were dismissed by the Council. In four days Tim's work permit is expiring. It will be his final day in Uganda should Immigration fail to renew it. Surely the Lord will not allow the enemy to be victorious in this situation. We do not know how to pray about Uganda anymore. The Spirit groans within us as He intercedes for us before the throne of God.

When four days pass by and we call Stevensons, the operator answers and says that the line to East Africa is down. How about that! There is no way now to find out Tim's condition as today his work permit expires. The devil is fighting back in whichever way he can! When we do not hear from them, I try phoning again three days later. The line is still out, the operator informs me. What a disappointment! We had made prior arrangements that today would be the day that we call them as it is Karen's birthday and they would all be together at Stevensons. A day later, I phone Bob Edwards in Nairobi, Kenya, and the call goes through. He lets us know that he just arrived back from Kampala and it looks good. The CID has not yet finished investigating the case, therefore the deportation order by the Commissioner is still on hold. He says that Kirk has been a great help to Tim and Colleen. He has given them a UNICEF vehicle to move around with as their new Nissan Patrol is still with customs. We continue to pray for Uganda.

It is twelve days later and after many failures, before we make contact again. We already are sleeping when Colleen and Tim call us tonight. Their phone just started working. We talk for an hour. They are still waiting on the Vice-president for his decision, but it looks good. The case was mentioned on the radio in a positive way. Another fifteen days slip by before we hear again from Colleen. It is on Marion's 60th birthday. All the grandchildren, including Tim, get on the line and wish her a happy birthday. It is nice to hear from them again. Their case is still in limbo. They share the news of a soldier from Rukungiri, whom I knew very well, who was shot and killed by bandits. The bus that he was riding in, which was on its way to Kampala, was held up and he was singled out and shot. He was a close friend to the two dismissed church leaders. Did God allow this to take place for a reason? Was he up to some mischief? Death threats on Tim, and his family, have been circulating around Kampala for some time.

Six weeks pass by when Colleen phones and asks us to write a letter to the Vice-president of Uganda appealing to him to have our name cleared as the two dismissed men have now dragged us into the arena of combat. They have requested Immigration not to allow us into the country for any reason! The secretary to the Vice-president is assisting Tim in his case with Immigration and has asked for this letter. Kirk, who is presently visiting us in Zambia, with his family, helps us draft it. When completed I fax the letter to Colleen and Tim. They will deliver it to the office of the Vice-president.

On the 6th of August, 1991, seventeen days after writing the above letter, Colleen and Tim read in the newspaper that the Commissioner of Immigration has been removed from his post. They are elated! Their phone, which happens to be working at the time, does not stop ringing all day. So many want to congratulate them and to just say that they are happy for them. What about Tim's passport? Three days later the Vice-president hands Tim his passport and asks him to go to Immigration and start applying for his and Colleen's work permits. What a turn of events! The following day they have them, in time to catch that scheduled flight to Zambia that they had by faith booked earlier. They land in Lusaka and are welcomed by a thankful Mom and Dad who are so happy to have them in their home once more. "Thank you, Lord, for seeing them through this terribly long ordeal! Give them now a well deserved rest," is my prayer.

I recall a similar case that took place years earlier in my own life while still in Tanzania. It is recorded in my book *To a Land He Showed Us,* chapter 13. That case started in April as this one did, and then ended four frustrating months later, in August, as this one just did. It is now a time for rejoicing! The devil put up a good fight, but in the end he has been defeated. Praise the Lord!

During their stay with us, Colleen comes down with malaria. The fever is draining her of whatever strength she still has left from her hardships in Uganda. Marion and I anoint her with oil and pray for her healing. The Spirit is present and I know that she is being healed. In fact, I feel the fever drop on her brow under my hand! We are touched as she pours her heart out of how she has always been faithful to Him, which is true, and never really bad, which is again true. Yet, she goes on to say, why does God allow her to pass through so much deep water? All I can answer her is that He has promised to be with us and to deliver us. And He just has.

My prayer is that the problem will be over with now, and will not carry on after they return to Uganda. The whole family have surely weathered enough storms already to last them a long time!

Twelve
The Battle Continues

We have taken Jim and Jeanne Weems with us to Kitwe for a service at the Kwacha East church. It starts at 10:30 A.M. Jim brings the message after the choirs have sung numerous songs. I give the altar call after he has concluded and many come forward for prayer. Then, the demons start activating and before we know it there are ten lying on the floor shrieking and kicking! Bodies are flying everywhere, people are trying to get out of the way of those possessed. I see Jeanne thrown back by an invisible force! The air is charged with demonic power! The powers of darkness are out in full force today. I had just started dealing with one demon-possessed person when all hell breaks loose! The demon in this person is not responding. It is doing all the talking and does not listen to me. I detect that this demon is out to keep me busy, so that I cannot attend to others. I leave and start looking for those who need deliverance from their demons.

There is complete chaos! Who needs my attention first? I guess whoever is the nearest to me does. Jim, Jeanne, and Marion are helping as much as possible. When finally the demons begin to vacate their hosts and things begin to quiet down in the place, I return to the first one I had started with and drive it out. It leaves quite willingly since there is no reason to delay me any longer. I am soaking wet when finally all are delivered from demons! This is the first time we witness ten demonstrating at the same time! We have had only three at once previously. We leave for Lusaka without taking time to wait for food to be served.

Jim and Jeanne Weems are traveling with us to Eastern Province. We are going to hold seminars in Petauke and Katete Districts. Lungu, of course, is along as well. We meet several road blocks along the way and hand out tracts to those manning them. On the way we stop off at Mtumbata for a short service. Lazarus Chisanga, who is a teacher here, is also the pastor. I share on Christ dying for us so that we may live. Many come for prayer so it is a while before we can quit. They give us tea and cake made out of mealie meal (maize flour). It is 4 P.M. before we finally reach Chinzombo. We settle into our huts. The Weems have one and so do we. There is no need to set up our tents. We eat before the evening service. Many have already arrived from the surrounding churches. Jim preaches tonight. The church is full. Many who come for prayer meet outside as there is no room inside. We end up casting out demons from two women who are possessed and then binding the evil spirits who are oppressing another woman. There are others, but I tell them to wait until morning. They have waited this long, they can wait another few hours.

After breakfast, we have the deliverance service outside the church building. There are ten of them who need help, eight who are possessed and two who are oppressed. It takes two hours to deliver them from the powers of the devil. There were baboon, lion, snake, monkey, ancestral, and religious demons who came out of them! There was also one woman who had a mad spirit. This deliverance ministry takes a lot out of me physically. I feel like I have already done a day's work! But, spiritually, I enjoy it. I love giving the devil a black eye.

There are classes throughout the day with a break at noon for something to eat. Jim and Jeanne take their turn at teaching, as well as Marion and me. Oscar, who works at the Mwanjawanthu clinic, teaches on health in one class while Marion teaches the women how to bake sweet potato cakes. She also hands out a piece of clothing to each one of them. Some of the women who were delivered this morning have brought their charms to be burned. Marion assists them. I pass out TEE books to the church leaders who are studying to be pastors, and also teach them for an hour and a half. Jim has the youth during this hour. The last thing this evening is a choir contest. Jim and Jeanne are setting up their tent and are sleeping in it tonight. The hut was too hot for them last night. Also, the mosquitos had bothered them, especially Jeanne.

At eight, after our breakfast, I meet with the district committee. A few changes have to be made with the office bearers. When done, we begin the service. The Lord's Supper is observed before I deliver the message on "The Bronze Serpent." Very many come forward for salvation, others come for strength and healing. We also deal with two, one a man and the other a woman, who are demon-possessed, and then one woman who is demon-oppressed. In the name of Jesus Christ they are all delivered in short order from the powers of the devil. Then, I pray for the children who are being dedicated by their parents. There are 21 of them. After this, 22 couples come up to have their marriages blessed. I do them all at the same time, and it turns out very well. It is hot as we are all gathered outside. I get enough sun today! There are 540 people present. It is 2:00 P.M. before we are finished. It has been a full, full forenoon!

We eat and then at 3:30 P.M. we gather at the stream, where the last baptismal service was held, and I baptize 77 converts! Oscar assists me in bringing them up out of the water. It sprinkles a bit during the baptism. A splendid service as so many are men. As soon as I take a bath to wash off the muddy water, I meet with the district committee. I pray for the new officers and for the new pastors. I listen to their problems. Finally, at eight we are called to eat our last meal of the day. I turn in tonight satisfied with the happenings of the day.

I get up at six and pack our stuff into and on top of the vehicle. I take along three women to Mumbi, and one of them is Oscar's wife, Mailes. So I have to put more things onto the roof rack. The left front tire is flat so I have to take it off and put on the spare. I get going finally at 8:30 for Katete. We are loaded so I drive slowly through the bush on the way to Mumbi. Here we drop off the three women, who will now walk from here to Mwanjawanthu. Jim buys some medicine for his constipation before we resume our journey. Along the way, we discover the medicine that Jim bought is only aspirin! Well, at least, he should not have any more pain. We stop at Petauke but there is no place where I can fix my flat tire, so I will try at Katete. It is twelve noon when we reach Katete. We fill up with diesel and get the flat repaired. We eat at a small motel. It is clean but there is very little choice of food to eat. There is no chicken so I have beef. There is only Coke so I drink tea.

We arrive at Songwe village, the place where our services will be held, in mid-afternoon. They are not ready for us. But, they do manage to call the local people together for a service this evening. I preach on "Where Are You?" Close to ten come for prayer. One says she has demons. I tell her to come in the morning as it is too dark to deal with her. I need to be able to see her face. Marion gives the women some food to cook for us which they do. So we have something to eat before retiring for the night. We set up near the place of worship. The Weems are sleeping in their tent while we are sleeping in the vehicle.

It rains towards morning, but the Weems fare well in their tent in spite of it. Marion puts together something from her basket for our breakfast. Jim preaches in the first service. The place is full. The building used to be a bar, but the Christians are using it for a church now. The people from nearby Gareta village have come to the service as well. Many want salvation after the sermon so we pray for them. There is a lot of darkness in this area. I can feel it! There are classes the rest of the day with a break for the meal at noon which the women prepared for all of us. I end the seminar with a message on the Church of God. We pray for many who want to receive Christ into their hearts. There are six who are demon-possessed and we do not stop until they have all been driven out in the mighty name of Jesus. The demons really fought us all the way, screaming, shrieking, gouging, and kicking! Jim and Jeanne are awe-struck at how much power they do have. Also, there is one who is demon-oppressed. She too is delivered. It is too late for the baptismal service as it got dark on us. We will leave it for next time.

It rains during the night, and there are also strong winds. Fortunately, Jim and Jeanne moved into the building for the night with their tent. Just the same, their night was quite spooky because of their hair-raising experience with casting out demons. And the howling wind on a dark rainy night does not help any either. They thought the night would never end. Marion makes breakfast with the stuff I bought in Katete. The women here bring us tea to go with it. We have prayer and at eight we leave

Songwe village. On the way to Lusaka, we stop at a village beside the Luangwa River bridge and buy Jeanne a chitenge (piece of printed material). It is her birthday today! They return to the States next week. Will they return again? I do hope so as we need help.

Marion and I prepare our front veranda for the seminar we are holding today for our pastors of the churches in Lusaka District. Eleven attend, but two are unable to come. After the classes a district meeting is held and the chairman is elected. TEE books are handed out to the pastors. Marion serves them lunch at noon and then tea before they leave in the evening. The new chairman receives a bicycle so that he can make his rounds to evangelize and to oversee the churches in his district. The following day a baptismal service is held at a dam which is several kilometers outside the city limits. About 100 people are gathered and I baptize 47 believers. A cold wind is blowing so I am shivering by the time I am through. Lisa and Lily, two teenagers from Calgary, are present. They have come out for a month to see what missionary work is all about, and to contribute in whatever way they can, such as teaching and telling Sunday School stories to children. I had planned to take them up to Northern Province before they leave but a severe fuel shortage takes place throughout Zambia and I have to cancel the trip.

The National Secretary informs me that it was not he who wrote that letter to the Mission Board stating that the Hoffmans will be terminating their services in Zambia next year. Then who was it? No one wants to claim responsibility. It will all be revealed as soon as we receive a copy of the letter from the Mission Board. Weird phone calls have been coming in with no one at the other end, except one time when there was a grunt before someone

171

hung up. Again at 11 P.M. last night, the phone rang twice. Both times, after a few groans or grunts, the party hung up! I felt an evil presence. What is the meaning of this? The devil is behind this attack, that is sure.

I am on my way today to plant a church in Siavonga District in Southern Province. Lungu and a member from Garden congregation in Lusaka, who has a sister married to the headman of Pembere Village, are travelling with me. Marion is sitting this one out as her back, which she injured when she fell, needs more time to recuperate. We make good time and when we reach Chirundu, which is situated on the border with Zimbabwe, we turn left onto a gravel road and drive six more kilometers before reaching our destination. Pembere (rhino in their language) is a small village consisting of grass-roofed huts scattered among the trees. This is a parched land, very hot, and rains that fall too infrequently. Fortunately the Zambezi River is not far away, just two kilometers to the south. We are now in Gwembe Valley, the eastern end of the great Rift Valley, which finally comes to an end here at the Zambezi River, the fourth longest river in Africa.

It is not long before we discover that no one is a Christian here. In fact, no one can explain who Jesus is! Lungu and I talk to three men and end up seeing them accept Christ into their hearts. We are served a gruel made from sorgum flour, cowpeas, and okra before we meet under a shady tree for a service. Women and children are in attendance, about 85 of them. No men. After a few choruses led by Lungu, I share on "The Two Roads." Many want the prayer of salvation. After the evening meal, more of the same, there is another service. Men are present this time. I preach on "Where Are You?" Many again want to be saved. It has been a successful day, planting a church from the roots up. Thank you, Lord!

I have a good night in the Nissan Patrol. The doves are cooing everywhere in the surrounding dry bush this morning. I shave and wash my face with water from my thermos. Water is scarce here. It has to be carried in from the river. Food is also scarce so I check for fish at the river and find no one selling any. Then, I try at Chirundu market and there is nothing either. I come back with a few other things for the women to cook. There is no breakfast. In the forenoon service I pray for the same ones after my sermon as I did yesterday! May they understand what salvation is all about before we leave this place. It is 1:30 P.M. before we eat our first meal of the day. It is meat, which I had bought, and sorgum gruel. Life here is grim, the villagers are just squeaking out an existence. They must watch their crops or wild birds and bush pigs will eat their sorgum. Elephants compete with them for the wild fruit during the dry season. Lions still roam the area. Rhinos are no longer a threat, they have all been poached out. It reminds me a little of Mbugwe, where we lived in Tanzania.

We take time to pray for the headman's daughter, Phaidus. She is around 20 years of age and has demons which have been with her for years. I am asked to cast them out. I struggle with them for half an hour before they leave with the Lord's help. Then, her mother wants to be delivered. She has had hers for a very long time. It takes an hour to drive these out. Both women weep during the deliverance session, the demons are reluctant to leave. The evil spirits here are mostly ancestral and very stubborn. But, it is the same everywhere we go. The first few times it takes awhile, but then they realize that I am determined to drive them out and will not give up until they are out! The mother and daughter surrender their charms and medicines that they had gotten from the

173

witch doctor. Also, they surrender their skirts and leg ornaments made out of seed pods from trees, which they wear when the dancing demon takes control of their bodies in a wild frenzied dance. I trust this is a breakthrough. The village reeks of darkness!

Five men accept Christ while I visit with them in the evening. One of them is Benson. After the service tonight, which is around the log fire again, he is chosen to be their church leader. I had preached on "Who is Jesus?" where again many were prayed for their salvation. We also take time to burn the paraphernalia belonging to the two women who had been delivered earlier. They had brought it with them from their huts. Before retiring into the Nissan for the night, I have a splash bath. I take it behind the vehicle. The moon is full so there is plenty of light. Tomorrow I plan to say my goodbyes and then leave here early.

We are loaded for our trip to Eastern Province! The roof rack is full and so is the inside of the Nissan Patrol. Lungu and the Kellseys are traveling with us. Gary and Betty are spending three weeks with us before travelling up to visit the Stevensons in Uganda. It is a nice day. We get through the danger area without a problem. From the Luangwa River to Nyimba, Renamo rebels from Mozambique have been attacking vehicles along this section of the Great East Road. Just last week several buses and lorries (trucks) were shot up and passengers were robbed. There have been killings as well. Some believe those responsible are Zambian bandits who know that the Renamo will be blamed. Before starting this journey, we had asked God to protect us. And He has! Thank you, Lord.

We reach Chinzombo village at 15 hours. We visit until supper which is at 6 P.M. An hour later we meet for our service which this time is in a grass enclosure that they have erected around the church. Five choirs sing for us. It is a good beginning to our seminar here in Petauke District. I preach on "You Must Be Born Again." Many come forward for repentance. There is a demon-possessed woman who has been reacting during the message but I have ignored the demons. This can wait until tomorrow as it is already dark. We will deal with them when there is daylight. I visit some with the chairman, Oscar, before turning in for the night. We are sleeping in our hut, the one they built for us, while the Kellseys are staying in another one. There is a smell of dung in here tonight! It looks like this is where they also keep their goats when we are not present.

After a few songs, Gary preaches in the service after breakfast. Quite a few respond when the altar call is given. Then, we go into classes. Marion has the women, Lungu the men, Gary the youth, Betty the children, and I have the pastors. They write their TEE tests. Out of the ten pastors, there is only one who fails. He will have to study the book again and rewrite the test in the next seminar. I teach until it is time to gather for the noon meal. Having eaten, we again meet for classes for a couple of hours. Marion and Oscar treat the sick before we start our service at 4 P.M. There are 600 present. I preach on "The Temptations of Jesus" and many youth come forward for prayer. While praying for the sick, an epileptic asks to be delivered. There is no demonic reaction so it must be a physical affliction. Trust that he has been delivered from any further attacks.

After this we tackle the demon-possessed. I do not get through the line-up as darkness sets in. But seven of them are delivered. There is a man and a woman who both have a mad spirit. Then, there are those who have snakes, lions, monkeys, baboons, ancestral, traditional and religious spirits! It is an hour and a half of battling with the powers of darkness before the seven individuals are set free from them. Gary got up to help us when we came to the mad man since he turned out to be very violent! Marion, Oscar, Lungu, and myself had trouble hanging on to him. It's unbelievable how strong these demons can be. There is yet a district meeting after supper before we can get to bed. It is already 22 hours when I crawl into the sleeping bag. It has been a full day!

After breakfast, we meet with the demon-possessed whom we did not have time for last night. There are five of them. The demons are easily driven out from four individuals. The fifth person has a demon which acts like death. The lady becomes a corpse, stiff throughout her body, eyes rolled back, and tongue curled into her mouth. There is no response from her for an hour! When it is time to start the service, we carry the woman into the empty church building. The meeting can now commence in the enclosure outside. I keep Lungu and Oscar with me to finish what we have started. I will not leave this woman as I had to do some time ago with the woman at Garden in Lusaka who had the same kind of demon. I now switch from commanding the demon to come out, as it is not hearing us, to commanding it to wake up! There is movement in her stomach immediately! It is only a short time when it comes out coughing. The woman is finally delivered. Praise the Lord! She walks out into the service for all to see the miracle that has taken place in her life.

Gary preaches and we pray for the many who come forward. The Lord's Supper follows and over 125 participate. There are 700 people present for the service. I pray for the 30 children who are being dedicated, and then for the seven couples who want their marriages blessed by the Lord. One old couple have been married for 40 years already! It is very unusual to see this, as one or the other would have passed on by now. There is no baptismal service as water is scarce here this time of the year. There is a choir contest after our noon meal. Six choirs compete. Marion and I help to judge the contest. We still have a service this evening in Katete District, where we also will be having a seminar, so we load up and take leave.

We reach Songwe village at 5:30 P.M. and find a grass enclosure and a church building made from poles and grass waiting for us. A nice surprise! It takes until 9:00 P.M. before we are served our supper. Then, an hour later I preach my sermon. The church is full. There is only one kerosene lantern in the building, and it stands on the pulpit beside me. Looking ahead into the darkness, it looks like they all want prayer when the altar call is given. So it is 11:00 P.M. when we retire.

Marion and I spend a good night in the Nissan. It's not that cold. We hear the choir from Gareta church singing when they march past our vehicle and Kellsey's tent at 5:30 P.M. A woman shows up and tells Marion that she is expecting a child that she had asked for when we prayed for her the last time we were here. She adds that she got pregnant that very month! Praise the Lord! It is her first child. Through the years many women who could not have children bore them after Marion prayed for them. This happened over and over again in Tanzania, Kenya, Uganda, and now it is also happening here in Zambia.

Gary preaches at nine, and then at ten we divide into classes. At noon we eat chicken again. We have been getting chicken at every meal. I like it. Otherwise it would be pork, which I do not care for. Most of the villagers here raise pigs. They look like they have been crossed with wild pigs. There are more classes in the afternoon. I teach on the ordinances as tomorrow we have the Lord's Supper and baptism. There is still a church meeting before supper where there are a few changes made in the committee. It has been discovered that two of the deacons are polygamists and one deaconess is a second wife in the home. Gary preaches his second message today at the seven o'clock service. Pray for those who come forward. We retire at 8:30 tonight. Rather early!

It is windy all night. A mist pulls in this morning but dries off by mid-morning when the sun gets warmer. One woman begins to react before the service. The demons start to tremble and then throw her to the ground. Lungu and I take charge and drive them out in the name of Jesus. Then, the demons in a second woman begin to manifest themselves. They too are driven out. We end up praying for two others who are demon-oppressed. This does not take long. The service finally gets started and I preach on "Listen to Jesus." I pray for those seeking help. Also, I have special prayer for those who need healing. Before closing the service, the Lord's Supper is observed. About 80 take part. There are close to 200 in attendance. There is a stream near the church and 97 follow the Lord in baptism. This is the most thus far in Zambia. We eat and then get ready to go. We give out TEE material, Bibles, and songbooks to the leaders before leaving for the next district.

We arrive at Kalume village in Chipata District at 3:30 P.M. and find the people still preparing for the seminar. They are in the process of erecting a flimsy enclosure out of sticks and grass on top of a termite mound that is to serve as a bath house for us. They are really backward here! While we wait, Kellseys set up their tent and we prepare our bed in the Nissan. We rest a bit as well. We eat some of the goodies Marion has brought along for emergencies such as this one, as there is no supper here tonight. Then, we join others at the logfire just as the sun is setting. Some have arrived from the large village of Lufu, a three hour march from here! I preach on "The Sower and the Seed" beside the fire after a choir from Kalume and one from Lufu sing. We turn in at 9:30 P.M.

Marion and I have a good night's sleep in the vehicle. We have tea for breakfast. Classes begin at ten o'clock, after the service where Gary preaches. There are over 100 in attendance. During the course of the forenoon, I discover that all but three do not know how to pray! It takes half an hour, after our classes, to teach them a simple prayer! Darkness is so thick here, especially at Kalume village. They serve us goat meat and nsima at noon. After eating, we pray for the demon-possessed. All five are delivered from the demons, which turn out to be mostly ancestral demons bearing local names. There are two others who are oppressed by them. It does not take long for their deliverance.

After this there is a baptismal service and 34 are baptized in the nearby river. It is a beautiful place. The river flows along between some rocks and large boulders. Charms have to be removed from many of them, as it had to be done during the baptism in Songwe village yesterday. One charm, the woman claims, shows that she is a virgin! It's hard to believe as she is in her twenties already. Following the baptism, there is a meeting where Stephen Mwanza from Lufu village is chosen to be the leader in this district. I enroll him the TEE program. The last service is beside the logfire again. I preach on "What

179

Do You Think of Jesus?" Lungu and the Christians sit around the fire and sing lustily into the night! It is keeping me awake so I get up at 11:00 P.M. and stop them. Otherwise they may have sung all night.

Up at sunrise we pack our stuff together, and have breakfast which Marion makes from the food she has brought along. We give out some Bibles to the church leaders and song books before starting out for Lusaka at eight o'clock. We stop at Katete and hold a service with some people next to a shop beside the Great East Road. I deliver a short sermon and pray for those who want salvation. It is a new congregation and it is starting off very well. A leader and five of the deacons are appointed. An hour later we continue with our safari and reach Lusaka at 5:00 P.M.

I travel to Mwajuni, 20 kilometers north of Lusaka, for the service this Sunday. Marion is resting today. When I arrive, there are at least 25 gathered under the tree. I preach on "Jesus is the Light." Several come up for salvation and for healing. One is demon-possessed so I pray for her deliverance and cast them out in the name of Jesus. She explains that she has been going to the headmaster of the nearby school for help. She says that he uses what he calls holy water to assist her. Instead of the demons vacating her, they only demonstrate when she is at his place. The demons tell her at night to go to him. That is strange! Will a demon lead anyone to someone to be cast out? The headmaster must be in union with the demons. She has been going to him for months. I advise her strongly not to go to him again if she wants to be completely rid of the demons. Otherwise, they will return with many others. I reach home after one o'clock.

In a trip up to Northern Province, and while at a seminar in Mbala District, I bring up the letter that was written to the Mission Board concerning my termination next year. Those on the Executive Committee claim no knowledge of it. There is nothing more I can do but wait for further developments on their part. I continue to teach and preach at the seminars while in Chinsali and Mpika Districts, after having left Mbala District. I must continue to fight the good fight of faith!

On the way to Chinsali I take the short cut from Kasama and find it longer than the map shows. Because of it, I reach the Chambeshi River at 6:05 P.M. and the men refuse to ferry us across on the pontoon. They inform us that they quit work at six. It is not far across the river. So near, and yet so far! I make my bed inside the Nissan. Lungu, London, and Tyson are sleeping on the ground outside. All because of five minutes, we have to spend the night here at the river's edge without supper! It is cold inside the Nissan. The three men outside have mosquitos to contend with as well, besides the cold damp air. At 6:15 A.M. the men with the pontoon finally stir themselves and begin bringing the ferry across. Fifteen minutes later we leave the river behind us.

After picking up a woman with her child at Mufumbushi, London and I continue with our journey to Lusaka. About 110 kilometers south of Mpika I barely miss hitting someone who changes direction in the middle of the road! I slam the brakes and swerve so as not to hit him. The man is carrying a sack of maize on his shoulders. He drops it and throws himself to the side, and escapes being hit by the front bumper. I stop and see him stand to his feet. He surely must be bruised from the fall he took on the tarmac when he slid across it onto the grass shoulder. London advises me to continue since I did not hit him. At Kapiri Mposhi, I drop him off and the woman with the child. I reach home without a further mishap.

The battle with the evil one continues on. I must keep on my full armour!

Thirteen
Many More Victories

We arrive at Lufu village in Chipata District in the afternoon. The Christians have erected a nice church building. A nice surprise! They are calling the church here Kawawa, the name of the stream below. It is after supper, and already dark, when we hold our service. I preach on "Jesus is the Way" and many accept Christ. The church leader at Kalume, who was appointed on our last visit, died a day ago. Witchcraft is suspected, and of his own making. Marion and I are sleeping on the floor in the pastor's house tonight. We had planned to spend it in the tent we brought along.

Rats are scurrying back and forth during the night. One of them scampers across Marion who is sleeping beside the wall! A mosquito troubles us as well. In the morning we eat nsima and rape, which is similar to spinach, along with peas for breakfast. I give Stephen his TEE test before the service. Lungu preaches and I help him pray for those who came forward. Then, I teach on what the Church of God believes while Marion looks after the children and tells them stories from the Bible. I quit at noon. It was an informative time as we discussed their beliefs in witchcraft. There is much darkness in this district. The Ngoni tribe here was once part of the Zulu tribe from

South Africa. The chief each year, in a big ceremony, drinks blood from the bullock.

It takes until 3 P.M. before we get back inside the church as they are late with food. There is a district meeting and Stephen Mwanza is appointed as the chairman. The district presently has nine churches. Before the baptismal service, I share on baptism and pray for those who want to repent. A woman suffering from epilepsy asks for prayer. She feels a seizure coming on but after prayer she recovers and is able to go through with baptism! Twenty-eight are baptized in the Kawawa River. It is 6 P.M. when we get back. The evening service begins an hour and a half later. It is actually too late already. The children make a lot of noise and women walk out before it ends. I do not stay around after the service as it is 10:30. I go to bed right away.

The rats again make plenty of racket during the night. One ran past us last night while sitting in the other room! Stephen and his wife accept them as part of their surroundings. We are served our breakfast while sitting on a mat which is spread out on the floor. There is no table. Marion treats quite a few of sick people this morning, while I pass out Bibles, songbooks, and other literature to the church leaders. Also, I enroll three new TEE students. I give money towards the well in the village for some bags of cement to repair the inside of it. Marion and I sing a duet in the service. We pray for the district leaders, dedicate children, and observe the Lord's Supper before I deliver the message. Several come up for salvation and for healing. After our noon meal, we pack up and leave for Katete District.

The seminar will be held this time at Gareta village instead of Songwe. Before we eat tonight, a hut nearby burns down to the ground after the grass roof catches fire.

We walk over to take a closer look. The church roof here is being built out of grass as well. They have a latrine and shower made from grass and sticks. They are more private than at the last place. Lungu preaches tonight. Ten come for salvation and two for healing. We ask a demon-possessed person to wait until tomorrow. Marion and I put up our tent tonight.

We get very little sleep because we are pitched too near the sleeping quarters of the men and boys who talk and laugh most of the night. Breakfast consists of rice and tea. I preach on "The Parable of the Sower" in the morning service. After praying for those who want salvation and healing, we deal with the two who have come for deliverance, including the one from last night. The religious demons come out almost immediately from both of them. I am pleased with the quick results. Then, we break into classes from 10 A.M. until 1 P.M. We eat after that. They serve us nsima and chicken. Marion opens a can of beans she has brought along to go with it.

There is a baptismal service and 28 follow the Lord in baptism. Marion stays behind and shares with the women as they shell ground nuts. After the baptism there is a district meeting. There are seven churches so a chairman and his committee are elected. After eating our evening meal, we take time to listen to testimonies and to hear the choirs sing. We quit at 22 hours. Marion and I have to move our tent tonight as white ants (termites) are crawling around underneath the floor. Fortunately for us they have not yet worked their way through to start damaging our belongings.

This morning we find a new batch of white ants under our tent. We give out the TEE books, Bibles, and songbooks to those who need them. After breakfast, we meet for the service. Pray for the district committee and

185

for the 28 children being dedicated. Before the message, we have the Lord's Supper. I preach on "Choose You This Day Whom You Will Serve." Quite a few come forward for prayer. There is one demon-oppressed, and two demon-possessed who have come for deliverance. There is a snake demon in one of the possessed, plus some religious ones. The second one is possessed with ancestral and religious spirits. The religious demons use mainly the name Mary or any of the Old Testament characters. It does not take long for us to cast them all out. Praise the Lord! We conclude the service at 11 A.M. and leave soon afterwards. It has been a good seminar!

At Katete we stop and purchase two bikes at one of the shops run by Asians. They are for the Chairman of Chipata District and the Chairman of Katete District. It takes a while before they are road worthy. We each have a soft drink and biscuits while we wait. Soon we are on our way, without the two chairmen. They are paddling back to their villages. At Petauke I fill the vehicle with diesel. We turn off the main road and carry on till we reach Mwanjawanthu village. By now it is 5 P.M. Oscar and his wife, Mailes, live here and we visit with them all evening. There is a borehole here with a pump that has been standing idle for most of the year. I try my hand at fixing it with my wrench from the Nissan tool bag. After a while I get it to pump. There is a water shortage here so we pray that this pump will keep working. Marion shares our leftovers with Oscar and Mailes and we eat. We talk until 10 P.M. before retiring for the night.

We all have a good night of rest. It was quiet with no singing and talking around us outside. The pump is still pumping water this morning! The Lord has performed a miracle for them. Thank you. I give four students their TEE tests after breakfast. Oscar and Mailes are two of them. They each pastor a church. Ever since her father had invited them to attend a seminar at Chinzombo, where they subsequently accepted Christ, they have been serving the Lord. Mailes had seen the change that had taken place in her mother's life after being delivered from 12 demons in the first seminar held by the missionaries Stanley and Marion Hoffman. The church here at Mwanjawanthu needs grass for their roof. The walls are already done. I give them money to buy some.

We travel on to Nyima Mwana where we have a church already started. Oscar is with us to show the way. We meet with those in the village and after a few songs, I preach on "Spiritual Warfare." Most of the thirty or so present respond and repent of their sins. The district chairman then accompanies us to the next village where the headman, who is a woman, lives. She has been refusing the believers there from attending our church at Nyimba Mwana. Lungu enters her boma, which is a cluster of huts enclosed within a wall of wooden slabs, and talks to her first. Then, I enter. She denies threatening our people. We have a good visit. I pray before we part company. She is noted to be a medicine man who sells concoctions to the demon-possessed, but is losing customers because we keep casting out the demons!

We carry on to Mtumbata and reach the village at 1 P.M. The pastor, Lazarus Chisanga, and his wife give us dinner. Then, he and another pastor write their TEE tests. After this there is a service where Marion and I sing a duet before I preach. Many come up for prayer, plus one who comes up for healing. When supper is over there is another service. It is dark and the people gather in front of the house. There is a lot of singing. Finally, Lungu shares and many of the youth ask for prayer. We are sleeping in our tent tonight.

It's a windy night. Even this morning it is still blowing hard. It was not cold in the tent though. I pack up before breakfast, then we leave after eating. I take along Lazarus and his wife to Petauke where I buy him tires and tubes for his bike since he wishes to help Oscar in planting new churches. A couple of women catch a ride with us to Lusaka. On the way, we stop to visit a new church we are starting in Mpansha village situated near Rufunsa. I preach on "Jesus is the Way." I pray for those who have come for salvation. One demon-possessed woman wants deliverance. She has two different demons. It takes ten to fifteen minutes to cast them out of her. The first, a religious demon, kept saying "Naught! Naught! Naught!" The last one says "I'm going! I'm going! Yes! Yes! Yes!" This happened at Gareta in Katete District as well. The demon there said the same thing, but added "Bye! Bye!" before leaving. After the service has ended, we assist in choosing the church committee.

We go to see the chief and we are kept waiting outside for some time before he makes an appearance. The customary clapping of hands takes place. We kneel on the ground until he takes a seat beside his house. He proves to be a disagreeable old man. Says that he has enough churches in his chiefdom. Only three, it turns out to be. Just the same, he concludes, I should write him anyway for permission to start a church in his chiefdom. We leave him. Lungu says that he does not have that much power. We should just go ahead. We reach Lusaka in the evening. Marion and I are drained from our trip. So is Lungu.

Three days later, Lungu brings me the news that the wife of the church leader at Kalume Village in Chipata District—who passed away last week because of his own witchcraft backfiring on him—is now dead too. She died of the same poisoning. It appears they purchased some medicine from a witch doctor to protect themselves from getting bewitched. Instead, they die from it! The children are very sick and may die as well.

This Sunday we are going to Kanyama, one of our churches here in Lusaka. Afunika Tembo is the one who started it and is presently still the pastor. The service is in one of the classrooms at a school in this crowded part of Kanyama. The classroom is full. Over 100 are present. I preach on "The Sower and the Seed." Quite a few come for healing, and for salvation as well. Then, there is a wedding which I perform. It is a very plain ceremony! The bride is Monica, Tembo's sister. She does not wear a white gown, just a colorful chitenge. Her husband is Geoffrey who works for us on the yard. Marion speaks to the women afterwards about a project. She is going to help them with used clothing as well.

We are traveling to North-Western Province this time. Our first stop is Solwezi District. We have been here before. We arrive in time for a short service. After the choirs sing for us, Lungu brings the message. It is 7 P.M. by now and very dark. We assemble at someone's house for supper. We eat some meat from a warthog that had been poached. It is here that we will spend the night in one of their rooms and go to bed without a wash. Marion and I bunk down on the floor and sleep in our sleeping bag. Lungu is sleeping in another room with a man who has come from Kabompo. He is David Leyo who has come to discuss our visit to his district.

The room we slept in last night had white ants above us in the grass roof. From all their chewing, we had white dust falling on us all night. Our bedding this morning is covered with it. In checking the Nissan, I discover a nut missing at the bottom end of the shock absorber on the driver's side in front. I take the vehicle to a workshop where they have the parts I need. While under the vehicle, the mechanic finds as well a bolt missing on the bracket that holds the muffler, and then another one which fastens the gearbox to the frame. Fortunately, they have the proper bolts and nuts. A good thing this is taken care of here in Solwezi before carrying on to Kabompo where the road is gravel and rough all the way.

While I am away in town, Marion and Lungu hold their classes. When I return, I have mine. For two hours I teach on sins. I do not get beyond the sexually immoral sins as there is a huge discussion on this topic. After we get something to eat at 14 hours, we go to hunt for some cold drinks in town. None of the shops has any, so Marion and I have to settle for one that is warm. We hold a service when we return to church. I preach and quite a few seek prayer. There are four who are demon-possessed. They have mostly ancestral spirits, but a few have snakes as well and roll around violently on the dirt floor. One young woman from the choir has a mad spirit. It tosses her about as if she is a mop! We have all to do to keep her from injuring herself. It hates the name of Jesus. But in the end, it gives up and leaves. Praise the Lord!

During the night, rats keep making lots of noise in the next room where the owners have stored their mealie meal. A good thing they moved it from the room we are sleeping in. I had asked them to do so. I foresaw this happening. Every now and then, a rat runs along on top of the wall that separates the two rooms.

It is soon light and we are up and packing for our trip to Kabompo District. It will be our first visit there. At 8 A.M., after tea and bread, Marion and I leave Solwezi. David Leyo is traveling with us and will do the interpretating for me. They do not understand Nyanja in North-Western Province. Here they use three other languages—Kaonde, Lunda, and Luvale. This means we must carry the different translations of the Bible and hymnbooks when we travel in this province! Zambia is difficult on missionaries and evangelists who want to spread the gospel throughout the country. There are at least seven languages he must learn before he can communicate with villagers in all the provinces and districts without an interpreter!

The road is not too rough and we make good time. We stop for a soft drink at Kabompo town, which is situated beside a river with the same name. Kabompo River is suppose to be the deepest river in Zambia. It flows into the Zambezi River. We reach Mumbeji village in the afternoon. This is where David lives. He works for the Agriculture Department and stays in one of their houses. There are reasonable facilities here, such as an outdoor toilet and shower made out of bricks and cement. Marion and I take a bath soon after our arrival. We set up our tent as we want to sleep in it tonight. I picked up some flea bites at Solwezi. I do not want the same thing to happen here.

There is a service tonight in front of David's house. I preach on "You Must Be Born Again." Have prayer with those who are seeking salvation and healing, before I deal with the demon-possessed woman who happens to be David's wife. She has three demons. The first one says he is a soldier from England. When he is ready to leave, he adds that he does not want to be in blacks anyway! The second one is a snake demon and is very active, twisting and writhing on the ground. It takes all four of us to control her! The third one is an ancestral spirit. It takes about 20 minutes to drive them all from her. There is truly power in the name of Jesus Christ!

It is a warm night. We do not have to close the flap on our tent. Lungu and some others are sleeping outside on the ground. I can hear someone snoring nearby. David's wife is okay this morning. She feels much lighter now since getting rid of those demons. After breakfast Marion and I take a load of people to Kabompo to register the Mumbeji church. Here in Zambia we have to register every local congregation with the government. It is to the police first and then to the Council. Whilst this is going on, I look for diesel, I discover it is twice the price here than in Lusaka! When the papers are ready for the registrar in Lusaka, we carry on to Manyinga.

When we reach Manyinga, we unload our passengers. Then, we drive 52 kilometers north, on the road that leads to Mwinilunga, to a village called Lwasongwa. David and Lunga are with us. There are two leaders up this way that need to attend the meeting today. The drive is through a remote wooded area. What a beautiful place! The Lunda tribe who live in here have poached out all the game as we do not see one animal. Even the monkeys are missing! No birds either! If this were Mbugwe, Tanzania, there would be plenty to see. The Lunda collect wild honey. We buy some from a local who is standing beside the bushroad.

When we return to Manyinga, the district meeting starts and it lasts until after dark. There are already seven churches here, so a district committee is elected with David Leyo as the chairman. After supper I preach on the Church of God. There is prayer for those who are seeking the Lord. Marion and I are setting up our tent and will sleep in it tonight. Tomorrow, we start on our way back home. There is a drinking party nearby and they beat the drums pretty well all night. Marion wakes me up from a deep sleep when a drunk stops near our tent. He must have wondered where this thing came from since it was not there the night before!

On our way to Lusaka we stop for a while in Solwezi to purchase the roofing sheets for the church, and to have something to eat. We stop at the Changa Changa Hotel, an inexpensive place for our meal. Then, we continue on. Our next stop is at Kitwe where I have a short visit with London before we retire for the night in Lothian House, a cheap place for guests who are traveling. Towards morning I have a dream. In it I am hanging onto a tree trunk. Looking down I see black snakes just below my feet hanging onto the tree as well. They appear docile, as if they are sleeping. What do I do? I wake up just then. Is it a sign that I am to be careful of those I will sit with in the meeting today? I pray for His wisdom and protection during that time.

After breakfast, Marion and I go to Kwacha East church where the Kitwe District meeting is to be held. I give two of the pastors who are present their TEE tests. Finally, the meeting starts. There are some of the key leaders noticeably missing. Why? It must be God's will. The meeting goes along well and we are able to wrap it up in less than three hours. There is a cloud hanging over this district and most of its leaders. Only time will reveal the reason. I can wait. We reach Lusaka after dark. We travelled 2,250 kilometers on this trip.

The Executive Council is meeting today. Most of our District Chairmen and Executive Committee members are present. On the agenda are the letters written by four members of the Executive against the missionaries. They had gone to the Mission Board and to Immigration. The issue is discussed at length. The Council decides that all four are to be suspended until when the Assembly meets in two months time to discuss the matter further. No letters are to be written by them anymore. If they do, they are to be reported to the police! Thank you, Lord, for your guidance in this all important issue! This has been one more victory for the work of God in Zambia. Marion's and my future here with the Church is more secure now. It is a good meeting overall. Oscar acted as the Secretary while Lungu acted as the Chairman.

Three weeks pass by and then one day, Marion and I notice that our equilibrium is not normal. Also, our throats are very dry. This has never happened to us before. What is strange is that it has affected both of us at the same time! Neither of us has any fever. Yesterday, I had a similar attack and chalked it up as maybe malaria coming on. Marion only had a dry throat. But, today both of us have the same symptoms. Have we been bewitched by the group who have been suspended? One of them tried before to bewitch me and it backfired on him. We join hands and Marion prays, rebuking Satan in the name of Jesus. It is not long after that we notice our dizziness is gone, and so is our dry throat. Praise the Lord! It must have been Satan who attacked us, but he has been defeated through the power of prayer.

Two days later, we have an attack of dry throat and dizziness again. It is not as severe as it was a couple of days ago. We pray about it and it leaves soon after! The next day I feel a dryness of the throat returning and the beginning of dizziness. I rebuke it immediately. It does not get ahold of me as it has done on previous occasions and leaves almost right away. Satan is still prowling about. The enemy is up to something. These attacks that Marion and I are getting are not normal as we get them at the same time, and then they disappear at the same time when rebuked in the name of Jesus. Continue to help us, Lord!

There is no further attack for the next two weeks. But, then they resume again. The second attack is much more severe with me than with Marion. I am quite disoriented, and even my memory is affected. I cannot remember directions at times, and also to finish a sentence I forget before I get through! We pray, rebuking Satan's power. It takes longer for me to recover this time. It is several hours later before I am back to normal. This is a strange affliction! We are sure it has something to do with the group wishing to deport us. One of them told us soon after we moved to Zambia that two of the missionaries of a church where he had belonged to died after being bewitched. Some leaders in the church did not want them anymore and so bewitched them in order to get their property. Is this what they want of us? We ask you, Lord, to defeat our enemies!

It is more than two weeks later, when we again are attacked by this strange affliction. It appears three times in four days, and then stops the day before the Assembly meeting. But, in the forenoon of this meeting, I have a mild attack. My throat gets dry and leaves me when I rebuke it and claim victory over the enemy! The decision taken by the Executive Committee two months ago is reviewed. The ones who were suspended do not sit quiet but are very vocal. We are shocked at the behaviour displayed by these so-called church leaders! But, before the meeting ends tempers cool and one of the leaders ask for forgiveness. It seems the whole thing that turned these men against me was that I chose to live in Lusaka instead of Kitwe when we moved to Zambia! From there on they began working against me. During the elections that follow, new leaders are elected onto the Executive Committee. Only one keeps his office. The Lord be praised for the outcome!

Lungu, who is the Legal Representative, delivers a letter to Immigration which contains the note of apology by the one who had written their Department earlier about cancelling my work permit, plus the minutes from the Assembly meeting which state their approval of our working in Zambia. Then, two days later, I receive a letter from Immigration asking me to come and see them, bringing along my passport and work permit. It is dated two weeks ago. When you are asked to bring in your passport and work permit, it means only one thing. You are about to be deported! I remember an earlier case while in Tanzania when I was nearly deported. I had been asked for my passport at that time as well by a government official. That experience I have shared in my book *To a Land He Showed Us,* chapter 13.

I show the letter to Lungu and he tells me not to go, that he will take care of it. Because it is a weekend, it is four days later before he goes to Immigration. There he discovers that it is a woman who has summoned me to appear before Immigration. She asks where the missionary was, and why he had not come. Lungu brings her up to date and explains all that has transpired since the writing of her letter. He also tells her that there is a letter of apology on its way from the one who wanted me deported. After this she relents and hands over the matter to the main Immigration Officer who tells Lungu that he has no problem with the missionary, and it is up to the church whether they want him or not. So the matter is solved.

Months pass by and we no longer are harassed openly by the ones who had tried to deport us. And, Marion and I no longer are attacked by that strange affliction! A miracle has taken place! The devil has been defeated through prayer and perseverance. Victory has been ours because of Whom we serve! He takes care of His own.

Fourteen
Demon Possession

When I receive a call from the Lord to take up residence in Zambia in order to plant churches and train leaders in that country for the sake of the gospel, Marion is hesitant about the move. She wonders why I would leave Uganda when the Lord is still using us so mightily. Did I think my work was already finished? I tell her that we will not be leaving the church in Uganda leaderless as Tim and Colleen are very capable of filling in the gap that we will be leaving. Besides, what about Zambia? They have no resident missionaries? Marion starts asking the Lord to give her a sign. It is not long before the Lord shows her the following passage: "Forget the former things; do not dwell on the past. See, I am doing a new thing! Now it springs up; do you not perceive it? I am making a way in the desert and the streams in the wasteland."—Isaiah 43:18–19. Well, that convinces her that God has something more ahead for us to do and that she should not dwell on past achievements.

What about that new thing it is speaking about? It appears to have something to do with opening up a way into spiritual dry places and bringing the water of life to those perishing there. If we did not perceive it immediately, we soon do after moving to Zambia and reaching out with the gospel into new territory. We discover so many oppressed and possessed by demons and evil spirits! Before long we are involved knee-deep in a ministry that is relatively quite new to us, namely casting out demons. Yes, we did come across them in Tanzania and Uganda but not on the scale as here in Zambia. It becomes a common sight at the end of our services to deal with a number of demon-possessed who need to be delivered from the powers of the devil. Where once people lived in the desert and wasteland of spiritual darkness, today are walking in the Way and enjoying the Water of Life, Jesus Christ!

What were their lives like when we found them! Allow me to share some unique experiences we have had with demons that are not recorded earlier in this book.

After a service in Solwezi District, we start to pray for the demon-possessed. There are eight of them, three of which are very powerful. One has a mad spirit and talks to me in Swahili, a tongue unknown to the host. Another one has an unclean spirit. One of the possessed knocks me over backwards and in the process I rip open the trousers on the inside of my leg! Five demons come out of her. She had been delivered before, but had gone back to the witch doctor for medicine to get pregnant. Still another has a lorry demon and makes the exact sound of a truck. She sits on the floor and shifts gears. I am wet with perspiration when we get through.

This evening in another service two of them manifest demons while praying for their needs. Before we can get through to them, a third one joins in. Three are manifesting demons at the same time, and all are teenage girls from the choir! One of them is so strong that I am thrown around quite a bit. At one time she ends up on my lap. There is a spirit of lust in this one. They possess religious spirits as well. Earlier, while sitting in the choir, one of these young women kept saying, "Hallelujah!" over and over again. But it was in a voice not her own. The religious demon in her was saying it. Someone not knowing the difference would say she was actually praising God. It takes an hour to cast all of the evil spirits from these young women.

Marion gives out medicine for an hour here in Zambezi District. It takes a lot out of her. Finally, we get around to dealing with the oppressed and the possessed. One woman is brought to us who is often seen running naked in the bush. She has 35 of them! How do we know? The demons in her tell us how many there are. Many of them are snakes and mad spirits. She is tossed about by them and it takes five of us to handle her. The demons kick more than I have ever seen before. One grabs Jordan's ear and kicks Lungu under the eye. I do some ducking myself to avoid getting kicked. I have to be constantly alert. At one stage when her mouth is wide open, there appears to be a snake's head sticking in her throat! I am sure it is the devil trying to frighten me away. It has the opposite effect and I am determined more than ever to drive him out! The demons speak a lot. When I ask them questions, they reply in English. After she is delivered, she drops to her knees and thanks the Lord with uplifted hands! She weeps when Marion puts her arms around her. It has taken us an hour and a half to drive them all out. The following day she again thanks us for setting her free. It is the Lord who did it, we were only His instruments.

In Kabompo District, it takes quite awhile to drive out the snake demons from two women. One of them is a 12-year old girl who has five of them. They writhe on the ground and it is difficult to hold them. The demons finally leave as she belches them out one by one! Another two women believe they have been bewitched so I pray for the spell to be broken. One had stepped on some charms and was now suffering pain in that leg. While all the sons of the other woman die immediately after birth, the daughter lives. In another service, a woman who is possessed with four demons has one that is a mad spirit. It has a very evil look, the worst I have ever seen. A battle ensues where the demon would have defeated us had it not been for the blood of Jesus Christ covering us. He is defeated and driven out with the name of Jesus Christ!

After each sermon we have demon-possessed people to deal with. The first one this afternoon that we start with has a violent demon which is very strong, but comes out in five minutes! Then, there is a six-year old girl who has an ancestral spirit which takes us a little longer. The ancestral spirit usually weeps as it does not want to leave. It has probably been there a long time. Someone who is not aware of this will feel sorry for the person and stop, thinking that it is the host crying. There is also a young man who has an ancestral spirit and is delivered as well. But the person who takes a lot of our time is a woman who has four different kinds—religious, traditional, ancestral spirits, and a mad demon. We are tossed around for some time. It takes an hour to cast them out.

Before supper at a village where we are having the seminar for Mwinilunga District, a woman walks to fetch water from the river. A large snake crosses the path in front of her. She falls down immediately and demons commence to react inside her. Some women find her and drag her to where we are seated. We commence binding the demons in her. There are six of them—a lion, a snake, one who is unclean, one mad, one religious, and one traditional. She has a real variety. It takes half an hour to drive these all out. The Lord is great! After the service, we cast out demons from six people. One spits out four of them and they come out as froth! One asks me to pray for her temper. While doing it, demons manifest themselves! They will not leave until I recall the woman and get her consent for them to leave. Then they come out. There are six of them!

There are four more to be delivered here in this remote village. It takes quite a while with two of them. One has a spirit that is deaf and dumb. When the host, who is a woman, recedes into a "sleeping" stage, I am able to bring her out of it. It is often very difficult to do this as now all communication with the demon has been severed. I get the spirit to communicate with me in English. The woman knows no English! The demons know we are in a hurry and therefore use delaying tactics such as going to "sleep." We do not give up, but it takes one an a half hours to do the four. Satan is not going to give up territory here without a fight. And so the battle goes on!

When we arrive, we go into the service right away. After my sermon, quite a few come for salvation, for healing, and for strength from the Lord. There is a teenage girl who is possessed and it takes us an hour to drive out all six demons. They are religious, traditional, ancestral, and snake demons. They speak in English and Swahili to me! I am beat when it is all over. We are the weakest since the time we drove out the demons from 16 people at Chinzombo in Petauke District a few years ago. Not eating food all day, driving on poor roads, and going into a service immediately does not help any.

Here at a service in Chavuma District, a three-year old boy is brought forward for prayer by his mother who says he has a bad temper. As soon as I lay my hands on him, there is a demonic reaction. He begins to struggle and attempts to bit me! It takes several of us to hold this little boy! Finally, the demon says to us, "I'm going now!" It is repeated several times before the demon leaves. There is a remarkable difference in his countenance. This is the youngest one I have cast demons from! There is also a young man suffering from epilepsy. I pray for him and he is healed! After the service when I am seated in the shade under a tree, the three-year old boy comes up to me without his mother, places his hand on my knee and watches me enroll some new orphans for Kinderhilfswerk. What a change has taken place in this boy. Praise the Lord!

Many come forward for salvation and healing after the message in Katete District. Also, four are demon-possessed. One of them is a girl, about 10 years old, who has three traditional spirits with local names. One other woman has snakes, and another baboons. Praise the Lord, all are cast out! All afternoon Christians have been coming in for this district seminar. They are carrying firewood, meat, and mealie meal on their heads, singing lustily as they file on by us. We have 800 in the service which is held in a large grass enclosure. After the sermon and prayers, we again find ourselves casting out demons.

There is a young man with a mad spirit who puts up quite a fight! He jerks around those who are holding him as if they are children. But what a change after the demon is out! Many women have religious, traditional, and ancestral spirits who weep a lot before leaving. Two possessed react before we can finish the one we are dealing with. Another two are repossessed before they can walk out of the enclosure. The air is heavy with demonic power! The two are brought back and we drive them out again. One woman has an unclean spirit and makes a bowel movement during exorcism! She is removed to the shower stall where we complete the job of casting out the demon. A total of 13 were possessed and three oppressed! Surprisingly, we got through it in two and a half hours.

We have three who are possessed in our seminar at Petauke District with snake and lion demons, traditional spirits, and a mad spirit. The woman with the mad spirit is very powerful and it takes four of us to control her. Three demon-possessed are delivered from lion, snake, monkey, religious, and traditional spirits in another service. Four more women, in still another service, are possessed with animal demons—the lion, monkey, and snake. It seems here in this district there are so many who have these kind of demons. There are these kinds of animals around in the bush. Demons from them have no difficulty in finding neglectful humans to host them.

I preach on Judgement Day and many come up for repentance. Also, four demon-possessed. Two of them have lion, monkey, and snake demons. The other two have religious and traditional spirits. One of the last two also has an ancestral spirit who used to be in a witch doctor. This one takes a little longer to deliver as she has had them all her life, and she is now about 50 years old!

Then in Nyimba District, we cast out demons from five people. There is one who has nine demons! One of them speaks Arabic! This means that the demon has dwelt in an Arab for some time and picked up their language. Then, in another service, one woman goes into what appears to be tongues. But after testing them, we find they are demons. We begin casting them out of her. Before it is over, she has become quite violent! After this one is delivered, another woman manifests demon possession. From her we cast out two of them.

While in Chipata District, we deal with someone who does not fall over but remains standing upright while the demons are being driven out. This is the first time this has happened to me. There are four of them and they are burped out one-by-one! A lion and three traditional spirits. The latter give me their names. There are a lot of traditional demons in this area. When dealing with three others at another meeting, they come out immediately when I command them to do so. Each person has two or three of these traditional spirits. The whole time taken to cast them out is the least ever in all my deliverance ministries thus far. Unbelievable! Must have been a couple of minutes only with each person. Thank you, Lord!

Here at one of our services in Lundazi District, we also find traditional demons. From one old woman we drive out several of them and each one gives us its name before leaving. In another woman, we discover five demons who speak to us in Arabic! Their names are Arabic as well. This one also has three traditional spirits. It takes us almost half an hour to drive all the demons out of these two women. At another service, we deal with two more old women and it takes half an hour to drive out the traditional and religious demons who said they are Peter, Maria, and Joseph! One has five demons and the other four. There is a third possessed woman but she leaves before we can get to her. The demon did not want to lose its dwelling place.

After the service the following day, I spot her in church and remember that she has not yet been set free. So this time the demons do not get time to lead here away and we drive them out of the woman. She has two demons. Another woman then comes forward for deliverance. This one had two of them—a traditional one and a religious demon named Maria. There is also an oppressed woman who wants deliverance. Snakes bite her on the legs, she claims! Her grandchildren help drive them away. Pray for the blood of Jesus to cover her and claim victory of the oppressing demons!

Next a three-year-old boy is brought forward for healing. He is retarded. When only a few weeks old, he had been taken to a witch doctor. As I begin to pray for him, the boy goes wild! I bind the demon and command it to come out in the name of Jesus. Before long, he becomes quiet and he has peace. The demon is gone. Praise the Lord! Then, a six-year-old boy is brought up who has the fits. When he responds with a demonic grin to my questioning, I begin casting out the demon. After a while he can stand and I walk him up and down the aisle of the church. Praise the Lord, the boy has been set free! I also pray for a sick woman with a swollen knee. At the same time the Lord heals hers, he heals my knee as well! Suddenly I can bend my knee and kneel on it without a problem. Thank you, Lord! (Two days ago I had tripped on a broken step and really banged my knee!)

The Luangwa River is near to where we are holding our seminar in Chama District. In fact, we are now in a hunting block. After one of the classes, we have two demon-possessed to deal with. One is a girl from the choir who has two traditional demons who make her dance. The other is a young man who also has a traditional demon that makes him dance and beat special kind of drums that the much feared Nyau dancers of the Chewa tribe use in their ceremonies for special occasions. Both of them are set free in less than an hour. The young man kept burping out his demons. After the evening service, one woman has four demons that need casting out, two of them being lions. One roars so fiercely that it could have passed for a real one. It is the toughest lion demon yet I have encountered! One other person has traditional demons. Both are set free from demon possession.

206

Our services here in Mambwe District are held just 16 kilometers from the Luangwa National Park gate. We pray for those who come for deliverance after the message. One man grunts like a baboon and the demon is cast out. There are plenty of them in the nearby park. A woman with traditional spirits is set free as well. Before we can enter the next service, a demon-possessed starts manifesting. As soon as the person is set free, more follow. There are three possessed with dumb spirits. The most I have ever seen at one go. They answer me by raising a finger or two when asked how many of them there are. One of these, a teen-aged girl, also has a mad spirit. One other person has a religious spirit called Ruth. There are traditional and ancestral spirits in most of them. When all is over, I have cast demons out of six possessed people and prayed for one who is oppressed. This has taken us only an hour. It is very hot here in the bush!

While up in Chinsali District, we experience some different demons. At one service the woman with two demons is delivered immediately. But a second one refuses at the last minute. She says they help her! In a later meeting, we deal with 12 possessed and five oppressed. It takes two hours to cast them all out. They are traditional, religious, and ancestral spirits. One person is possessed with only one demon, but it leaves as soon as I command it to do so. It takes less than a minute. One demon even said, "Hoffman, why have you come to disturb us?" I wonder where I have run into him before since he knows who I am. I have been around.

At another deliverance service, the first woman who comes forward has five demons—three traditional, one ancestral, and one Mount Kilimanjaro. The names of the tree traditional spirits are: Mulenga, Mwila, and Mwenya. The toughest one is Mulenga. Once he leaves, the other two come out easier. It takes at least half an hour to drive them all out. It is under a hot burning sun. The second person is a very skinny woman yet the demons she possesses prove to be very strong. They are Mulenga and a mad one. It takes ten minutes to drive them out. The third person is a man who has a religious spirit called Mark. It also takes 10 minutes to set the man free. The demons in all three people were quite talkative and conversed with us! They answered my questions each time.

In a seminar at Mpulungu District, we meet three women and one man who are demon-possessed. In two of the women and in the man, the demons react violently. There are seven traditional demons in the man, one of them keeps spitting. They give us their names when asked to do so. The third woman is old and has a demon that stutters! All four individuals are delivered from their demons within an hour. In an evening service where about 1,000 people are present, I cast demons out of a woman whom the demons throw to the ground. Three others have traditional and ancestral demons, plus Kilimanjaro. They all leave in the name of Jesus. While praying for a pregnant woman who says she has chest and back pains, demons manifest themselves. they throw her down and really rack her body. I am able to cast them all out in about five minutes. Praise the Lord! They were hard on her, and on me. In trying to cushion her as much as possible so that she will not lose her baby, I twist my knee. What will those demons try next? I will not let this keep me out of commission!

At Mporokoso District, a man possessed with five demons is set free in five minutes. Praise the Lord! One of the demons came from Mount Kilimanjaro in Tanzania. Each demon told me his name when I commanded him to do so. After our meal tonight, a mentally deranged person comes begging for a shirt. The pastors push him outside where others now laugh at him. I follow the man and talk to him. The Spirit of the Lord comes upon me and I rebuke them all and pray for the man. He accepts the Lord! A miraculous change comes over him and he speaks to those around him about Christ! Praise the Lord! The man, who was deranged, now joins us in the evening service.

Among the eight who are demon-possessed, three of them are men, which is quite unusual. One has a dumb spirit which takes some time to drive out. A second young man has a violent spirit that almost gets away from us. He kicks so hard that he falls down. We now can deal with him. The demon leaves as soon as he knocks the man down. One of the women is so strong that in her twisting and turning she lands on my lap with me sitting on my backside! The demons are all driven out of her.

In a following seminar, I cast out demons from two more women. The first one has six of them— traditional and Kilimanjaro. She does not know English or Swahili, yet the demons speak to me in these languages! It takes about 20 minutes to get rid of them. The second woman has eight demons—six traditional, one religious, and a mad one. The demons are strong and she has to be pinned down to control them. They reacted while we were still dealing with the first woman. It takes half an hour. A good thing I ate before the service. I suspected there may be some demon- possessed. I got caught at the last place without eating something and the demons really drained me that day!

In Mpika District, I meet someone who is possessed with three demons. They give me their number when I ask. Another person has a demon who speaks in Swahili and tells me the places he has been in Tanzania! Mount Kilimanjaro is one of them. Both women are delivered within half an hour. In the following deliverance service, one oppressed person is prayed for and four others have their demons driven out. One of them is thrown to the ground just as we are finishing with the oppressed woman. She rolls and screams. It takes us a while to control the demons since we had not yet gotten to her. It is always better when the host asks for deliverance instead of us coming in after the demon has surfaced. It turns out that she has eight demons that we drive from her. There is a man who has been crippled by demons, plus he has a mad spirit. He is delivered! It takes about an hour to get all four people delivered from the powers of the devil.

Here in Isoka District, during a deliverance service, the demons in a man and a woman leave immediately after I command them to do so. The third one, a woman, says she is only oppressed with dreams. But it turns out that she has five demons! They are very talkative and stubborn. One is a babbling demon, the first of this kind for me. It is probably a religious spirit. One demon even claims to be Christ! I tell him he is a liar. He does not argue. One other demon wants to know why I am mad at them? Surely, they should know by now! It takes over half an hour to drive them all out.

What about Lusaka District, especially in the city? As has already been seen in an earlier chapter, we have dealt with demon possession in most of the churches in Lusaka. So I will just add a few more cases that need sharing. At one service a demon in a woman tells me that there are ten of them inside. One is a snake, two lions, and the rest are either religious or traditional spirits. It takes about 15 minutes to cast them out. In another meeting, a young woman says snakes appear in her dreams. I

210

plead the blood of Jesus over he and command the demon no longer to oppress her. There are two others who are possessed. One has ten of them—ancestral, religious, and a snake demon. They are very active! One demon in her has the woman clap hands, pat me on my chest, and call for her son saying he is sick. It is all an attempt by the demons to divert my attention. Maria is called upon to assist them by a religious demon. Even the name of Jesus is mentioned by another religious demon. It takes quite a while to drive them all out.

The second possessed woman has five demons. After the first one, an ancestral spirit who sheds tears, is cast out; it appears she is now delivered. But when asked to follow me in prayer, she cannot say that the blood of Jesus Christ cleanses us from our sins. This happens four times! There were still four lying spirits in her! The powers of darkness are ever trying new tactics in an endeavour to keep possessing the people. They are not anxious to vacate their hosts. But, praise the Lord, with me it is not succeeding! In another service, there are two women who are possessed with religious spirits. The older one has Isaiah and Maria. The younger one with a baby on her back has Marko. They come out after dealing with them for only a few minutes. An older woman whom we had met earlier is delivered of a traditional spirit and a baboon demon. To my surprise they both come out rather quickly. The baboon demon she had brought with her from the village out east.

A lot of people are waiting for us as I reach the place of our seminar here in Mongu District. They sing and dance around the vehicle! Marion is sitting this one out. There is a famine right now in this area and the food we are going to be eating is what I had sent here. The 20 bags of mealie meal had to be brought in by ox cart from the tarmac road which took most of the night. The vehicle could not bring it this far because of all the sand found here in Mongu District which is part of the Kalahari Desert. I will be sending in another 100 bags of maize, as the only thing to eat around here are mangoes. When the water in the Zambezi River recedes, a large plain develops. Many of the Lozi then move onto it and live there with their animals. Then, when the rains bring up the river and the plains again flood, the Lozi move to higher ground led by their king, the Litunga, in a ceremonial voyage with canoes called the "Kuomboka."

Tonight there is an ngoma nearby. The drums and the ululating are interfering with my sleep. It carries on until 8:00! I learn this morning that they were driving out the demons from someone. Have they not yet heard that they can be driven out in the name of Jesus? In one service we are dedicating 87 children to the Lord! Some of them are still wearing charms which we remove. Then, we start on the demon-possessed. There are 18 who are possessed and nine who are oppressed by demons. Many of them are men. Quite unusual! Two more do not stay but leave before we can get to them. It takes an hour and a half to set them all free from the powers of the devil. Many have traditional spirits, snake demons, and dumb spirits. A few have lions and monkey demons. I am surprised at the number of dumb spirits in this area! Even a woman, who complains only of having fear in her heart, manifests a dumb spirit.

Through all these experiences of binding demons and casting them out in the name of Jesus, I have gained some knowledge about them. They are able to impersonate a wide range of animals, objects, and people. There is a rank system where some are superior and stronger than others. They do not give up someone easily and will try to re-enter their previous hosts. They do not like to hear about the blood of Jesus and are frightened of the Bible when it is placed upon the possessed person. Demons will try to outsmart you in any way they can, lie to you, and use delaying tactics. They do remember you when you meet them again.

I do not believe that there is a demon in every hiccup, sneeze, or behind every bush. But they are ever present to oppress or possess human beings. Born-again Christians cannot be possessed when the Holy Spirit occupies that first place in their heart. But a Christian can be oppressed should they become lax in their walk with the Lord. Demons are in the world to carry out the bidding of the devil. They are a force to be reckoned with. The sooner we are aware of this, the better we will be when it comes to dealing with them.

Fifteen
Mediums and Hosts

Just as sure as a spiritually born-again Christian can be filled with the Holy Spirit, so too can someone who is not born-again be filled by one or more evil spirits. On my travels thus far you have witnessed many who were possessed with demons, or evil spirits. What kind of evil spirits they were was dependent in which area the people were residing. If it is in a remote village then Satan will match up or disguise his demons to impersonate any ancestral spirit that the inhabitants will be worshiping, plus any wild animal in the vicinity that the witch doctor or medicine man will use to bring fear into their hearts.

I should add at this juncture that demons can also possess or reside in animals. Did not Jesus send a large number of them into a herd of pigs? (Mark 5:11–13) I have read of accounts where lions after being shot countless times kept on charging until they had mauled the ones hunting them. Those who survived, and onlookers, both reported that the lions behaved as if they were demon-possessed! It is not strange then that we have often come across demons roaring as lions. They had at one time resided in lions and could now impersonate them. The animal, or reptile to be more exact, that the demon will impersonate more often than any other animal or human is the snake! That should not come as a surprise, should it? The first incident of this is recorded in Genesis 3:1–7 where Satan possesses the snake and speaks through it.

Since this phenomenon of spiritual possession was in existence in the beginning then it should not seem strange that it is still existing today. God and Satan are still competing for the souls of mankind. Satan uses every kind of trickery there is in order to deceive us into following him. He is more successful with certain techniques in areas of this world than in others. While the roaring of a lion or the hissing of a snake coming from a person in America may not seem as if the person is possessed with a demon, it certainly is the case in Africa. Satan must use what is acceptable and practiced by the populace. It cannot be too far-fetched or else the people will not fall for it. And so it is that ancestral worship is one of the practices he uses very successfully to his benefit to keep the black African in the shadows!

I want to share some findings that many of the tribes here in Zambia still believe and practice today concerning spiritual possession. Mostly they are from the Tonga in Southern Province and the Nsenga in Eastern Province. We have national co-workers who come from these tribes and some of them have assisted me in learning more about their beliefs. Listen to what they say.

There are spirits whom the Tonga call "basangu" and the Nsenga call "ombeza" who search out someone to possess. Recurrent dreams in which a spirit appears is a sign that a future possession will take place. When this happens the person is seized with convulsive tremblings, cries out in a strange voice and drops to the ground senseless. The spirit, or demon, then speaks through the possessed person should anyone address it. Those present when the possession takes place may greet the spirit with

215

clapping and singing. The spirit may then give its name and why it has come.

The basangu or ombeza are closely tied to the social life of the people. Some say they were once early prophets, while others believe they have always been spirits who have gone from one human to another. Those possessed with basangu or ombeza are true mediums for they mediate between the spirits and the world of the living. The messages they bring from the spirit world are of public importance. The one possessed with basangu or ombeza is the only agent through whom these messages can be transmitted. It may predict epidemics, droughts, floods, and other disasters. It may complain that old rituals are being neglected, customs changed, and taboos broken. The famous rainmaker Monze was one of those who was a basangu medium.

Those with basangu or ombeza possession claim foreknowledge of events. They know everything in the minds of those who come for their advice, including what is going on in their homes. They have a knowledge of many languages, and have extraordinary powers. While in a state of possession, they are able to dance about on their heads, balance objects at impossible angles, and carry impossible loads with no outward sign of strain. At the Choma Museum one can see on display huge eight-foot steel balls which were once used for clearing bush. They were attached to a chain between two tractors and then dragged along the ground. I personally was told on numerous occasions by someone who resided at Choma that there had been a man who lifted one of these large balls over his head, not jut once but at different times! An impossible feat under normal circumstances. But, for a basangu medium, it is possible I am told. Then, a missionary friend witnessed in a village outside Livingstone a man walking about and leaping 20 feet into the air! Unbelievable, but true. No wonder then that these mediums are able to rouse such respect!

The medium summons the people when his spirit has disclosed a message for him to deliver to them. He sits in his doorway while they stand or sit on the ground facing him. He begins to breathe deeply and then breaks into falsetto. After he has made his pronouncement, the people clap. Should the people on their own come to seek advice, the medium must then awaken the spirit. The people assist by clapping and calling out to it until the spirit has arisen. When the medium falls into a rigid trance, the spirit then takes control and makes the proclamation. When complete, it again becomes inactive. The medium now sits dazed, his face changes expression, and the voice becomes more his own. Some have no memory of what they have said or done during the trance and depend on those present to brief him of what transpired. The spirit remains with the medium even when it is not active.

Should the spirit fail to awaken when it is summoned through the clapping of hands, then smoke is used. Medicine is burned and as the smoke fills the room, the spirit is forced to speak out. Fumigation is commonly used to dispel unwanted spirits from those whom they have occupied. While working among the Waburunge in Tanzania, we often heard of how the Muslims drove out evil spirits from their followers by using smoke and banging metal cans together. These sounds would awaken us at night when we resided at Aimabu. Their screams could be heard a distance away as the spirits came out their victims.

Some basangu or ombeza agents (mediums) carry on in death, as in life, their roles of leadership. Shrines are

217

built at the grave sites which form a center of attraction for ceremonies and rituals to the rains, the harvests, and the averting of disasters. It used to be that each Tonga neighbourhood had at least one of these shrines. This may still be the case in some places.

There is also a form of demon possession which the Tonga call "masabe" and the Nsenga "mashawe." It is the most common and more spectacular. Masabe derives its name from the masabasaba, leg rattles of large seeds from certain trees used in some of the dances. When shaken they give forth their distinctive sound "saba-saba-saba." Masabe or mashawe is a spirit that enters people and forces them to dance. There are animal demons, ancestral spirits, and masabe or mashawe which represent objects such as an airplane, a lorry (truck), a guitar, or any new thing entering their neighborhood. In earlier years, most possessing spirits and demons were drawn from the animal world, almost always from those representing species which are dangerous or frightening. It is interesting to note that no antelopes are included in the masabe dances, nor any animal commonly hunted for meat. Where larger game and more dangerous animals have disappeared from certain areas, there the animal spirits have lost their popularity.

They differ from the basangu or ombeza in that the masabe or mashawe seek for agents through whom they can express their own desires while the former possess mediums in order to control or help people. The possession of masabe or mashawe is a private experience and is meant solely for the one possessed. Failure to carry out the orders of the masabe or mashawe reacts upon the possessed, for masabe or mashawe affect only their own carrier, whereas failure to carry out the instructions of the basangu or ombeza can react upon the people rather than upon the agent who is just the carrier of the command. Masabe or mashawe and basangu or ombeza possessions are manifested in very different situations. Instead of just the medium facing the people empowered to make some announcement, the masabe or mashawe medium along with other demon-possessed in a dance ceremony can purpose together to cure a particular person who has been struck down by another masabe or mashawe. During the course of a ceremony, one demon such as the lion may enter any number of carriers, or mediums. Also, any one medium may be entered repeatedly by different demons, indicating each new arrival by some characteristic action of that particular object or animal. Drummers and singers then shift to the appropriate music. the newly possessed individual begins the dance associated with his or her spirit. Others join this person and in turn may be possessed. Each masabe or mashawe has its own dance. The spirit and dance are called by the same name. Many women are possessed at least once. A few seem to look upon possession as a career, and as a new dance begins they are found among those who first are possessed by the new demon.

Possession also takes place spontaneously during a dance among the onlookers. Some women refuse to go near the dances for fear that they will be seized by a demon. Once a woman has been possessed and then delivered from a demon, she can be drawn to the dance where repossession can take place once more. If she attempts to resist the drums and stay away, she feels her heart beating uncontrollably! Until she joins the dance, she can expect this excitement to increase. For this very reason our converts, after having their demons driven out from them, are given strict warnings to stay away from these dances.

Those who have been possessed tell us that first there is a tingling in the arms and legs, a rapid beat of the pulse, and the throbbing of the heart. Then comes blackness just before they lose consciousness. While in this trance, they drop to the ground. Their body is entirely rigid. The spirit, or demon, now takes control. When ready, the demon will withdraw and the dancer returns to normal. Or, the demon can be cast out through exorcism.

Because of not being able to get out as much as those in the towns and cities, the village women find possession dances a welcome escape from their hum-drum daily routine. It is therefore the women who are more liable to be possessed by evil spirits than the men. The most common reason for this is, I am told, is they harbor more hatred and brood longer over petty wrongs done to them. Men tend to protect themselves more from all this with the medicines they have acquired. Women are more vulnerable since they are usually the ones who have started the quarrel among themselves. More often than not, it is a close relative who will send a masabe to possess the one she has differed with. Motives do not have to be sizeable, they can be just some little thing, like refusing to assist with food or clothing, or failing to show respect. A mother, grandmother, sister, sister-in-law, aunt, or a clanswoman can be one of the masabe or mashawe senders.

Some animals that a masabe or mashawe will possess are: baboons, monkeys, mongooses, hyenas, jackals, leopards, lions, elephants, pigs, ducks, cranes, and the turacos. There are spirits which take on the characteristics of a train, airplane, lorry, motorcycle, bike, motorboat, tractor, pump, or guitar. Others are the soldier and the policeman. Each one before possession by one of the above will have dramatic dreams about it. So vivid that they easily submit to its entry.

I should add that there are mediums who have incorporated some aspects of Christianity into their framework so as to infiltrate the Church. There is the angel masabe or mashawe. Angel has its drum rhythm, its songs, its bead wristlets, its medicines, as does any possession dance. People are content to be entered by angel spirits and its acceptance is spreading among certain churches. There are also the names of biblical characters, such as Saul, Ayubu (Job), Lazarus, Mary, Joseph, Marko, and others who are being used by the masabe or mashawe. One even announced himself as Jesus. I promptly told him he was a liar to which he made no reply. His effort to deceive me failed.

Animal demons involve impersonation of the animal. Someone who has one of these spirits imitates the call of that animal, such as the grunting of the lion, the screeching and scratching of the monkey, the hissing and twisting of the snake, etc. Sometimes food is even provided for them. Maize cobs are thrown before the one possessed with a baboon demon, who then eats them in baboon fashion. The elephant will lumber on all fours swaying from side to side while the crane waves her arms in a graceful twisting motion. Train dancers hoot and clank like a locomotive. Police dancers use a whistle to give drill orders. The one with a soldier demon will march stiffly and salutely smartly. (I came across one of them while in Tanzania.) Foreign dancers speak in the language of their spirit's homeland. (I have been addressed by a few speaking in Arabic, and yet the individual knew not one word of it when the spirit was inactive.) There are spirits who speak falsetto when they call out to those around them.

Some possessed dancers only do a simple shuffle while others dance backwards very rapidly. These that do the latter will finally fall to the ground and roll about uncontrollably, swinging heels over head. It ends with the body going rigid into a curve supported only by the heels and top of the head! Most dances, no matter how sober they may be, end in a frenzy! The rhythm of the drums increases creating a faster and faster pace. Feet move at incredible speeds, arms and heads shaking, the whole body vibrating! This takes place after the demon has taken control of the dancers.

When these demon-possessed individuals show up in church, the evil spirits often are activated by the anointed message being preached in the service. Their main purpose is to disrupt the service so that no one will repent and receive Christ as their personal Saviour. We prefer not to deal with the possessed until after having prayed for the sinner and the sick. But should the spirits become too restless and noticeably disturb the service, we take charge over them and drive the demons out of the carrier.

The reaction of the demon-possessed is much the same in most cases. While kneeling, the body becomes stiff, and eyes stare straight ahead. There follows a cry and the person falls to the ground. We try to help break the fall as much as possible and lower the rigid body carefully. Without our help, the possessed drops with a thunk. If the possessed is a woman, then one or two of her friends will gather around to arrange the garments so that her writhing will not lead to indecent exposure of the body. From the time the person falls, his or her own personality becomes inactive until the spirit or demon who has risen to take control departs.

We now commence commanding the masabe or mashawe to depart from the medium. The spirit may or may not comply immediately. Instead he may engage you in a conversation in order to use up your time and tire you out so that you will discontinue your exorcism. Even though I am so tried at times, especially after having dealt with several hard cases just before this one, I do not give in. The demon knows that this method can work and often it has with some preachers. Otherwise the demon would not try this stunt. The demon has said to me on several occasions, "You are going to give up, you are going to get tired." He was wrong. It was he who got tired and vacated the host.

If there is a snake demon, it will commence to hiss and twist about making it difficult for us to hold the person it is occupying. In fact, when the rolling starts, you are forced to let go. It is now impossible to hang on. When the rolling stops, we again lay our hands on the person and continue our exorcism. When the snake masabe or mashawe finally is driven out, the person will sit for some time staring vacantly in front of him or her, ignoring everyone else. When the transition is complete, the person is asked to kneel and we have a final word of prayer with him or her. Those who have been possessed before will pass a lot quicker from one stage to the other, from being under the control of an evil spirit to being oneself again.

There is another type of possession which is simply the possession of a ghost. No clear explanation was given as to who they are and where they come from. They are either ghosts originating from the local forgotten dead, or are spirits who have fallen into the control of sorcerers.

A ghost enters its victim for the purpose of killing. A sudden violent illness is therefore attributed to ghost possession among the Tonga. Treatment is carried out in private and involves fumigation and the clanging of metal cans in an attempt to force the ghost to leave its victim. Before it flees it should call out its own name and the name of the sorcerer who sent it. Once released, the victim should show immediate improvement.

Ghost possession differs from basangu or ombeza possession, and masabe or mashawe possession, in that it is wholly undesirable. Whereas the above mentioned mediums expect a long-term relationship with their spirits and demons where they can reap some personal benefits from being possessed, victims of ghost possession seek only to expel them and to prevent their re-entry. Ghosts have no mediums, only victims. And these must be short-term ones, for either a ghost is expelled or the victim dies!

The Nsenga have a master demon known as Mfumu Mpasi, the king of lions. This one stems back to the days of the early kings who were not buried but laid inside caves. Two bowls were placed at the entrance, one containing uncooked mealie meal soaked in water and the other one with red ochre in water. The lion who approaches the cave and stops to eat the mealie meal is said not to be possessed with a demon. But, should the lion drink the red liquid, he is a killer and has a demon, and Mfumu Mpasi is his name. He usually has 12 other demons with him that he is in charge of. We have driven him and his entourage out of many whom they had possessed. Praise the Lord!

The Apostle Paul said that we wrestle not against flesh and blood but against the powers of this dark world and against the spiritual forces of evil. This portion of Scripture is recorded in Ephesians 6:12. It has become very meaningful to me since coming to Africa, especially here in Zambia where demon possession is very common.

We have met many who have been hosts or carriers of evil spirits, and many who still are! We are often surprised and shocked when in a worship service a demon is activated in someone who is singing in a choir, or who is a layman in church. Demonism is not a lost art out here, but a very real part of everyone's life. And it is against this power of darkness that we, who are in the light, are to fight against! Because of engaging the demons so often and driving them out of those possessed by them, they have been waging personal attacks on me and Marion in order to slow us down. But greater is He who is in us than he who is in the world! Therefore, we press on in our fight against the powers of this dark world.

Many have learned that God has a Spirit who will help them in their needs if they will but believe in Him, leave behind their beliefs based on fear, and accept Jesus Christ into their hearts. They have been miraculously changed! They no longer host demons, but have become agents of the Holy Spirit. Praise the Lord! This is what keeps us going, knowing that His Word will not return void but will bring forth fruit in due season if we faint not. Amen!

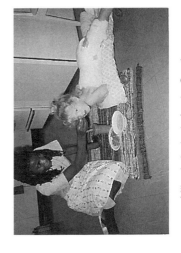

Mikaela looked after by Sarah.

Natasha and Tiffany with Opa.

Shaina and Mikaela recuperating.

Mikaela with her Opa.

Mark and one of his many flats.

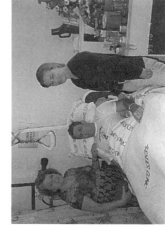

Mark recuperating from his hunting accident.

Kirk and Mark out hunting.

Mark and one of his buffalos.

Mark and a zebra kill.

Kirk finally got his sitatunga.

Mark and his sable trophy.

Kirk with his record trophy greater kudu.

The tsessebe I got at Bangweulu.

My kafue lechwe trophy.

The brindled gnu (wildebeast) I dropped.

Colleen gets an impala after 23 years of not hunting.

Our empty lot at Avondale in Lusaka.

Tim speaking at the sod-breaking ceremony.

Hon. Penza, Minister of Finance, doing the honors.

Dedication of the multi-purpose building.

Colleen's Nursery and Preschool at Avondale, Lusaka.

Marion with Sarah and Monica in the kitchen.

Marion's Tailoring School at Avondale, Lusaka.

Marion busy with her computer.

Cruising down the Zambezi River.

A double rainbow at Victoria Falls.

Kirk, Suzie, and the girls.

Three generations—with Mark and Sean.

Marvels present at Mailes Ndao's ordination.

Graduates at Marion's Tailoring School.

Church choir at Avondale Church.

Marion ordained on the same day.

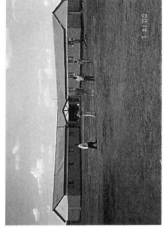

The hostel in Avondale, Lusaka.

Our home in Livingstone.

The multi-purpose building in Avondale.

Another staff house going up in Avondale.

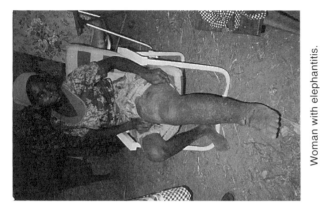

Woman with elephantitis.

Fresh caterpillars ready for cooking.

Care for a fried grasshopper?

Sixteen
Customs and Traditions

Zambia is a vast, thinly populated, tree-clad plateau in the heart of Africa. Grassland with clumps of trees, or wooded savanna, covers much of the country. There are some areas of swamp, while evergreen forests grow in the drier, sandy southwest. The year we moved here in 1989 the population was 7,420,000, while Uganda's was more than twice as much at 16,700,000. Yet, Zambia at 752,614 square kilometers is at least three times larger in size than Uganda, which is 236,860 square kilometers. Once known as Northern Rhodesia under British rule, Zambia gained its independence in 1964. In spite of a large percentage of the population claiming Christianity as their religion, traditional beliefs still abound.

There are many traditions and customs that keep Christians from practicing freely their newly found beliefs. Growth is therefore minimal because of the katundu (luggage) that they carry with them from their old life. I want to share a few of those practices which I would like to see banished so that more time can be spent in walking with the Lord.

*   *   *

When a Nsenga girl reaches the age of puberty, she

breaks the news to her sister, or a female neighbor. That person then notifies the mother and asks her to confine the girl in the house. It is now time for her to learn many things: how to look after herself, how to respect her elders, and how to prepare for her future husband. There are also traditional beliefs and customs that go back in time she must now be taught. The teacher who will undertake this role is chosen by the mother. Often it is the grandmother if she is not too old and if she lives in the immediate vicinity.

The period she will spend in the house is dependent on the girl's own behavior. It may be from one month to three months. It can even be longer if she is a slow learner. The Waburunge in Tanzania often keep their girls confined to a hut for up to two years!

When the young girl has completed her confinement, a ceremony takes place to announce to the neighborhood that she has now reached womanhood and is available for marriage. Before the girl is placed on top of a stand which has a platform, called a chisaka by the Nsenga, a younger girl climbs up first and starts dancing. This is a signal that the ceremony has begun. There is much singing and dancing among the spectators. When the confined girl is about ready to come out, the young girl on top of the chisaka is removed by a young boy and escorted to the hut where she is waiting. The girl exits wearing beads around here neck that cross in front of her. When on top she commences to dance. Spectators cheer her on and throw money at her feet.

At the end of the ceremony, the girl, who is totally exhausted by now, is escorted back to her parents' house. The crowd disperses. In some neighboring tribes, it is much like an auction where the highest bidder whisks away the girl to his house where she may or may not remain to become his wife. She has now become a woman. Not so with the Nsenga. The girl may guess that there is a suitor, unknown to her as yet, out there in the crowd but she is not whisked away.

The girl will from now on no longer romp around with the girls as she did before her confinement but begin to perform the duties of a grown woman. She has passed from childhood to womanhood during this period of confinement.

*   *   *

Many villagers still practice traditional marriages which the church must recognize or else homes will be broken apart. If not, the man may use it as an excuse to leave his wife of many years and choose a younger one when he becomes a member of the church, stating that he chose his first one when he was still a pagan. All the couple needs to do is have their marriage blessed when they join the church. It is not necessary for them to be remarried.

Traditional marriages may differ in some points but basically they are the same with the majority of the 70 plus tribes in Zambia. When the man sees a woman he would like to marry he takes over a small gift to give to her. This may be done secretly or through a friend. If she accepts it, then the courtship commences. The girl will show the gift to the grandmother who in turn takes it to the girl's parents. When the two lovers meet the second time, she is given another gift. Now, she tells him what her relatives think of him. If all is well, the wedding plans are set into motion by the man's relatives.

Several of his relatives now bring a gift to the girl's

mother in order for the marriage discussion to begin. Without the gift there is nothing to talk about. No bride price is discussed at this meeting. That is for another day. When that day does arrive, the bride price is struck and the men on his side are sent to deliver the dowry which has been agreed upon.

On the day of the wedding, the bride arrives covered from head to foot in chitenge material. Or, she may wear around her waist a short skirt of reeds with beads around her head and across her body. Her breasts are covered with a tiny cloth. Walking behind her, the bridal party usually carries a live rooster and a cooked chicken, mealie meal, salt, cooking pots with sticks, a towel, a razor blade, cloth, and small pot. As they approach the compound of the groom, all start to sing and fall to their knees. They then crawl the remaining distance to his hut. Inside the man is waiting for her with some of his older relatives. Once she is inside, the elders leave and the two are alone.

That night the couple shave each other's private parts with the razor blade. The hair is saved and placed in the small pot along with the blade when done. This will be inspected in the morning to see whether the union took place. Then the hair and the blade are disposed of by them. The cloth used for wiping is kept by the couple.

During the morning the couple are visited in their hut by the elders from both sides. The girl cradles her husband in her lap to show her love and care for him. She takes some prepared food and feeds him with her hands. He does the same for her. The marriage is now complete. There is much ululating. The couple come outside and more words of advice are offered by the relatives. Then all disperse and leave the newly married couple to start life together.

*   *   *

A child does not necessarily inherit his or her father's property. Among the Nsenga it is the child of his sister who will inherit the property. When sick the uncle takes the child to the doctor and not the father. The uncle will come over when the child is sick and tell the parents that their child needs to be taken to the doctor, or witch doctor. The father then trails along behind.

When an infant dies, the elders will gather to determine which one of the parents is to blame for the death. They will be questioned as to whether they had sex within three months of his birth. This is the period where there is to be no sex between the couple. If they did not, then when they had the first sexual act, did they smear the semen from the man over the baby's body in order to energize the child? If they failed to do this, then it is their fault and they will be fined which may amount to several goats. The uncle on the mother's side will take the goats.

Should the child come down with measles, no sex is to be performed. If the baby dies, then the mother is questioned whether they did have sex. If she answers in the negative, then the father is to blame. He must have had sex outside with someone else and he is fined. Whether he did or did not is not the point. He must shoulder the blame. There is to be no sex for three months after the death of a child.

Should the death of a twin occur, the parents in the Nsenga tribe will place the fruit of a sausage tree beside the child in the coffin so that it will not be lonely. Otherwise, the spirit will come back and haunt the living twin.

At the grave site when an infant is buried, its soap, cup, dish, and toy are broken and stuck into the mound of clay signifying all ties have been broken. Nothing remains behind to sadden the parents as they try to readjust their life without their child. If this is not done, then the spirit of the child will come back to haunt the parents. The soil, before it is thrown onto the coffin, is touched by the relatives. This is to signify that the spirit of the child is free to sleep in peace. At the grave site of an adult, his or her Vaseline, soap, and favorite plates are put inside the coffin or broken and placed on top of the grave.

Young children do not attend funerals. They are kept away and do not know what takes place at the burial site. When adults die, children are told they have moved away to another area.

Funerals bring together many relatives, neighbors, and friends who stay to eat and drink for days. No one dares stay away for fear of being accused of bringing about the death of the deceased through witchcraft. Every death is attributed to some form of witchcraft. Therefore, immediate relatives make special effort to be present. This brings an extra burden to the bereaved in feeding the crowd at their home. Everywhere there are groups sitting around and doing nothing to help provide food and assist the women folk with the cooking.

When finally all have left, the elderly women come and prepare some herbs boiled over a fire in a smaller container where salt has been added. After this act has been performed, the mother is now free to cook on a fire. Until now she has been prohibited to come near the cooking fire. If this is not done, then the spirit of the child is not happy and the mother may die as well because of it.

*   *   *

When the man dies, the relatives on his side will

show up and grab everything, including the woman's clothes, and leave her with nothing. Why? Because she is to blame for his death, even though the doctor's report states otherwise. On the other hand, should the woman die, this ruling does not apply. He can donate or give away any item from his late wife if he so wishes. It is not compulsory.

The relatives grab the property because they believe everything belongs to the husband. When the man dies, the woman immediately is asked for the bedroom keys and the bank account book should they be that well off. They get the woman to sign for the dead husband and as soon as she has the cash, they take it from her. "She is left to sit in the sun" is a Nsenga saying. There is nothing else left for her to do but return to her mother along with the children. There is no property snatching when a woman dies.

A law has been instituted to prevent this happening but it is still practiced openly in the villages. There are lawyers, the woman is told, who can assist her. But she cannot afford hiring one, and so the practice of property snatching goes on.

*   *   *

When the husband dies, the wife must go through a cleansing process which involves several rituals she is to perform. She is to wear a black head scarf and white beads on her wrist specially made for her by his grand-mother. The woman from now on walks barefoot and does not sit on a stool or chair until the cleansing ceremony takes place which is to sleep with her brother-in-law, or a cousin on his side, in order to remove the spirit of the dead husband from her. Without doing this, his spirit will be around to haunt the woman until she is driven insane.

The waiting period today with the Nsenga may be only three months, but in the past it could be as long as a year. The woman cannot wash her clothes until the cleansing has taken place. She is not to sleep with a man, nor get married, and must wear a pad. Beer is brewed for a week from grain that has been sprouted and fermented during this time of waiting.

The cleansing act consists of the man, who is either a brother or cousin of the dead man, shaving off all her body hair, except on the head, before having sex with the woman. If the man is not married, then he will have to be shaved as well by her. But if he is married, then he already will have been shaved. He needs to keep this act a secret from his own wife. After the sexual act is performed, the spirit of the dead husband is now released to go its way.

The following morning, the relatives go to the burial site and place beer and mealie meal with water at the head of the grave which is facing east. This is so that his spirit will not follow them. The woman now removes the white beads and leaves them at the grave. The same day, the woman's head is shaved in the presence of relatives and friends by an elderly woman from his side. The pad is now removed and disposed of along with all the hair by burning them or burying them. The spirit of the dead man is now sleeping in peace as the woman has followed all that was required of her by his relatives.

Should a wife die, the husband will need to sleep with his sister-in-law, or a cousin, in order to get cleansed. The woman who is to sleep with him must be single and will be chosen by her relatives. The sexual act will be performed in the dark and as secretly as possible in order to protect the girl from future suitors. But the man may choose to marry the girl himself if he has any feelings for her. After the sexual act, the spirit of the dead wife is now released from the home and departs.

Three months to a year later, the relatives meet at the grave to erect a marker or tombstone. They throw money on the mound and place mealie meal at the head of the grave. Clan cousins pick up the money as they have been doing all the work cooking for the group.

*   *   *

Traditions and customs of the past that interfere with Christians in their walk with God are harmful and not helpful. No matter what face we put on them, the Gospel can not condone them. Until Christians take a stand against these practices, darkness will continue to keep them from enjoying the fullness of His light. They will keep living in the shadows. For many they are long shadows.

Seventeen
Back on the African Savanna

Hunting! Fourteen years have slipped by since I last tucked my khaki pants into my hunting boots, laced them up, buckled on my hunting knife, slapped on my bush hat, picked up my rifle, and lit out on a hunt for game on the African savanna. Why has it taken me so long, you may ask? Do I not like to get away into the bush anymore? Let me tell you I miss it a lot! But circumstances have prevented me from doing this any sooner. Our years in Uganda prevented me from owning a gun due to the unstable situation of the country during our years there. Anyone with a gun was a prime target for thieves. Then, there was no legal hunting during that time as well. And, so, any hunting I did was from the easy chair repeating my own experiences while in Tanzania and Kenya to anyone who wanted to listen. Those were wonderful years for me that I spent in the African bush.

Since those hunting days, Kenya has closed hunting down, Tanzania shortened theirs to six months, and Uganda has not reopened at all. Now where do I fit in? I am used to a full year of hunting anytime I wished to venture out for meat on the table. My license gave me a full menu to chose from. Even Marion could join in with her own license to add to mine. Game was plentiful. How exciting it was to see animals in the wild wherever you looked. I did not have to go far to bring down an antelope. What has happened to all the game? Less hunting is being done by hunters such as myself, and yet the number of animals has not increased out there on the African savanna. The hunter today must be prepared to travel miles, spend a number of days on the trail, and spend a large amount of dollars to bag his trophies. Very few hunt anymore for meat. Too expensive! And, so, they chase trophies they can take home to mount on their walls.

I now live in a country that has a hunting season from June to December. There are very few open areas where one is able to find any wild animals around to shoot for meat. Those that can be found are so spooked that you need a rifle with a scope in order to bring it down. They are that scared! The local population has hunted them to near extinction. It is well known here, and in the neighbouring countries, that Zambians are poachers. No one has hunted the once numerous black rhino for years and yet there is not one found any longer in Zambia. This includes the parks. The only ones found alive yet are the white rhino that were recently imported from South Africa and placed in the Mosi-Oa-Tunya National Park just outside Livingstone. What about the elephants? I have not seen a big tusker yet, even at the famous Luangwa National Park, since moving here. Even if I did see one, I cannot get a license for it anyway. They are for the poachers to slaughter.

Yes, my desire for hunting has been dampened since those earlier years when there was excitement running through my veins because of what was waiting for me out there on the savanna and in the bush. Herds of animals roamed the plains! But what is out there today for a hunter like me? Only disappointment. Oh yes, if you hire a professional hunter and pay him a large sum of money, he will take you to places where you can still hunt the animal you want. But for us who do our own hunting, life is no longer the same. At least for me. I have had a good life, maybe not as good as those who came before my time, but I have wonderful memories of my hunting days. And, so it is that I sit often and recall those experiences, and excitement again pumps through my veins.

I do want to share the hunting experiences that are worthwhile repeating that I have had thus far since coming to Zambia. They will not be as exciting as those I wrote about in an earlier book *In the Tanganyika Bush* of my time in Tanzania. Those of my hunts in Kenya are in another book *Tracks in the Dust*. The following accounts of my hunts include one or both of my sons. Very seldom have I gone out alone. Why? Time. I am so busy that hunting is no longer the release from the crowds it used to be. I wish it were, but as I already have mentioned, hunting no longer holds the excitement it used to.

It is my first hunting safari (*ulendo* in the Nyanja language) here in Zambia. I have agreed to join Colin Green in order to learn where this open area is where one can still hunt without having to apply for a permit to a Game Management Area (GMA). Zambia has divided most places outside of parks where game is still found into GMAs. Marion gives us something to eat before we leave at 13 hours. The place we are heading for is 250 kilometers north-west of Lusaka. The last 90 kilometers of it is over a dirt road which is very rough in sections. En route we come across a lone sable antelope. Colin does not stop. "There will be others," he says. I hope he is right.

It is 6 P.M. when we reach our destination. Our camp is on the south bank of the Kafue River not far from the Kafue National Park. An excellent spot! It gets dark quickly. We eat our supper in the light of a pressure lamp.

248

There are several tents with cots inside them at this camp site which belongs to Colin's friend, John, whom we found waiting for us. I have brought along my sleeping bag and will be bunking inside one of the tents with Colin. I hear a hyena after we crawl into bed. There are lions in the area I am told.

Up at 4:00! After a cup of tea and a guava, we leave camp. It is soon light and we keep driving on until noon. During this time we see only reedbuck. Colin shoots one of them. Plenty of tsetse flies, though. They are everywhere, inside and outside the Landcruiser pickup. Their sting is much like that of a horse fly. Sleeping sickness is still found in Zambia because of this pesky fly which is its carrier. We have come to a waterhole surrounded by a growth of heavy trees. We are greeted by the carcass of a buffalo, already half eaten by lions. The tongue and the insides are missing so it may have been killed by a poacher who left the scene as soon as the pride of lions appeared to claim the meat.

We see some warthogs but they do not stop running when they spot us. There is a roan antelope but no one has a license for one. Tracks of elephants cross the trail we are on. Then, there are tracks of lions as well. When the radiator starts steaming, we stop for it to cool down. During this time we have something to drink. I share the roasted ground nuts Marion sent along. Too hot to stay out on the savanna at this time of day, so when the vehicle is ready we wend our way back to camp. We eat our meal at 2:30 P.M. Colin and John do some fishing and catch four of them. On our evening drive, when things have cooled off some, we see no animal that one of us has a license for. So nothing is shot. After a wash in the river tonight, we eat some of the meat from the reedbuck that

Colin shot this morning. The hyena lulls me to sleep to-night.

We wake up at five, and a half an hour later we are on the road. A herd of buffalo is spotted as they are about ready to cross the track in front of us. They are making their way to the heavy stand of trees that connects with the park. As soon as they see us, they take off in a cloud of dust! The two men take after them on foot and I stay behind with the vehicle. While waiting, I watch an eland make its way across my front and disappear into the bush. No license! But when a small herd of sable make an appearance, I become interested. I pick up the small gun left behind, a .270 calibre rifle with a 120 grain bullet, and begin crawling up to them. I manage to creep up to within 200 yards of them when I also notice some hartebeest with them. The black male sable is well hidden by the female. Then, the herd spooks and both the sable and the hartebeest take off at top speed. I look around me and see a vehicle passing nearby. Too bad! Had it been my gun, I would have shot earlier and not come this far. It is a 30.06 calibre rifle and would have been enough to bring the animal down.

The men return and say they wounded one of the buffalo. They climb inside the vehicle and return into the bush to follow their trail. When it is impossible to go farther with the Landcruiser, we continue on foot. After a couple of hours of fruitless searching, it is decided to give it up. The lions will have fresh meat tonight. "Let's return to the vehicle," we say. But where is it? We finally split up. John takes his two Zambians while I go with Colin. We walk for miles in the bush. Then, as we wander into an open glade (*dambo* in Nyanja), we meet up with John and the vehicle. He had just found it and fortunately for us we come upon them when we do! A minute later and we would have missed each other as sound does not travel far in this heavy bush. Talk about good timing!

Back in camp we stretch out for a well deserved rest. It was hot walking back in that bush. There was no breeze at all. The drinking water we had with us was warm. When evening comes, we take a drive. A warthog is spotted. He has no intentions of stopping. Then a hartebeest comes into view. Colin takes a shot at it and hits the tree instead! We return at sunset empty-handed. No meat today to show for all our efforts, whatever they may be.

Again we get up at five and light out for our last attempt at getting some meat before heading for home. It is still dark when we leave camp. It is cold standing in back of the open vehicle. I have been sleeping in my clothes inside my sleeping bag since I have come. It has been that cold! But, it warms up quickly once the sun is up. By noon it is hot! There are no buffalo along the dambo this morning as there were yesterday. We drive for some time before a warthog is spotted. This one stands long enough for Colin to drop it with his first shot. We carry along a trail that should have plenty of game. But there is nothing! Lots and lots of tsetse flies though. They are everywhere. No one is spared from their drilling for blood. Some that I kill are full of it! Mine?

We end up back in camp at half past eight. We load up our things and an hour later, after a bite to eat, we head for Lusaka. We take the meat of the warthog along and the reedbuck which had been cut up and drying on a line. Colin has also salted and peppered the meat which he is turning into biltong. We make good time and reach home by 2 P.M. My first hunt in Zambia, and I come back without even firing off a shot! Imagine?

My second attempt is in the same area. This time it is with Colin again. Mark and Gary Kellsey, who is visiting

251

us from Canada, are traveling with us. Again, sable are spotted as we get closer to the camp site. And, nobody has a license for one! They are expensive. Colin drops a warthog before we reach our destination. After unloading our camping equipment, we take off for more meat. We see more sable. Then hartebeest are sighted and Mark tries his hand at shooting one. He shoots several times but misses. Next he runs after an impala but cannot get close enough to fire off a round. The animals here in Zambia, at least in this area, are very shy of humans. It must be due to all the poachers roaming the bush.

We return to camp at dark empty-handed. The supper is made from the vegetables we brought along and the liver from the warthog. We sit around and talk until 9 P.M. Then we turn in. I am using my sleeping bag, leaving on my clothes except for the shoes as I did on my previous ulendo. The night does not feel as cold though.

It is still dark when we decide to get up at five. After tea and some bread, we commence our hunt. There are no buffalo where they are supposed to be. We keep driving. We do not see anything for hours except duiker and oribi for which no one has a license. Finally, we run across a herd of hartebeest and Mark takes after them. This time he drops two of them. That takes care of his and my licenses. When we fail to see any reedbuck, we return to camp and skin out the two animals and hang the meat up to dry. At 3 P.M. we return to the hunt. When we see a herd of impala, Colin tries for the buck but misses. Besides sable we see hartebeest but they are a no-no now. Before returning to camp, we load up some kuni (firewood). There is plenty of it lying around in the bush.

The two guinea fowl that Colin shot earlier today are cleaned and cooked for supper. Gary cuts himself with the ax while preparing some dry wood for the fire. It is quite deep. Mark looks after it. There were a lot of tsetse flies today. They are even biting tonight! They do not like to quit. A crocodile is hanging around in the river. It has been cleaning up on the bones and scraps we have been tossing away. Let us hope he will not come for the meat that is hanging on the line!

But the crocodile does come and carries away one of the rib cages while we sleep. We may have lost more if Mark had not awakened at 3:30 to check. He promptly moves the meat on the line back onto a tree. At sunrise we pack our stuff back into the vehicles and after something to eat we commence our trip back to Lusaka. Of course, we hope to do some hunting along the way before leaving the game area. Colin, who is in the front vehicle, draws first blood when he shoots a reedbuck. I finally get my turn and drop an impala. It is a fine male which fell at my first shot. We clean out both animals before loading them onto Colin's open vehicle. It is now on to Lusaka. We reach home and it is dark before all meat gets cut up and packaged ready for the freezer. Marion will not let me off that easy. "You shoot it, you help put it away!"

Two weeks later we are back in the same hunting area. Mark and Kirk have joined Colin and me on this hunt. We split up as soon as we enter the land of the tsetse flies. They are hopping mad today! I take Kirk with me and Mark goes with Colin. We come across warthog and impala. Kirk shoots an impala but misses the warthog. When we reach camp we find Colin just pulling in with Mark. They too saw some game and Colin has his impala in the vehicle as well. After unloading our stuff into the tents, we skin and cut up the animals. The meat is hung up on a limb to dry. Then, we return to the hunt. Kirk shoots a warthog and Mark gets a duiker. It is now too dark to hunt any longer and we return to camp picking up kuni on our way. The rest of the animals are skinned and the meat hung up to dry. Supper is late. We chat until 10 P.M. before retiring.

The night is not really cold. The reason may be that it turned cloudy overnight. Mark got up at 3:30 to check the meat. He heard the crocodiles and saw their eyes in the light of the torch so he stayed up the rest of the night around the campfire. We leave camp at daybreak without eating. When we come up to a herd of hartebeest, Kirk drops two of them with a shot each. Mark and Colin miss their shots at impala. We return the meat to camp at noon. We eat some lunch and then work on the meat. Get it all done and hung by 2 P.M We return to the bush once more. There are some puku but no male among them. I take off after reedbuck but am unable to get close enough to where I can place a clear shot at the buck. Mark has a shot at a nice male reedbuck with a good set of horns but misses. Too high! He has not had any luck today at all. Bring back more kuni for our fires. We hit the sack early tonight.

I hear a hyena during the night. Mark wakes up at 4:00 to find out if we are interested in checking whether the buffalo are at the waterhole where we found some of their tracks yesterday. Colin tells him we are not going. So we do not get up until sunrise. We load up our stuff and the meat as we are moving out today. We have a bite to eat before leaving the camp site. Kirk and Mark take my vehicle and I ride with Colin. On our way out we see a herd of sable plus a lone roan. When we come across some reedbuck, Colin drops one. Mark misses his shot. We skin out the animal and cut it up. The meat is hung up to dry out for a while before loading it. We reach home in the late afternoon. Kirk has had a good hunt while Mark has not been on at all this ulendo.

This next hunt takes place on the Kafue Flats bordering the Blue Lagoon National Park. I am taking Kirk and Mark with me for the Kafue lechwe which are found in large herds on the north side of the Kafue River. It is only 15 kilometers from Lusaka. The last 40 are quite rough and impossible to drive during the rains. Once we reach the herd, numbering in the hundreds, Kirk drops a nice buck at 250 yards with his one and only shot. It takes an hour to skin it and cut up the animal. We eat the lunch Marion has sent along before we make our way back to Lusaka. Kirk has had another successful hunt. But then he has always been a good shot, even back there in Tanzania.

My son-in-law Tim is here and I wish to take him along on this hunt that I have planned for the open area beyond Mumbwa and beside the Kafue River. Colleen is staying behind with her mother. I had wanted her to go along but she is not quite over her bout with malaria. Mark is coming along as well. When we reach the hunting area, I have Tim try out the rifle he will be using. He fires off a couple of rounds and when he is satisfied, we continue on our way to the camp site. It is dark when we reach it. Colin Green is waiting for us. We have chosen a spot farther down from where we have been the last three times. Tim and Mark will be sleeping in the tent we have brought along while I will be sleeping in the open with Colin in his enclosure he has made out of guni sacks. We hear hyenas as we eat our food and settle down for the night.

Just after midnight I am awakened by an animal walking around near the river. I cannot see anything in the light of my torch. I return to my bed on the ground. It is 5:00 when I wake up again. The night has not been cold at all sleeping out in the open. We get up and have our tea and some buns. Then, we drive out into dark. As soon as there is light, we spot zebra and Mark drops one big stallion. We gut it before loading the animal. Next, Tim brings down a reedbuck, followed by Colin with an impala. We end up in camp by 11:30 with our load of meat. Tim helps Mark skin his zebra before we eat something light.

When we are back in the bush, we continue our search for sable. They were so numerous on our last hunt but they are not to be seen this time when we have a license. Too many hunters have come and gone since then. When a bush pig shows itself, Tim fires a round after him. He misses. We get back to camp by dark without a kill. We eat supper and talk awhile before retiring. We ran into a lot of tsetse flies today.

I hear some footsteps again during the night, as the night before, so I get up to look. It is 2:00. I do not pick anything up in the light of my torch. What animal is it? We are up early and leave at 5:45 after our cup of tea. Again we check for buffalo but they are nowhere in sight. Our search for a hartebeest for Tim ends in failure. We return to our camp at 10:30 and begin dismantling it. We need to be back in Lusaka by tonight. Once our stuff is loaded, we turn our vehicles homeward. Of course, if we see anything that is still on our license, we will take time to shoot it. I had wanted a puku but the ones we have seen thus far have been female.

When we meet some reedbuck, Tim shoots his second one. It has a better set of horns than his first one. We cut it up and load the meat. Then, a lone male sable is spotted! I take out after him on a run. When I get to about 200 yards from him, I fire. To my surprise the bull goes down as if axed! But before I can reach his side, he gets up and strangely does not run off. The gun I am using is Mark's

.243 rifle which does not make enough damage, as I am learning, on a big animal like the sable. I placed several more shots into him before he finally drops dead. An hour later we have the animal skinned, cut up, and loaded. It is now 6 P.M. We reach home three hours later. The women are waiting for us but the children are in bed. It is almost midnight before we can crawl in between the sheets.

Today, I am after my first Kafue lechwe. Mark and Kim are accompanying me to the Kafue Flats. When we reach the place, we also discover hundreds of zebra spread out as far as the eye can see! But I do not have a license for one. I am after lechwe. I spend an hour looking over them for a good set of horns. There are hundreds of lechwe mingling around on the muddy flats. I finally decide on one buck but he is 350 yards away! I fire off a round. It is high. I have allowed too much. The next shot hits him in the lungs. It takes one more in the spine to bring him down. The horns measure almost 33 inches each. We take out the stomach and take all the meat with us. A successful hunt! And it is only 4:30 when we reach home.

Mark is anxious to get his first buffalo. So we plan an ulendo to an open hunting area just north of the Lower Zambezi National Park. I am up at 3:30 and pick him up half an hour later at his place. We travel east on the Great East Road until we reach the game post where we pick up two scouts. They guide us into the bush where there are buffalo to be found. When we reach a place where we cannot travel any farther because of the rough terrain, I stop the vehicle and as I step out of the Nissan I am almost bitten by a puff adder! The scout who is climbing out right behind me sees the snake next to my feet and grabs it at the neck just before it can strike. He then calmly tosses it aside. That was almost too close!

After two hours of tramping up and down hills and searching for water holes, we return to the vehicle exhausted and empty-handed. The only animals we saw were a duiker and a bushbuck. And lots of tsetse flies! We move on to another spot. I stay with the Nissan this time and Mark takes off with the scouts on foot. They return two and a half hours later without seeing a buffalo! We decide to call it a day and start out for Lusaka. Before we hit the Great North Road we come across a herd of roan antelope with a nice male among them. We drop off the scouts at the game post.

My next hunt with Mark is on a game farm near the Kafue River outside of Kafue town where they want a wildebeest and an impala culled from among their animals. It is not an ulendo that takes us into the broken countryside filled with tsetse flies but an easy leisurely drive on the African savanna. Just the same it must take a good clean shot so that the rest of the herds do not panic and scatter whenever they next see a group of humans pass through this midst. Mark and I are driven out and when we approach the wildebeest, I am dropped off so as to approach them on foot. When I am within a comfortable shooting range, I plant a 30.06 slug in a wildebeest's rib cage and the animal drops dead from a heart shot. It is over that quickly! What about the impala for Mark? After some searching, the buck he is after does not show himself. So he leaves without his trophy.

This ulendo will take us into the Mulobezi GMA which is situated west of Kolomo and straddles the southern end of the Kafue National Park. Marion is coming along plus Mark, Kim, and their daughter Courtney. It will be a nice outing for us all. A good change for Marion from the crowded city life. We are able to make an early start and at Kolomo we fill up with fuel including some extra jerry cans. Then it is off on a dirt road which has several bad dips in it. At one of them the roof rack which is loaded down with tenting equipment slides ahead. Now we are unable to open the doors! The clamps are in the way. After some effort I get mine open.

It is a 150 kilometer drive before we finally arrive at a site where we pitch our tents. It is a nice spot among some fever trees and near a river which still has some water in it at this site. After we have unloaded all the stuff off the roof rack, we are able to slide it back into place. Marion cooks our evening meal on an open fire and we eat it as the sun sinks beyond the horizon. As soon as it is dark, we hear a hyena. We had seen sable, hartebeest, impala, duiker, and warthog along the way as we were coming to this spot. We may have a good hunt here in this GMA.

Just after midnight we hear elephants nearby making a lot of noise in the riverbed where there are several waterholes. The hyenas keep howling most of the night. Towards morning a bushbuck barks right next to our camp. We crawl out of our tents when it is still dark and have a bite to eat before loading our vehicle for the hunt. Then, it is off to look for game. We soon discover the animals keep their distance. They run as soon as we approach them. Mark is interested in buffalo but nothing is seen of them. There are sable but no big male in the herd. We return to camp at noon.

In the afternoon Mark and I strike off in another direction. We come across more game on this route, but as soon as you step out of the vehicle they are off as if stung. After he fails on his first try at a sable bull, Mark succeeds on the next male we come across just as it is getting dark. We have to cut it into two before we are able to lift it into the vehicle. We skin it out and cut it up after we get back into camp. We eat by the light of the pressure lamp. The women along with Courtney had a relaxing afternoon. We turn in late tonight.

It was a rather quiet night, except for an occasional howl of a hyena and the bark of a bushbuck. We saw the buck and two females last night when we were coming back to camp. Mark was not interested in him as he had a broken horn. We leave at sunrise and check out a couple of waterholes for fresh buffalo spoor. Nothing. We drive off in another direction. Soon we run across fresh buffalo tracks and Mark takes after them on foot. The scout and the skinner follow him. I stay with the vehicle and it is a long wait. They are gone for hours. When they return Mark reports that they had caught up with the herd but failed to drop one of them. After the buffalo had seen him, they took off and disappeared into the heavy undergrowth. We return to camp.

After our meal, put together by Marion, Mark and I return to the hunt. We see very little game where we had seen so much yesterday! As we keep looking, a warthog pops into view. I take a shot and hit him but he keeps going. I run after him into the bush and end up tracking him a short distance through tall grass before dropping him with my second shot. We drag it out of the bush and then on to the vehicle. On our way back to camp, we load some firewood on top of the roof rack. We reach camp just as it is getting dark. It is a nice evening with a cool breeze blowing. A shot is heard not far away. It is a poacher we are told. Marion and Kim heard one last night as well before we got back to camp. The hyenas are at it again tonight. Before we retire, we stick all the meat inside the vehicle so that the hyenas will not be able to drag it away.

An animal does prowl around outside our tents during the night. But everything is here in the morning.

Nothing has been taken. The night had been cold and we had to throw the extra sleeping bag on top of ours. We are up at six, and a half an hour later Mark and I leave camp. Marion, Kim, and Courtney are managing on their own while we are gone. We make a large loop south of the river without coming across any fresh spoor of the elusive buffalo. There are other animals, such as the roan, sable, eland, impala, and oribi. There are no wildebeest. That is, until the end of the loop. They are too far for any decent shot. I try to get closer to them but they do not cooperate. We give it up and carry on until we spot another herd of wildebeest in the middle of a dambo. I decide to go after one of the bulls and commence my stalk. It is a long crawl through dry grass and brush before I reach the edge of the open glade. The one I want is 200 yards away standing broadside to me. I rest the 8mm rifle on a dry log and squeeze off a shot. The bull drops without knowing what hit him. A good shot! We take the animal back to camp for skinning and for cutting up the meat.

We try again in the afternoon for Mark's buffalo. I load up kuni while he looks for spoor in the surrounding bush. After two hours of fruitless searching, we return to camp. There is still some day light, so Mark and Kim go out for a stroll. They come back with a spur-wing goose which Kim shot. They make for tough eating unless cooked well. Marion did one for me which I had brought home one day in Tanzania. That one had tough meat! We talk awhile before turning in.

We hear baboons, a bushbuck, and a leopard during the night. I heard him cough six different times before he faded out of earshot. The leopard loves baboon meat and that may be the reason for them being so noisy. Letting him know they are standing together against him! We load up the vehicle after breakfast and then begin our trek back to Lusaka. We are full! I take it easy all the way back to Kalomo and make it without having a flat tire. Then, we are on tarmac the rest of the way to Lusaka. We reach home by sunset. All the meat gets put into the deep freeze before we can call it an end to this hunt!

Kusaka nyama (hunting animals) can be fun, or it can be work, depends on the outcome I guess. For me here in Zambia, it has mostly been the latter.

Eighteen
Ulendo Wosaka!

As safari is the Swahili word for a journey, ulendo is the word in the Nyanja language. This language is spoken quite commonly throughout most of Zambia. To hunt animals is kusaka nyama in Nyanja. Therefore, ulendo wosaka means a hunting journey. This what I am sharing in this chapter, as I did in the previous one, about my hunting trips, or ulendo wosaka, into the Zambian bush. Let me continue reminiscing.

I am up 5:30 and prepare myself for my ulendo to the open area south of the Kafue River. Half an hour later I get Kirk out of bed and we have breakfast. Then, we pick up Mark at his house and take off for our next hunt. After we turn off at Mumbwa and get on the dirt road, we have a flat tire just beyond the tsetse fly post. A sharp rock has ripped a hole into the side of the tire. It is now quite useless. We stick on the spare. From now on we will be traveling without a spare tire!

As soon as we reach the hunting area, we begin seeing nyama. We keep driving on until we reach our camping site beside the river and set up our tents at the spot we did last year when Tim was along. It is now midday. We eat the sandwiches Marion has sent along. They taste good out here in the bush! Then at 3 P.M., we go on a drive. There are some animals about. Kirk finally shoots an impala standing on the other side of a ravine. I cannot cross it with the vehicle. Mark goes to his aid while I try to find a way around. When I do, I am unable to locate them. I have lost my way! After a futile search, I return to the place I had been. I find them waiting for me. They had carried the buck across the ravine. They are happy to see me as they thought I had gotten lost! Was I?

We bring along some kuni on our way back to camp which we reach just at dark. Marion sent along some steaks and we make them for supper. There is a bushbaby crying out there in the forest tonight. The boys talk until late but I turn in early.

During the night Kirk hears an animal dragging away his impala skin and gets up to retrieve it. He does not see what animal it is. It is a restless night for the boys while I sleep fairly well. This morning we eat some bread with our tea and then leave before sunrise. We do a lot of driving during the day and come up dry. There is some game but it is very spooky. I try a shot at a reedbuck 350 yards away with my 30.06. The bullet strikes the ground below the animal. There is no second chance as the buck sprouts wings! Kirk has no luck as well. We see kudu but nobody has a license for them. There are puku in the distance but it gets too late to go after them. We end up bringing no meat back to camp, only firewood. We make the fillet from yesterday's impala for supper. There is an elephant breaking off branches across the river from us. It is not as cold here at night as it is in Lusaka.

The elephants were again feeding nearby during the night. We could hear the ruckus. Then, at dawn they cross right by our camp! They ignore us completely. None of them is carrying any big tusks. What a pity. After a bite to eat, we go hunting. We are not successful until midday. The first animals we drop are puka. Kirk and I each get one. I had to shoot mine through some brush as it was hiding from me. It turned out to be a good shot. After this I shoot a duiker while Kirk gets a grysbok. Finally, I drop an impala. Since I have lined up my 30.06, it has been right on. I have gotten all three animals today with one shot each! Before this I had shot at a puku three times, missing each time. I tried out the rifle and found it was shooting six inches to the right at 150 yards!

Before we head back to camp, Kirk takes a shot at a reedbuck and misses. We bring back more kuni. Everything is as we left it. We thank the Lord for watching our camp as we were gone all day. The meat is hung up on a branch to cool off during the night. We have had a full day and we are tired tonight. We turn in after a good meal put together by Mark. The bushbaby is starting early. We can hear it crying back in the tall trees along the river's edge.

We spend a quiet night. The elephants are around again but they do not make much noise. We see their tracks everywhere. We have loaded our tenting equipment and all the meat by 8:00. We then start out for Lusaka. Kirk is still looking for his first reedbuck. He finally has a chance at one but misses with both shots. It just isn't his hunt this time to get one. He will have to try in another hunt. We reach Lusaka and find Karen and Kim at our house. I thank the Lord for assisting us to reach home safely without a spare tire and for not having a flat along the way!

Kirk is looking for a kudu and it must be one with trophy-sized horns. A tall order so I take him out to the Bruce-Miller Game Ranch situated just west of Choma. Big ones are known to hang around there, if not on the ranch, then in the immediate vicinity. By the afternoon we are at the home of Ian Bruce-Miller and before long he is driving us around in search of the ever shy greater kudu. We come across many female and young but no full grown male. Soon it is dark and we return to his house where we join him and his wife at the evening meal. We are spending the night here and in the morning try again for kudu.

It is a cold night. We are served tea before setting out at daybreak on our hunt. We see more female kudu. Then we turn our attention for a trophy reedbuck. Kirk needs one and it is not long before he has an opportunity to line his sights on a beautiful buck. The reedbuck drops with his first shot. Kirk is pleased with the horns, which measure almost 16 inches. We return to the house for our breakfast. Before long we are back in the bush searching for a male kudu. At 1 P.M. one is spotted in the company of three females. Kirk leaves the vehicle and starts stalking him with Ian at his side. When he is about 250 yards from the kudu, Kirk aims at the bull and fires. The kudu do a disappearing act!

Kirk and Ian run up to the spot where they had last seen them and find not one kudu but two lying dead at their feet! The bullet had shattered right after hitting the bull in the neck and then veered off to one side hitting a female who happened to be standing just before him to one side. Three fragments of the bullet had entered her, killing her on the spot as well. Kirk was ecstatic! There are handshakes all the way around. The horns measure 59 inches, the second longest gotten in Zambia thus far, Ian informs him. I am glad for him in getting this fine trophy. And, I am happy to have been there when he shot it!

Our next hunt is back on the Kafue Flats. Before Kirk and his family head back to Uganda, Kirk wants to try for a trophy Kafue lechwe. Mark, Kim, and Courtney come along on the hunt. The road to the flats is very bad at this time of the year. A fire has just burned out most of

266

the grass and reeds along the river making it a very dirty drive. Because of the drought this year, we come across many skeletons of zebra and lechwe. There is still plenty of both species left throughout the flats near the river. We make our approach cautiously.

When we are within rifle range, Kirk shoots one that appears to have a good set of horns. It does. They measure almost 35 inches! Then it is Mark's turn. He lets Kim shoot it for him. She does okay and hers are just under 30 inches. Finally, I have my turn and drop one that turns out to be as big as Kirk's. Great! We all did very well on this hunt. We give the scouts one animal and bring the other two home. We are all covered in dust, especially me. I am all black!

I am on my way back to the open area south of the Kafue River to hunt for reedbuck, impala, and hartebeest. I have taken Afunika Tembo along with me. He claims he has been on hunts before with other Europeans, even in Mozambique some years back. There are no problems along the way and we enter the hunting area around 10:00. Immediately we meet a stranded Land Rover with two Zambians who had spent the night beside their vehicle. Their battery is dead so I give them a tow to start it. After a short distance, their engine dies. I spend the next hour trying to keep their vehicle running but give up finally when the towing cable keeps tearing and their vehicle keeps stalling. They have some friends at the fish camp beside the river and they ask us if we could inform them of their dilemma. We said that we would try but when we get there no one is around.

We search for hours but do not come across the game we are wishing to hunt. Only a warthog, impala, and baboon are to be found and they run in the direction of the park as soon as they spot us in the bush. Very disappointing! There are quite a few kudu around though. We see two big bulls with their huge spiraled horns. We watch them for a while through our binoculars. Beautiful! Why did I not bring a license for one? Finally, at 5 P.M., we come across a reedbuck and I drop him with my first shot. When a second one poses for a shot, I drop him as well. We now have meat. Tembo helps me skin them out and we take the meat with us to camp, which we set up nearby. We have small tents along and pitch them before it gets dark. Our meal is eaten by the light of my trouble lamp connected to the car battery. It has been a full day, and hot on top of it, so we turn in early. Tembo takes an ax inside his tent. "It's for protection," he says.

No hyenas come around during the night to snatch away the meat that Tembo has hanging on a line. I wake up several times during the night to check but see nothing. Tembo has made a fire but it is not that bright. I only hear a night jar and the whistle of a reedbuck once or twice. What a quiet place! We crawl out of our tents at 5:30. We eat something and then load up our tents and meat before heading out. We come across reedbuck but no hartebeest. Usually they are plentiful around this place. Goes to show how mobile game can be. Here today and gone tomorrow! We drive on to where we had seen the impala yesterday. They are there but again we cannot get near enough to them. I try for some time to close the gap between us and get into a position for a shot but it is not to be! They again hike into the park. And so it is that we have to call it quits at noon and head on back home. This is the first time that there have been so few animals around.

My next ulendo is to an open area south of Kasempa in North-Western Province. Mark arrives at sunrise and we load his vehicle. Half an hour later we drive out the yard. We reach Kaoma just before midday. We have a bite to eat at a small restaurant run by a 350-pound woman. The two men we have along, to help us with the skinning, eat with us. After we are done we take the sandy road leading up to Kasempa. It is a poor road, nothing more than a trail. As soon as we cross from Western Province and enter North-Western we are in hunting territory. Mark and Kirk hunted here three months ago. We carry on until we reach the Lumba River where we expected to set up camp but find all three sites already occupied by hunters from Kitwe. We are now 150 kilometers due north of Kaoma. The east side of the road that we are traveling on is a GMA. We can hunt only on the west side without having a permit.

Mark and I carry on along the road looking for another suitable place to set up camp and run into rain. It comes down heavily and the two in the back have to crawl under the tarp that is covering our camping equipment to keep from getting wet. We do not see any animals so we keep going until we arrive at Shongwa, a camp for game scouts, situated at the north end of this open hunting area. We set up our camp as it is now nearing sunset. It did not rain here so the ground is dry. Mark and I are sleeping in our tent while the two men will be staying in a shelter that the scouts here use as a kitchen. We eat very little as the scouts sit around visiting with us until way past dark. It is very humid tonight as we turn in.

It cools off during the night. I do not sleep too well as I did not bring along my safari mattress. I keep turning all night. I am up at daybreak and eat a light breakfast before leaving camp to look for game. Two scouts are coming along to help find the animals we want. We drive over some rough terrain covered with short pointed termite mounds. Then, we spot a small herd of hartebeest. There

269

is only one male among them. I approach them on foot and when they are ready to run, I take a shot at one of them and miss. They are off in high gear! During this time Mark, who is with the vehicle, has a flat. When we have the tire changed, we continue our search for hartebeest. The area is empty of game! It is much later before we come across another small herd that is resting in some tight bush. Before they can take off, I quickly fire off a round at the male. This time I hit him and he goes down! He is a nice big bull with a good set of horns.

On the way back to camp, we have another puncture. While we skin the animal and cut up the meat, the two punctures we had this forenoon get repaired. The meat is hung up in a tree to dry out. There are lots of tsetse flies in this area as well. It showers some. We do not eat much. We're not hungry. We return to the bush towards evening. Only a few duiker and a couple of female reedbuck are spotted. It is dark when we return to camp. We eat the stew that Marion sent along. It is still cold in the cooler. It is again humid tonight.

We are up at dawn and dismantle our tent. We pack up our vehicle after a light breakfast. It is time to leave this place. The flat that we had yesterday evening has to be redone this morning. When it is fixed, we make our way back to Lumba River. On the way we run over a black mamba. The snake measures 10 feet long! Mark has to finish it off with a .22 rifle as it is far from being dead. Ten kilometers before reaching the Lumba River, Mark turns off onto a loop through the bush. It is a dry run. No game. After we reach the Lumba, he again takes another swing through the bush. We do not come across anything worthwhile, only some impala and they were all female.

The hunters from Kitwe are still camped here. There are others beside them. We pitch our tent beside some water and away, as far as possible, from the other hunters. It is a very hot day so we rest in our tent until 4 P.M. Then we strike off in a westerly direction following the river. There is no game except for a bushbuck which Mark spooks up from the riverbed. He shoots it. We get back to camp at dark. Our fellows heat some water for us and I take a bath, my first on this trip. I have not shaved since leaving home. I left my razor behind. I have only a tin of fruit, some ground nuts, and date cake that Marion sent along before turning in.

A nice cool night as we leave open the flaps on our tents. Frogs and night birds serenade us all night long. I do sleep quite well. We are up at 5:00 and pack our stuff for another exit. We have cold cereal for breakfast. We plan to take the road from Kasempa to Mumbwa today so it demands an early start. At 11:00 we reach Kasempa. We fill up with diesel and eat something at a small restaurant. They only serve nsima and chicken so all four of us order a dish of it. Before leaving town, Mark talks to the game warden about hunting in the Lunga-Luswishi GMA since we will be passing through it. He is agreeable but when we reach the game post 100 kilometers from Kasempa, the assistant game warden refuses. We hang around camp hoping the game warden himself will show up. But he does not by dark. We have to put up here for the night.

There is a small guesthouse here on the banks of the Lunga River. When we inspect it, I find the smell of bats in the rooms too overpowering. It does not bother Mark so he chooses one of the rooms for the night. I set up the tent for myself and will sleep in it. A crocodile swims by in the river just below us when we park the vehicle next to the guesthouse. The flies are really bad here in camp. They are large and very sticky. They get onto the meat that we are hanging up for the night under the grass roof which serves as a kitchen. We light a fire in it so that smoke will keep them at bay. It has been a miserable day.

During the night a huge crocodile comes up out of the river. He has smelled the meat. As he meanders toward it, he discovers my tent standing in his way. He stops and at this moment Mark hears something and steps out of his room to investigate. He spots the crocodile near my tent and gives a shout which wakes me up. Through the open flaps of the tent, I see a crocodile in the bright moonlight turn direction and take off. He makes a beeline for the river. The shelter where we ate our supper is in his way. He charges into it, scattering our coolers and cooking utensils all about! What a racket! There is a three-foot wall that circles the shelter and he climbs over it to get back to the river. There is a big splash as he finally hits the water. Would the crocodile have pulled me out of the tent had Mark not come out when he did? Crocodiles have been known to do that. More people in Zambia are killed and eaten by this reptile than any other animal. I would say I have just had a close call with death!

This morning we cross the river, drive a short distance, and visit with a South African who has built a lodge overlooking the Lunga River just north of Kafue National Park. From him we learn that government officials have been hunting, shooting up the game, and then hauling them out in lorries. No wonder we do not see many animals! After we return to camp, we load up and leave for Lusaka. We carry on in a southeasterly direction on the road that leads to Mumbwa. It skirts the eastern boundary of Kafue National Park. There should be plenty of game to see, but there is not. But we do have another flat tire on the way! We reach home at 6:00 P.M. There is still meat to be cut up for the deep freeze before we can call an end to this not so successful hunt.

Kirk is visiting us again and during this stay he and Mark want to go hunting for the black lechwe in the Bangweulu Swamps. I am going along. Both of their vehicles are loaded down with fuel, camping equipment, and food, plus two workers. After a cooked breakfast that Marion has made, we commence our ulendo. At Kapiri Mposhi it is discovered that the fuel tank on Kirk's vehicle is leaking. We patch the leak with a bar of hand soap and then cover it with putty. It does the trick. I learned this years ago and have tried it ever since and it works each time.

At noon we arrive at the Livingstone Memorial that is at Chitambo's village. It is here where Dr. David Livingstone died May 1, 1873. His heart was buried here under a tree while his remains embalmed and then carried by faithful servants to the coast where he was placed on a ship and transported by sea to England for burial. For me it is a dream finally fulfilled to stand at the spot where the great missionary and explorer knelt in his prayer and where he surrendered his soul to the Master for his last journey. His body was found in the morning still on its knees at this very site. The hut is gone and so is the tree. But his memory is not. It is a memorable experience for me!

We carry on towards the swamps. At 5:00 P.M. we reach the place where Mark and Kirk hunted two years ago. There are huts made out of grass especially erected for hunters at the site so we do not set up our tents. Mark and Kirk prepare the evening meal from the groceries we have brought along. It is dark by the time we eat. We turn in early tonight. I am using my sleeping bag and pillow which I have brought along.

I sleep well, until daylight! Mark and Kirk had a good night as well. It is nice and quiet out here in the swamps. After breakfast, we drive off scouting for tsessebe, an animal that resembles a topi. It is not long and we come across a large herd of them. I try a shot at 300 yards with Kirk's 7mm. It drops with a single shot! The horns measure more than 17 inches. Not bad. Half a hour later Kirk shoots one as well. It has a set of horns which are bit longer than mine. It is on to the flood plains after this to look for the black lechwe. They roam in a large herd out here much like the Kafue lechwe does on the Kafue Flats. We come across several herds. There are too many to choose from. I finally settle for one with nice black markings standing 125 yards away. I again use Kirk's gun and the buck drops with one shot. The horns measure over 24 inches. We return to camp with the animals. A good morning's hunt, reminding me a bit of those hunting days back in Tanzania!

We rest in camp for several hours before venturing out again. We pick up kuni as we go along. There are oribi but the boys want something with horns at least six inches in length. The ones we see do not come close to that. Later on in the afternoon we strike out for the swamps to check for sitatunga. When we get there, we split up. I tag along with Kirk to take film while Mark takes his tracker. There are several machans (raised platforms) scattered throughout the swamp. We crawl up one of them. They are quite sturdy in spite of appearing to be the contrary. Kirk and I wait until it is dark but fail to see one sitatunga. We make our way back to the vehicle and return to camp. Mark is there. He saw a female. It is late when we hit the sleeping bag.

Kirk and Mark take off for sitatunga before sunrise. I get up at sunrise and start packing the meat into one of the vehicles, along with the trophies, to take back home before they start to go bad. I do not stop along the way and reach Lusaka in the mid-afternoon. What about the boys? They return two days later. They each get their sitatunga, nice ones at that! Plus they each get their oribi and Mark his tsessebe. A very good hunt indeed. One of the best for us in Zambia thus far.

For an outing, Marion and I take Helga Stalts, who is visiting us from Canada, out to the Bruce-Miller Game Ranch and have her try her hand at hunting African game. Also, it gives me a chance to bag an animal or two. We drive over there in the afternoon and enjoy the outdoors for a while before the sun sinks out of sight. Ian has Helga shoot off a few rounds at a target, to get the feel of the rifle before the hunt tomorrow. She does quite well. We are given a good meal for supper. Soon after we retire to our bungalows. A good thing there are nets over our beds as the mosquitoes are plentiful tonight.

There is a beautiful sunrise this morning. At 7:00 A.M. Ian picks us up and we are off on our hunt. Marion is not going along. Instead she has chosen to do some fishing at the dam. Someone is going to show her where to go. When we spot an impala herd, Ian escorts Helga into the bush and they stalk the buck until she has a clear shot at the male. It drops from her first shot. She is elated! She did just great. And it is her first animal on a hunt in Africa! What more can you ask for?

After we drop the impala off at the yard for skinning, we return to the bush for reedbuck. When we come across a nice male, I drop this one with one shot as well. It is decided that we should go for a third animal. We see some nice kudu but they do not allow us to get near them. They are always staying out of range! Then, one stands long enough for me to plant a slug in his chest. But it is a little high and he keeps going. I chase after him. His adrenaline is working pretty good now and it takes several shots to put him down for keeps! It takes some time to load him because of his weight. But in the end we manage to get the carcass onto the back of the pickup.

When we get back to the yard, we find Marion waiting. She has caught no fish. She failed even to get a nibble. After all the meat is cut up, we load it up and travel back to Livingstone. We again have lots of meat to put into our deep freeze. It has been a successful hunt!

I make another trip to Bruce-Millar Game Ranch four months later. This time I have my daughter along and her husband. It has been 23 years since father and daughter have hunted together in Africa! The last one was in Kenya. It is like old times riding in the hunting vehicle on our way to sight in my .300 rifle. Tim stayed back at the house as he still has a fever from his recent bout with malaria. Ian sets up the target and I hit it right on at 25 yards. Colleen has her turn and she does the same. She has two more tries at the target. The second one at 50 yards and then at 75 yards. Both right on, in fact, and the last one is a bull's eye! So I did a good job at sighting it in yesterday with just looking down the borehole. Ian then takes us for a drive to see if we can come across any kudu. But we do not see any. We do not mind. Colleen and I are having a nice chat even though it's getting cool sitting in the back of the open vehicle. It is like old times!

Ian takes Colleen and me out to the hunting area soon after 6:00 A.M. Tim stays behind as he still has a temperature. We are looking for kudu but try as we may there are none to be found. Just a glimpse of one once. It is decided to try for impala. When we come across a small herd, Colleen takes a bead at the buck and he drops from a heart shot at 75 yards. Very good shooting after all these years! She has not lost the touch. We take the animal back to the yard and we have our breakfast at the house.

We return to the bush. This time Tim is along. When we come across another herd of impala, Tim takes his turn at shooting the male. His first shot goes high, but the second one is right on. He does great for the condition he is in! We come across reedbuck but they do not stop long enough for a shot. A bushbuck stands for a while but Colleen cannot get the shot off in time before he disappears. We quit and come back to the house. We pack up and have something to eat. By this time the second animal has been skinned and cut up. It is time to go back to Livingstone. It has been a nice outing with Colleen and Tim. We need to do it again!

Nineteen
Tests of Faith

We all have had our tests of faith. No one any more than Job himself. He not only lost all his property and children, but also his health. Yet he hung on and in the end gained back more than he had lost! His own words recorded in Job 23:10–12, that he uttered in the midst of his trials, do come to pass. Listen to them: "He knows the way that I take; when He has tested me, I shall come forth as gold. My feet have closely followed His steps; I have kept to His way without turning aside. I have not departed from the commands of His lips; I have treasured the words of His mouth more than my daily bread." In the midst of trials when we are sorely tested, it is not always easy to look beyond them and believe as Job did that all will turn out for our best.

During our years on the mission field we have had our ups and downs when our faith got tested. I have found that when it came to my own welfare, I could handle it a lot easier than when it affected my family. The question is then, whose faith is being tested now? Mine? Or theirs? When this happens I try to do my part as much as possible and leave the rest up to them and to God. His will be done! This is especially true once my children have grown up and started their own families. They now are accountable for how they will react when the faith is tested. How hard that can be to the parent when the child does not react the way you think you would have reacted.

Karen McLain came into our family when Kirk married her in 1982 after a courtship that had a beginning back when they met in Kenya at Rift Valley Academy, a boarding school for missionary kids. Three years later she and Kirk went to work in Sudan with World Vision. When the warfare between the Sudanese government troops in the north and the animistic rebels in the south got too dangerous, World Vision ordered their workers to leave the country in 1988. Kirk and Karen moved to Uganda and he soon was working for United Nations Children's Fund (UNICEF), an agency of the United Nations. We were in Uganda during that time and we would meet on a regular basis. Their lives with the Stevensons were inseparable. We watched their first daughter Ashling come into their lives in 1987. She and her cousins Tiffany and Natasha were three peas in a pod. It left a hole in our lives when we moved to Zambia in 1989. We kept telling ourselves that God's will comes first.

After our move, each family had two more children. Shaina and Mikaela join Karen and Kirk while Jesse and Logan enter Colleen and Tim's lives. We try to go up to Kampala whenever there is an opportunity. Christmas was a must for family reunions. Then, the inevitable happens! UNICEF transfers Kirk to Malawi in early 1995. Karen is devastated. How can she leave the life she has grown so attached to? All her friends are in Kampala. She cries often on Colleen's shoulder. It is so hard to pack those last few items into her luggage and fly out to Lilongwe. Kirk had flown on ahead and was already at work in his office. Tim moves much of their stuff by road to Lilongwe.

One consolation for Kirk and Karen and their chil-

279

dren is that we are now within driving distance. It is just over 700 kilometers from Lusaka to Lilongwe. We actually get to see them more often now as they drop in on us for weekends. And when I visit the churches in Malawi, I stop off at their house for the night. The Stevenson family members are the losers. The cousins no longer meet on a near daily basis as they used to. Mark and Kim's two children, Courtney and Sean, now fill in the gap on this end for Kirk and Karen's three girls.

At noon on November 15, 1995, the phone rings in our Lusaka home and I answer it. It is a call from UNICEF in Lilongwe. I cannot believe my ears at what I am hearing! A woman on the other end of the line informs me that Karen Hoffman has been involved in a terrible auto accident and is in a critical condition! She goes on to say that the two girls, Shaina and Mikaela, who were traveling with her at the time were also injured. All of them are at the moment in the hospital at Chipata awaiting evacuation to South Africa by air. Kirk is on his way to Chipata by road and I am to come pick up Ashling who had stayed behind in Lilongwe to attend school.

After I hang up I relay the news to Marion. We are in total shock! Nothing like this has ever happened before in our family. I then phone Colleen and break the news to her. I am all shook up and Colleen tries to comfort me. I pass on to her the phone number I had been given for the hospital at Chipata so that she can keep in touch. We take time to pray and then I throw a few things together and leave for Chipata at 1:30. Marion has sent along some sandwiches and a drink which I eat as I speed along. I did not take the time before I left as I wanted to get started as soon as I could in order to reach Chipata right after dark. It is a six-hour drive under normal circumstances. I make it by 7:10. It is very dark when I reach the hospital. I find

Reid Brown, a friend of Kirk's from years back, waiting for me. He informs me that Kirk, Karen, and the two girls are at the small airport just outside of town. So we drive over there with both of our vehicles.

The SOS plane that had flown in from Johannesburg to evacuate the injured party is sitting on the tarmac. There are no lights anywhere on the small airstrip. People are moving around with their torches. I approach the plane and peek inside. I see Kirk seated beside Karen who is attached to a life-giving machine. She is unconscious. Shaina is lying there next to her and appears to be unconscious as well. I ask one of the medical personnel where Mikaela is and he points me to a vehicle. I find her lying on the back seat with her injured leg tied to a make-shift splint. She is in pain and crying. I try to comfort her by talking to her, telling her that Opa has come.

I talk to Mikaela until Kirk joins me. He has just come from being with Shaina who is drifting in and out of a coma. We hug and we both weep on each other's shoulders. When he has calmed down some, he tells me that it looks bad for Karen as she is in a coma and that seven of her ten ribs are broken on her right side. Her arm is also broken. Reid has already given her some of his blood as it is of the same type as hers, and it is a rare type, different from Kirk's. He says that Shaina has a bad head concussion and Mikaela a broken leg. The accident took place just a couple of kilometers north of Chipata when a lorry took the inside corner coming around a bend in the road, side-swiping the vehicle Karen and the children were in!

At 8:30 the plane is ready for the flight back to South Africa. The air strip is not made for night flights so there are no lights at all along the runway. I joined several others and we line up our vehicles, lights facing the runway, to assist the pilot in seeing where he is going. The takeoff is okay and the plane lifts off into the black sky. I sit watching with a heavy heart until the red blinking lights fade out of sight. What a sad parting! I turn my vehicle and follow Reid and his wife in their vehicle to the doctor's house for a briefing. The UNICEF vehicle with a medical person from Lilongwe is there as well, plus the one that brought Kirk. The doctor is a Belgian married to an Asian man who runs a workshop in town.

The doctor relates how she had tried her best with what she had to assist Karen. The broken ribs had badly punctured her liver causing internal bleeding and loss of blood. They had tried to set her arm. They have no oxygen available in the hospital. So they could only wait for the SOS plane to fly in. I ask her what the chances were for Karen. She replies, "A 50-50 chance." She actually shows more concern for Shaina. "She is drifting in and out of a coma" she says, "and they are getting deeper." Mikaela, because she is still young, should recover from her broken leg quite well, the doctor concludes. The two UNICEF vehicles finally leave for Lilongwe and I follow them. The border officials on both sides of the border had been told about the accident and so they were still open waiting for us at 11:15. An hour later we are in Lilongwe and I am led to Detlaf Palm's house where I am to spend the night, or whatever is left of it. The man works with Kirk in the office.

I wake up at 5:00 and phone Colleen. I bring her up to date as to what has happened since the last briefing that she received from Sharon Brown when she called the hospital earlier. I have a hard time to keep from breaking down. I ask her to call Mom as I am unable to get through to her. Detlaf leads me to Benson's house where Ashling spent the night. She is happy to see me. I tell her that her Mom had been in an accident and that her Dad has flown her and the two girls to a hospital in South Africa for treatment. She asks, "Will Mom die?" I am taken aback. I answer, "I do not know." I do not elaborate on the seriousness of it. I will have to do this slowly over a period of time. I drive over to Kirk and Karen's house and pick up clothes for Ashling and Kirk. I find the mattress that Karen had been lying on when she was driven to the hospital. It is soaked with her blood! I have the workers wash it thoroughly. Then I leave for Lusaka taking Ashling with me. We reach home before dark.

I find Reid and Sharon Brown with their two children at our house. Mark and Kim are present as well. Sharon gives us a letter that Karen wrote us just before leaving camp yesterday morning, only hours before her accident. The Browns now relate what had taken place since they were there and saw it happen. After visiting with Kirk and Karen at Lilongwe, they decided to drop in at Luangwa National Park and view the animals as it was not much out of the way. Since Karen has never been there too, she decided to tag along with her two girls in their vehicle. They all had a wonderful time! Her letter confirms it. The day then arrived for them to leave. They packed up their tenting equipment and started out, Karen for Lilongwe and the Browns for Lusaka.

As they approached Chipata where they were to part to go their separate directions, they came across a curve in the road. The Browns saw an oncoming lorry in the middle of the road so they took the shoulder to avoid getting hit. Karen was a short distance behind them and swung as well to the left in order to escape being hit by the truck which was at this point completely on her side of the road. He was taking the corner much too short! Looking back in his rear view mirror to see how she fared, Reid saw dust and pieces of metal flying into the air. "Karen's been hit!" he exclaimed to his wife. They swung their vehicle around and drove back to the scene of the accident. The lorry had stopped and those inside appeared to be shaken up. The box of the lorry had ripped open one-half of the 4-WD Land Cruiser on the driver's side and forced the top of the car to go backwards and to the side. How can anyone survive such a terrible crash?

The Browns unfastened her seat belt and pulled Karen out from behind the wheel. She was in excruciating pain and was bleeding profusely. Shaina, the three-year-old, who had been lying down on the front seat was then removed. There were lacerations on her face from broken glass. Where was Mikaela, the two-year-old? They heard someone crying in the back of the now-crushed body. She was discovered underneath the luggage and camping equipment. They saw that she had suffered a broken leg. A passing motorist stopped at the scene. He was driving a pickup. Reid pulled out a mattress from Karen's vehicle and laid her on it in the back of the pickup. Sharon sat with her until they reached the hospital. On the way, Karen told her how much her chest was hurting. (Because of the fastened seat belt she could not move over far enough to escape being hit by the metal box.) She also asked Jesus several times to help her. Then she sunk into a weakened state and said, "I'm going to die, Sharon."

At the hospital all three are admitted. Reid had been following with the two girls in his vehicle. (The Browns have a couple children of their own who were riding with their dad.) Kirk is notified and should be arriving in an hour. Karen fights to stay alive. When Kirk finally walks into the room, she tries to say something to him and immediately drifts off into a coma. Her will to survive has finally given out. A body can only take so much punishment. She has had more than her share today!

Marion, Mark, and I make plans to fly down to Johannesburg tomorrow to be with Kirk during this time of grieving. Colleen is also flying there to join us. I had called her earlier and we had talked. We are expecting the Lord to perform a miracle! Kim has been keeping in touch with Kirk by phone and the doctors have told him that Karen's brain is not functioning because of a lack of oxygen. This took place when she went into a coma while at the Chipata hospital. When the SOS plane came with the necessary equipment it was too late. "Kirk is devastated and needs our support," adds Kim. Ashling is holding up quite well. She does not know the whole story yet.

Kim drives us to the airport the following day and we land in Johannesburg on time at 3:40 P.M. Kirk is there to pick us up. He came with a taxi. We rent a car so that we can get around in this large city. Our first stop is at the Sandton Hospital where they have Karen and the two girls. It is a shock to see them in such a state. The last time I saw them it was on the Great East Road. I was returning to Lusaka from Malawi while Kirk and his family were on their way back to Lilongwe from visiting Marion at Lusaka. We had stopped and chatted some beside the road. I remember Mikaela was reluctant to greet me which disappointed Karen. She wanted so much that Mikaela would learn to love her Opa.

Now Mikaela is lying in a hospital bed with her leg in traction. Her leg has been broken just above the knee. While she was resting on a mattress in back of the vehicle, the metal body crashed against her leg that was probably resting on top of the back seat, and smashed the bone. Shaina has cuts on her face and stitches on her head where she received a concussion. Her head must have struck the gear shift lever since she was lying down when the accident occurred. She says that she bumped Mommy's head. So Karen was leaning way over trying to escape the metal box coming at her. Karen does not look like herself. This vibrant woman, once so full of life, lies before us now with tubes attached to her in order to keep the heart pumping. Unless the Lord performs a miracle, Karen is no longer with us. Her soul is with the Lord. The doctor informs Kirk and me that Karen is clinically dead! Kirk is taking it hard and I try to comfort him, while at the same time I too am in need of some comforting. Marion is holding her own.

At 9:30 P.M. Rolf Bohlin, a friend of Kirk's who is with UNICEF and in whose house we are staying, takes me to the airport where we pick up Colleen. We return to the house as it is now late. Marion, Mark, Kirk, and Ashling are all there. We talk until 2:00 A.M. before we climb into bed. It is a sad reunion for our immediate family. This is the first time we are facing a crisis of this magnitude! Lord, strengthen us for the task that is before us. We need all we can get.

Mark comes to our room at 6:00 A.M. The four of us—Marion, Colleen, Mark, and myself—go into prayer beseeching the Lord to perform a miracle by restoring Karen. Each one pours out their soul before the throne of God. The Spirit then overpowers me and I groan within me. He intercedes through me and my voice changes. I am transported to a place where I am allowed to see Karen! She is beyond a wall conversing with someone who is just hidden from view. There is an opening in the wall and she is standing just inside of it. I plead with her to return to us from heaven where she now has been for over two days. She does not turn her face to acknowledge my presence but keeps looking intently at that someone who re-

286

mains out of sight. Is it Jesus? It appears as if she is waiting for His permission to return to her family. I am granted only a side view of her, and with all my pleadings she does not look at me once. I turn my attention to Jesus and plead with Him to permit her to come back as Kirk and the three girls need her. There is no answer. I travail and almost faint from weariness. I cannot stop as my throat is controlled by the Spirit. Finally, it subsides and all is calm. It is now up to the Lord and Karen to decide whether our request will be granted. We must now wait and see.

Marion remains with Shaina and Mikaela while Colleen and Kirk accompany me up the stairs to where Karen was admitted. At her bedside, I pray for her recovery. Colleen also prays. There is no response from her. We spend some time in her room before leaving to go downstairs. Kirk now says that he has peace in his heart. He accepts the fact that her place is in heaven and that she will not return. Now the trauma of adjusting his life without her begins. Throughout the day he has to be assisted and I do what I can for him. Colleen and Mark help wherever they can. Marion is busy with Shaina and Mikaela. I am very tired at 4:00 P.M. and find an empty room to lie down for an hour's nap. We eat at the restaurant that is in the hospital. Marion takes a break from the children and goes up to see Karen. Ashling goes with her. Then Colleen and I sit with sadness beside her bed and try to remember the good times. How helpless we feel. We watch the needle on the life-giving machine getting ever weaker. Karen's state is deteriorating progressively. It will not be long before the heart will give out in spite of the machine. It is 10:00 P.M. before we all return to the house.

At midnight Karen's body gives up finally! A phone call had come from the doctor a half an hour earlier requesting that we come as her heart was fading fast. So Rolfe had taken Kirk and Mark to the hospital. I had wanted to go but was refused. So I remained with Marion and Colleen to talk with Ashling. We pray with her. She is accepting her mother's passing gallantly. We are up until 2:00 again before settling down for a few hours of sleep.

We are up at 6:00. Phone calls are made to relatives notifying them of Karen's death. Colleen calls Tim and tells him the heart-breaking news. Kirk learns that his mother-in-law, after hearing of Karen's accident, is on her way and will arrive tomorrow morning. She does not know that her daughter has already passed away. Marion and I spend the afternoon with the girls at the hospital. We had wanted to take Shaina up to see Karen yesterday but she refused. It appears she was upset that her mother had not yet come to see her! It is too late now. Ashling had gone up to see her twice. She even said goodbye to her last night. Mark is broken-up that no miracle took place. Colleen tries to comfort him. Finally, he gives in and weeps bitterly. I console Kirk with several passages of Scripture. Karen's body has been moved to the government mortuary for an autopsy due to it being an accident-related death. We are all with Shaina and Mikaela tonight at the hospital. When they are asleep we too return to the house and turn in. It is midnight.

Kirk, Mark, and Colleen pick up Glenda, Karen's mother, at the airport and bring her to the hospital where Marion, Ashling, and I have been since morning. She is accepting the death of her daughter quite well. The following morning when it comes time to view the body at the funeral home, the mother and Kirk decided not to leave the casket open for the girls to see their mother in death, mainly because there is very little resemblance to her former self. I read John: 1–4 and share on Karen being there now. The body will now be shipped by air to Dublin, Georgia, for burial at the family cemetery. Mark flies back to Lusaka in the afternoon.

The doctor tells Kirk that Shaina will need an operation. An X-ray has revealed an air bubble still in the vicinity of the concussion. They are going to open up the skull and put a plate under the cap to hold up the dent that she has where she hit against the gearshift lever or some other sharp object on the dash. Shaina comes through the operation okay. It is a good thing they performed it as more cracks are discovered on the skull than the scan had revealed. They have put in plates to keep the skull cap intact and in place. Shaina is in a much better frame of mind after the operation. It has done wonders for her. There is no more despondency. Marion and I have a chance to talk to Shaina about Karen and she realizes now that her mother has gone away to heaven and will not return.

Mikaela's blood count is still low so her cast will have to wait until she has had a blood transfusion. For one who is a hyper person, it has been rough having to lie on her back day in and day out with her leg held high in traction. Kirk has hepatitis so he cannot donate his blood. Colleen and I have the right blood type but have had malaria recently. But when the doctor hears that Mikaela is flying back into malaria-infested Zambia, he relents. Colleen is flying back to Uganda today so it falls to me to donate some blood of mine to Mikaela since I will be around should she require more. They actually do not find any malaria parasites in the blood that they give Mikaela. She now has my blood flowing in her veins Kirk remarks, "She will really be hyper now with Dad's blood in her!" There is a marked improvement in her condition the following day.

Ten days after Karen's accident, Marion and I find ourselves alone with Mikaela as Kirk, Ashling, Shaina, and Glenda are flying to the United States for the funeral. They will be meeting up with Tim in London who is going along to represent the rest of us at the burial. Marion and I move over to a lodge near the hospital so that we can be closer to Mikaela, who is now in a body cast. One of the nurses has brought over a skateboard and we pull her around on it. Eventually she learns to push herself around. I wrench my back but good one evening when I lift Mikaela from the skateboard to put her into bed. The muscles in my back on my right side go into spasms. Is it ever painful, much like a charley horse! A hot bath does not give me much relief from the pain. I have it looked at the following day by the physiotherapist who works on the same hospital grounds.

We look after Mikaela for five days at the hospital before the doctor finally gives the green light for her to leave. With medical assistance we are put on board in first class of the flight back to Lusaka. Mikaela is quite an attraction on board. The plane leaves one hour and 45 minutes late. This is due to a passenger who had checked in her baggage but then did not board the plane. After waiting for an hour, the flight crew had to look for her piece of luggage and then remove it. They were not taking any chances for it may contain a bomb! When we finally land, Kim and Courtney are there waiting for us. It cheers up Mikaela to see her cousin. We receive a fax tonight from Kirk. He and the two girls are fine. Tim is still with him helping him to sort things out.

We have a fairly good night sleeping again in our own bed. Sarah, one of our house workers, is assigned to look after Mikaela. This is her job now until she returns to Lilongwe. I call Colleen and she said that Tiffany is taking Karen's death very hard and asks a lot of questions. They had a nice memorial service in Kampala with representatives from UNICEF, Lincoln School, the international women's prayer group, the international fellowship group, and representatives from the church in attendance, in addition to the workers and some others. It was held in Lincoln School where Karen had taught during her years in Kampala. Money was donated towards a memorial for Karen. She said it was a very touching service, with many words of praise for the work she did while in their midst. Karen was well-liked and admired by the community in Kampala.

There is a Memorial Service here in Lusaka at the Kanyama Church where we dedicate a pulpit in her memory. It was built with funds received from the Memorial Service held at Kampala. She and Kirk had donated funds for the roof of this church earlier when she was still alive. From this day on the congregation here starts calling it the Karen Church of God. It is a very touching service for me. There are many choir numbers, solos, and a quartette. There are several speeches and a sermon. The service is three and a half hours long!

A month has gone by since Karen's death. Kirk and his girls are ready to return to Lilongwe. Marion is going along to help get things ready for our Christmas in Malawi. Karen had started on it and had been looking forward to having us all together at her house and then at a place on Lake Malawi. No one has the heart to cancel it. And so it is, we will carry through with it in her memory. The night before they all fly out, Mark and his family join us for the evening meal. While eating the soup that Marion has made from stuff she bought at a shop, bugs are discovered in it! I already have emptied my bowl. The rest leave theirs, except for Courtney who still wants hers. Mikaela has really gotten attached to Sarah. When Sarah gives her a hug and tells her that she will miss her, Mikaela pats her on the back and tells her not to cry!

We are up early as Mikaela is awake. We take her to our bed, as we have been doing for days now. Today is the last time we can do this as she is off to Lilongwe with her daddy and two sisters. I will miss her. We have grown very attached to each other. Kirk had said one day, "I wish Karen could see this!" Her wish has come true. Mikaela finally loves her Opa.

I drive by road to Malawi four days later and join the clan in Lilongwe. The Stevensons flew in two days earlier while Mark with his family turns up two days later. Mikaela is happy to see me. She is able to crawl around without the skateboard. Tiffany has to do some last minute shopping for Christmas gifts and so I take her around to the few shops they have in Lilongwe. Colleen and Marion prepare the meal on Christmas eve. It is very good, especially the turkey. Kirk is quiet because he misses Karen. We all do, and it is difficult to pray without weeping. But we manage to carry on and the kids sing before the gifts are opened. They are beautiful gifts! Kirk gives out those that Karen had chosen, even the one to himself that she had bought for him which Ashling knew about.

The following day we all leave for Monkey Bay on Lake Malawi where we spend several days on the beach. The day after Christmas, Kirk cuts away the body cast on Mikaela, leaving only the part that covers the leg that was broken. Tim completes the job a few days later. She is a very happy girl now! Mikaela is able to sit in the high chair at the table which she has not done for seven weeks. She must now learn to walk again properly. This will take time. On New Year's eve we try to stay awake until midnight but it is too difficult. Tiffany, Ashling, and Natasha fall asleep while I am telling them a story. But then Ashling and Tiffany wake up later and I have to finish the part they missed. Marion and I turn in at 11:30. At midnight I wake up and wish her a happy New Year!

There is a sadness to the end of the year. The death of Karen has really disturbed the family's closeness that we had enjoyed in the past. It will probably never be the same again. We all will need the Lord to help us in the coming year to adjust to her loss. May He give Marion and me the grace and strength we will need to cope with the extra load we have been handed. Lift our hearts, Lord, and put a song in our hearts!

Marion stays on in Lilongwe for six more weeks attending to the children as Kirk is away at the office all day. During this time, the ladies of the community and the church she attends rally to their aid and bring cooked meals to the house so that Marion is able to spend more time with the three girls. Four angels of mercy look after Mikaela's therapy, take Ashling to school, drive Marion shopping, and bring in the meals. Marion will never forget the compassion shown by these heretofore unknown ladies during those six weeks in Lilongwe.

Before closing this chapter which I am dedicating to the memory of Karen, I want to add that during our two weeks in Johannesburg, the Lord saw us through a strenuous ordeal that tested our faith and taxed us physically. We were in a strange country, far away from our fellow-workers and therefore without anyone to assist us in our bereavement. We could only comfort each other and look to Him for grace and strength. There were times I wished I could have sat back and be ministered unto as well. Fortunately I had enough in reserve to draw from without running out.

Why did Karen's sudden departure affect me so much? Maybe an experience from my own past had something to do with it. My own mother left behind five pre-school children when she went to be with the Lord! I was four years and ten months old, and grew up without experiencing a real mother's love. What is it like? Ashling, Shaina, and Mikaela will be asking that as well. Yes, Kirk has remarried. His wife, Suzie, is doing her best to fill that void in their lives. As for me, I have been able to make my way through the shadows. They were long, and in the process I have rediscovered a hurt that only those who have experienced it can really understand.

Twenty
All for the Sake of the Gospel

Traveling from district to district has been a big part of my ministry. First a church must be planted. Not just one but as many as it is possible so that there can be fellowship among the Christians. Our goal is to have at least seven congregations in a district so that they can officially elect a committee with a district chairman, or overseer. They can now assist the missionary in administering the district. I come and hold seminars and conventions to help strengthen the churches. The pastors are involved in a study program called Theological Education by Extension (TEE). There are many districts in Zambia and as we keep reaching into them, my travels increase in number and length. Often I am away up to ten days, with only a break of a few days to a week before I am off again in another direction for more of the same. The days are full from sunrise to late into the night. Preaching, praying, teaching, baptizing, dedicating children, observing Communion, blessing marriages, treating the sick, and handing out used clothing. No one is pushing me to do this. I have been doing what I have been doing, and will keep doing, all for the sake of the gospel!

In order to be able to do all of the above, we must have a reliable vehicle that will stand up to our strenuous schedule and to the roads here in Zambia. Spares are not always available either when there is a breakdown. It is, therefore, imperative that we have a new vehicle every term so that we will not be left stranded along an isolated road in a remote corner of Zambia. Yes, we order them ahead in plenty of time, but it is not always that they arrive on time. Marion and I have had to make do with taxis on most occasions. When we returned to the field in 1993 we discovered the new Nissan has as of yet not arrived. It arrives two months later! Taxis are now a means of getting around. Usually, they are on their last tire. One day we are with four church leaders who hail a taxi, a weather-beaten Fiat, to take us into town. They squeeze in the back and we sit in front with the driver. Every time he shifts, Marion has to lift herself up as she is sitting on the lever! It is embarrassing for her, I am sure. The next vehicle we take is not much better.

Marion and I are now off on another trip. This time to hold seminars in the districts of one of the Provinces. The vehicle is loaded in the evening so that we can make an early start in the morning. We are taking two bicycles, six boxes of Bibles, songbooks, TEE books, Sunday School material, tracts, and two large boxes of used clothing, plus our sponge mattress and sleeping bag. Our personal belongings and lunch will be put inside the Nissan when we are ready to leave in the morning. One or two others will be traveling with us, either to help translate or to teach.

The roads we are traveling in the beginning are tarmac which may have countless potholes that wreck tires, tubes, shocks, springs, and your back. It is also hard on the brakes and the clutch from shifting and slowing down for every one of the potholes. Even a wheel bearing has gone bad on one of our trips. Eventually we turn onto graveled roads that are very rough, and finally we are on bumpy bush trails before we reach our destination. There was one time we even had to make a temporary bridge in order to cross a river before we are able to carry on to Mwinilunga from Manyinga. We used rocks and wood that we found lying near the road. With God's help we made it across and held our seminar as planned!

If I am alone, I will be sleeping in the Nissan Patrol should there be no other sleeping quarters available, or if it happens to be too rainy for the tent. On a couple of occasions when the vehicle was too full with stuff I have brought along, I had to climb up on top, with just enough room to spare beneath the ceiling, and it became my bed. When Marion is with me, we spend the night in a hut which may have housed goats or chickens the night before. The smell is often unbearable. One night Marion coughed and coughed so we had to move out into our tent which had to be pitched at 1:00 A.M. The smell inside the hut was of manure and gave her an allergy. During nights when it is windy, dust blows into the tent or hut, and lands on top of us.

There are no flush toilets in the villages. They are just deep pits with not so large logs across the top and covered with sod. The latrines are enclosed with a fence made out of grass, reeds, and sticks. The doorway is very narrow and low so as to keep the goats and cattle from entering. I have to stoop over and turn sideways in order to enter one of these latrines. Any white shirt I am wearing will soon have dirty streaks on it. They are even more difficult for Marion. Bathhouses are grass enclosures as well. Our towel is used to hang across the opening, which has no wooden or grass door. The sky is the roof. The men, sorry to say, use this place as a urinal and before long the bathhouse smells like a toilet. The water brought for bathing may range in color from a clear to a brownish tint. It may have come from a running stream, shallow wells, or waterholes that have been dug into the dry sandy river bed.

Because word has gotten around that I prefer chicken to beef or pork, we can expect one less chicken scratching around on each compound when we arrive. Their staple food is nsima, ground up maize (white corn) that is cooked over an open fire and stirred into a gruel or heavy porridge. We are often served rice and rape (a green spinach) or cooked pumpkin leaves along with tea. When it is caterpillar season, they serve them along with the nsima. Of the two kinds I have eaten, the smaller ones are more palatable than the much larger ones which have a prickly hard crust and can scratch the inside of the mouth if not enough nsima is wrapped around them. White ants, when they are in the flying stage, and the green grasshoppers can be on our menu as well when they are in season. During the dry season many live on a wild fruit called masuku which the elephants love as well. They have a tarty taste to them and I usually eat my share. In certain areas game meat may end up on my plate as well, especially when they hear I am also a hunter and have shot wild animals.

There is no set time when the meals will be served. Whenever it gets cooked it is time to eat. The cooks do not have a clock to watch. So our classes sometimes must be cut short; or they have to be extended an hour or so. We have eaten meals as late as 10:30 P.M. Most evening meals are eaten in the dark around the log fire, or by candle light if in a hut. Whenever I remember to bring along the trouble light, we use it not only for the night service but also for our evening meal. But the drawback with this kind of lighting is that it attracts the flying insects and many will find their way into your dish and get eaten along with the food. Some of them have a bitter taste! Almost everyone knows that I love honey. This was true in Tanzania, Kenya, and Uganda. And now here in Zambia. Whenever we receive gifts at the end of a district seminar, more often than not there will be a container of wild honey for me. I have also bought it from the honey gatherers whenever I came across them walking alongside the road, or sitting up in the tree extracting it from a hanging log. These men appear to be immune to the stings from the bees.

Women are up before sunrise, getting the fires started so that water can be heated for bathing and for breakfast. Children, who are still on the breast, straddle their mother's back held there by a cloth tied around their middle. Some are screaming and the mothers are trying to calm them by patting the rump gently. The rest of us stir at dawn. After tea and bread, we normally have our first class around 8:30. Then, a worship service will follow at 10:00. This may not end at noon if there are quite a few who need demons cast out of them. I prefer daylight hours for driving out evil spirits. It is difficult to distinguish the features of the possessed when it is dark. The powers of darkness must not be given any advantage, if we can help it. Believe me, they love darkness more than light!

A district meeting takes place after the noon meal. During this time I have heard some unbelievable stories! Let me share one of them with you that Boscoe related at Mpulungu. He is giving an account of what he did with the money that was given for the roof of the central church. He actually went across the border into Tanzania, as he said he would, to buy the iron sheets as they are cheaper there. But when he arrives, he discovers they are more than originally calculated. There is not enough money now. No problem! Let me buy kapenta, small fish the size of sardines, and take them to the Copperbelt where they will fetch a large sum. So he transports them nearly 1,000 kilometers by road to sell in Kitwe. With the money now, he buys maize and transports it back to Mpulungu where it is in great demand.

But when he reaches home, he discovers to his dismay that the number of bags on the lorry do not match up with the number that were bought. It appears whenever the lorry stopped without his knowledge a bag or two was unloaded and sold for less to any passerby at the truck stop! What should he do now? The money is less now than when he started. There is someone who has an engine for sale. All it needs is some repairs and then it can be sold for double the price! He has only enough left for a down payment. The owner will wait until he sells it for the balance. He will be able to recover what he has lost and still come out on top. But there is one problem now? There is no buyer for the machine? The owner has now reclaimed it and will not release it until he has been paid. The story that Boscoe has just told us only Satan could have concocted! This is what happens when God's money is misused. I have seen this happen over and over.

After the district meeting there are more classes. They are broken up into groups—the pastors, the women, the youth, and the children. We stop before dark in order to give time for Marion to treat the sick or to pass out the used clothing. The women receive blocks of material for their projects to raise money. Saturday afternoons are usually reserved for baptismal services and for pastors to write their TEE tests. New books are given them should they pass. Bibles, Sunday School material, tracts, and songbooks are distributed to new pastors and churches. Communion is observed during the Sunday service, plus child dedication, and the blessing of marriages. Many who were married in their traditional ways, which we recognize, want now to make Christ the head of their homes and have their marriages blessed in the Church. Some of them are well up in age.

Poverty does strange things! And it shows up in many ways. One of them is when handing out used clothing. A stampede will take place if it is not kept under control. Marion and I have seen it happen on several occasions. No matter how many pieces of clothing we may take along, it is never enough. I doubt if a truck load of it would have sufficed! Clothes are sometimes a curse and not a blessing. Things can go along just fine until there are only a few items left. Then the remaining ones who still have not received an item will rush forward for something. Both men and women are struggling to get a piece. There is complete chaos! Unbelievable! A good thing has become a bad thing! To avoid this from happening again, we have had to resort to helping only those who are the poorest of the poor, the disabled, and the very aged. The district leaders point them out to us.

Since coming to Zambia we have had visitors fly in to visit both us and the work. While here, we take them along to participate in the city services and in the seminars up-country. We have already mentioned the Kellseys and the Weems. But there have been others. Reinhard Berle, Director of Kinderhilfswerk in Germany, has been here several times, once bringing along his Uncle Karl. He is assisting the church in Zambia with drilling boreholes (wells), relief work, and the supporting of an orphan program. He also has assisted in purchasing a vehicle and a house. Doug and Frieda Karau of Calgary, Alberta, who have been supporting our ministry since day one (July, 1959), were here for the month of August in

1994. It was a real privilege to have had them with us. They accompanied us for a week on our seminars in Eastern Province where they experienced firsthand the power of God at work. They also shared in Mufulira and Lusaka churches.

Someone whom I met at Alberta Bible Institute and who since then has been a fellow servant, Gilbert Sommert of Wetaskiwin, Alberta, came out to see us for two weeks in April, 1996. Josef Jakobsh of Vernon, B.C., and Ron Roesler of Kelowna, B.C., came together with him. All three men have been instrumental in raising funds for the work. They shared in Lusaka and then at a seminar in Mongu district. More recently, Warren Senft of Medicine Hat, Alberta, came in July, 1998 and stayed for five weeks. He had the experience of participating in seminars in Eastern Province, Kaoma and Mongu districts, plus in Lusaka. I also took him with me to a church in Zimbabwe where he delivered the message. Then, there was Helga Stalts, a registered nurse from Calgary who arrived in September, 1998 and stayed two months. She drove along to North-Western Province and worked with Oscar Ndao treating the sick in a village setting. She learned first hand what it is like treating patients with the very minimum amount of medicines. She assisted with office work as well.

Because of our building program that is ongoing here at Avondale, Lusaka, since 1996, we have had several work camps come out from Canada and the States to give us a hand. They stay for one to three weeks before going back. During this time they not only put in physical labor, but we have them take part in services at Lusaka and in one of the villages where they will also see how the rural Zambians live. It is a chance for church people from America to meet church people from Zambia and vice versa. They have come from Western Canada, Ohio, and Missouri. Our son Mark is the Project Manager. Many buildings have already been erected here at headquarters in Lusaka.

As soon as Mark makes a commitment to serve the Lord in which ever way he can, obstacles come his way. He likes to go out hunting now and then as you already have seen, either with Kirk, or alone. The following incident takes place while Marion and I are in Uganda with the Stevensons.

Tim and I had to attend a regional meeting in Nairobi so Marion and I had taken advantage of this opportunity to visit with our daughter and family. The day before we are to fly back to Lusaka, we receive a call at 6:00 P.M. from Kirk in Lusaka. He jolts us all with the news that Mark has been gored by a buffalo that he had wounded while out hunting! A plane has flown in to evacuate him to Lusaka. We are to pray as it looks bad! This we do as soon as we hang up. We are in total shock! Will he make it? Not many do when gored by a buffalo.

Kirk calls again at 10:00 to bring us up to date as to what had happened. But it is not until we hear it from Mark himself that we are able to piece together as to what took place out there in Zambian bush.

He is out hunting in the Luangwa Valley north of Nyimba when they sight a herd of buffalo. He had a license for one, so he and the scout take out after them, he with his .375 and the scout with his AK-47. The herd of about 15 make a hasty retreat into a thicket. Mark and the scout work their way towards the buffalo and when he spots a good-sized bull 40 meters away, he plants a slug just behind the shoulder. The thicket erupts with stampeding buffalo. There is dust everywhere. After waiting fifteen minutes, they commence their search for a sign of blood. They find it and follow the tracks of the wounded buffalo.

In five minutes they come up to him in some dense scrub. Mark gives him two more shots in the chest. The animal does not drop, instead he thunders off. There is plenty of blood now on the trail to follow. The bull is moving towards the river and into thicker bush. The men move on and then suddenly he is there to the right side of them! Mark pumps two more bullets into his shoulder as the buff barrels past them. Very slowly and cautiously they advance, the scout spread out to the left of Mark. Their guns are ready and cocked. Blood is everywhere. Then, the buffalo comes into view just 20 meters ahead of them! His back towards them. Mark sends another bullet his way.

The bull sways and looks as if he is finally ready to go down. Mark runs to the side of him so as to get a better shot and put him out of his misery. The buffalo turns his head and sees him. His nose comes up and he charges! Mark gives the bull a quick shot into his chest hoping to turn him but it has no effect at all. Knowing that he has time for only one more shot, Mark waits until the buff is five meters away and tries for a brain shot. The bull does not even flinch but keeps coming.

At the last second, Mark tries to side-step him, but the bull wings his head to follow him. As the animal turns, his horn pierces through the khaki shorts and rips open the lower part of Mark's abdomen! The horn then buries itself deep into his thigh. At the impact of the charge, Mark's gun goes flying out of his hand. His reaction now is to grab onto the horns. The bull commences to push him along through the thicket, cutting up the back of Mark's legs in the process. As the bull tires, he stops and his intention now is to crush into the ground with his boss the man that is still attached to his horns.

Before the buffalo can carry this out, the game scout comes running up to the side of the buffalo and opens up with his AK-47, shooting the animal in the head and neck. Nothing happens, so he runs to the other side and does the same thing. After about twelve rounds, the buffalo finally collapses. He drops next to Mark and they look at each other just inches apart! Snorting and eyes glaring, the buff still tries to hook Mark with his horns. The scout drags Mark away and props him against a tree. The buffalo finally gives up and dies.

Mark cannot walk, his leg looks a fright. Afraid that his insides may fall out of his ripped open abdomen, he lies still and raises his leg to slow down the bleeding. Next he makes a tourniquet above the wound on his thigh with his belt. Once settled, he sends the tracker back to the vehicle for some water, and sends the scout to a professional hunter's camp about six kilometers away for assistance. Mark at this point is not sure whether he will make it or not. It takes an hour and a half before a vehicle finally arrives from the safari camp to collect him. The professional hunter radios Kirk in Lusaka and reports the accident to him. Kirk sends a small plane out to the camp where Mark has been brought. Soon he is on the tarmac of the Lusaka airport. There he is stabilized by a medical team before transferring him to a larger plane and flown off to Harare. Within 12 hours from the accident, Mark is in the care of a surgeon at a hospital in Harare where we find him two days later.

We thank God for sparing his life. No intestines or vital organs were damaged when the horn entered and ripped open the abdomen. Also, his leg is not fractured, even though bone chips were removed by the medical team from the open wound in his thigh where the horn had entered. It had missed the main artery by a hair. A miracle!

But, Marion and I are in for another shock. This near escape from death does not save his and Kim's marriage. Kim announces that she no longer wishes to live with Mark. She refuses any counseling and just wants out! It is heart-breaking for Mark, their two children, and the rest of us. Upon her insistence, divorce has been granted and she has moved to South Africa with her new love. As for Mark, he has drawn closer to the Lord because of the two dramatic experiences he has had within a month. He is still working with us in the building program at the national headquarters, and is having to adjust his life all over again.

*   *   *

We are wending down on our tour of holding seminars, and both Marion and I are feeling the strain of the heavy schedule. This is the eighth day on the road and today we head back home. It has been a full week of teaching, preaching, and holding district meetings. Besides this, Marion has been busy with the women in their programs and I with the men in the TEE program. She passed out used clothing to the poorest of the poor and treated some sick with the medicine she brought with her. There was a woman with elephantitis. Her whole leg is infected with the disease. At another place we had a leper attend the service. He has already lost all of his toes and fingers. There was also a man suffering from river blindness, a crippled man, and a blind man being led by a boy.

At each place many children were dedicated, communion services were held, and new Christians were baptized in nearby streams. And, of course, many possessed with demons were delivered. No matter how exhausted we were, Marion and I carried on until all were set free from the power of the devil. Two days ago I got malaria but I refused to let it get me down. Marion is also suffering with stomach problems from eating some of the food they served us. It may have been from the goat meat we ate. We had them slaughter the goat that was given to us as a gift so that everyone could taste it too. I ate some of the liver for added strength.

On our way home we cross the Kabompo River on the pontoon which is hand-operated on cables. Then we take the bush road, a short cut on sand through a forest. This area is connected with the Kalahari which runs all the way south through Botswana, Namibia, and into South Africa. We must use our 4-wheel drive all the way. It is slow going and very rough in places. We stop at Kaoma to fill up with diesel. We had hoped to purchase something to eat at the little shop but there is nothing. The tarmac road to Lusaka is under construction in places. There is a 40 kilometers detour at one section which slows us right down. It is very rough driving! Finally, we reach home at 5 P.M. after being on the road for nine hours non-stop.

I have taken the journey quite well in spite of nothing to eat all day, but Marion is quite done for, as are the ones who have ridden back with us to town. There is no food waiting for us at home, so we go out for a snack. As we retire for the night, Marion breaks down and weeps during our prayer time. The care of the work is too great for her already. I must slow down. We both are exhausted and there is no one around capable of helping to relieve some of the load we carry. Share as we may with the churches in America that we need missionaries, there is no response. No one cares!

*   *   *

Today is our wedding anniversary! But I will have to wait until tomorrow before I see Marion and enjoy an evening together. I have been on the road for the past five days holding seminars. I have had a good night. I spent it in the Nissan. I did quite a bit of sweating due to the malaria still in my system. They bring me water to bathe at 6:00 A.M., which I need. I had gone to bed last night without one. I collected a lot of dust on the road coming to this place. Two hours later we meet at the church. I teach until 12 with a fifteen-minute break at 10:30. We eat at the church. Then I enroll the new TEE students and go into the district meeting. At 3 P.M. there is a service and I bring the Word of God. I pray for the many that come forward, including six children who are dedicated. Several sick need special prayer and one is oppressed by demons. There are also two possessed who are delivered. I notice two more women that have demons but they do not come for help. An old woman as she files by me after the service has a charm around her neck. I remove it with my pocket knife. She is still hanging on to her past beliefs and following the Lord with one leg! It has been a full day for me! I thank the Lord for His continued strength.

While waiting for supper, I make my bed in the Nissan and chew on my mixture of ground nuts, raisins, and sunflower seeds. I am looking forward to going home, having a bath in the tub, slipping between two white sheets, and snuggling up to my wife.

Today is my last day, and tonight will find me home.

At last! No more small kids standing around with their "How are you? How are you?" No more trying to eat a bar, cookie, or apple, without being spotted by one of these little tykes. At the last place, I had to resort to eating my bar in the latrine, of all places! Quite a feat! No more skimping on my drinking water, making sure it will last. How thirsty I have been at times, especially yesterday all afternoon and evening. But through it all I have survived and the Lord has blessed more than enough by giving me opportunities to preach and to cast our demons in His name. Thank you, Lord, for all these chances to be out in the Zambia bush for the sake of the gospel! Many of the miles I have travelled on this trip, I would only drive for His sake and never for my own.

Marion and I have done all that we can in trying to break down as many strongholds of Satan as we are able to in our human frailties. I do not believe that we could have done any more than we have. We trust that what we have been able to do through His power thus far in Zambia has helped to shorten the shadows that we found when we first came to this country.